Conversational Japanese

Second Edition

by Naoya Fujita, Ph.D.

ALPHA

A member of Penguin Group (USA) Inc.

ALPHA BOOKS

3 1907 00275 5857

Published by the Penguin Group

Penguin Group (USA) Inc., 375 Hudson Street, New York, New York 10014, USA

Penguin Group (Canada), 90 Eglinton Avenue East, Suite 700, Toronto, Ontario M4P 2Y3, Canada (a division of Pearson Penguin Canada Inc.)

Penguin Books Ltd., 80 Strand, London WC2R 0RL, England

Penguin Ireland, 25 St. Stephen's Green, Dublin 2, Ireland (a division of Penguin Books Ltd.)

Penguin Group (Australia), 250 Camberwell Road, Camberwell, Victoria 3124, Australia (a division of Pearson Australia Group Pty. Ltd.)

Penguin Books India Pvt. Ltd., 11 Community Centre, Panchsheel Park, New Delhi—110 017, India

Penguin Group (NZ), 67 Apollo Drive, Rosedale, North Shore, Auckland 1311, New Zealand (a division of Pearson New Zealand Ltd.)

Penguin Books (South Africa) (Pty.) Ltd., 24 Sturdee Avenue, Rosebank, Johannesburg 2196, South Africa

Penguin Books Ltd., Registered Offices: 80 Strand, London WC2R 0RL, England

Copyright © 2011 by Naoya Fujita, Ph.D.

THE COMPLETE IDIOT'S GUIDE TO and Design are registered trademarks of Penguin Group (USA) Inc.

International Standard Book Number: 978-1-61564-1-055
Library of Congress Catalog Card Number: 2010915382

13 12 11   8 7 6 5 4 3 2 1

Interpretation of the printing code: The rightmost number of the first series of numbers is the year of the book's printing; the rightmost number of the second series of numbers is the number of the book's printing. For example, a printing code of 11-1 shows that the first printing occurred in 2011.

Printed in the United States of America

Note: This publication contains the opinions and ideas of its author. It is intended to provide helpful and informative material on the subject matter covered. It is sold with the understanding that the author and publisher are not engaged in rendering professional services in the book. If the reader requires personal assistance or advice, a competent professional should be consulted.

The author and publisher specifically disclaim any responsibility for any liability, loss, or risk, personal or otherwise, which is incurred as a consequence, directly or indirectly, of the use and application of any of the contents of this book.

Most Alpha books are available at special quantity discounts for bulk purchases for sales promotions, premiums, fund-raising, or educational use. Special books, or book excerpts, can also be created to fit specific needs.

For details, write: Special Markets, Alpha Books, 375 Hudson Street, New York, NY 10014.

Publisher: *Marie Butler-Knight*
Associate Publisher: *Mike Sanders*
Executive Managing Editor: *Billy Fields*
Executive Editor: *Randy Ladenheim-Gil*
Development Editor: *Michael Thomas*
Senior Production Editor: *Janette Lynn*

Copy Editor: *Megan Wade*
Cover Designer: *William Thomas*
Book Designers: *William Thomas, Rebecca Batchelor*
Indexer: *Tonya Heard*
Layout: *Brian Massey*
Proofreader: *Laura Caddell*

This book is dedicated to:

My wife Naoko and son Hayato (Ken) for their love and support,

My parents, Akio and Shigeyo Fujita, for helping me become who I am,

The Tabuse and Kito families for their encouragement, and finally but not least important,

All my students, who have taught me how to teach Japanese!

Contents

Part 1: **Before You Get Started: The Basics**.........................1

  1 **Can I *Really* Learn Japanese on My Own?**.............3

    The Five Golden Rules...3

      Rule 1: Be Confident! 4

      Rule 2: Be Brave!..4

      Rule 3: Be Persistent!..5

      Rule 4: Be Creative!..6

      Rule 5: Be Japanese! 7

    How to Use This Book...7

    The Top Ten Reasons to Learn Japanese........................8

  2 **Behind the Language** 11

    Geographic Facts About Japan 11

    Who Are the Japanese?...12

    Japanese Society 13

    Communication for Peace and Harmony......................14

      Principle 1: No Matter Whom You Talk to,

      It's Safe to Be Polite..14

      Principle 2: Be Humble When Talking—a Good Listener

      Is a Better Communicator 15

      Principle 3: Know the TPO 15

  3 **Japanese Sounds: As Easy as *A, I, U, E, O***............17

    Keep Your Mouth Open, Please: Syllabication 18

    All the Possible Japanese Sounds...............................19

      The Two Standalone Consonants...............................21

      Tricky Sounds 21

    My Husband Is a Prisoner? Importance of Long Vowels........24

    Japanizing English Words 24

    Japanese Is a Calm Language 26

Part 2: **The Survival Skills: Grammar** 29

  4 **Speak Like Yoda: Basic Sentence Structure** 31

    Godzilla Ate John, or John Ate Godzilla?....................31

      A Quick Grammar Review......................................32

      Particles..33

Particles: Tiny but Mighty! 34

    -ga: *Subject Marker* 35

    -o: *Object Marker* 36

    -ni: *"toward"; "in"* 37

    -mo: *"also"* 37

    -kara: *"from"* / -made: *"up to"; "until"* 38

    -de: *"by means of"; "at"* 38

    -to: *"together with"* 38

The Concept of "Topic" 40

Simple Is Beautiful 41

Review Quiz 42

Answers 43

5   Everything You Need to Know About Conjugation 45

Conjugation Is No Headache! 45

    Verb Predicate Conjugation 46

    Adjective Predicate Conjugation 50

    Noun Conjugation 53

Answers 56

6   Other Grammar Essentials 59

TE-Form 59

    Continuous Action 60

    Connecting Predicates 63

    Other Instances When You Want to Use the TE-*Form* 67

How to Describe Something or Someone 68

    Adjectives 68

    Nouns 69

    Na-*Adjectives* 70

Asking a Question 72

    ka 72

    Wh-*Questions* 73

Review 74

Answers 75

7   Numbers 79

Basic Numbers 79

    10 to 99 80

    100 to 9,999 81

    Beyond 10,000 84

    Big Numbers 85

What Is a "Counter"? 85

Review 87

Answers 87

Part 3:   Getting to Know People **89**

8   Greetings 91
       Greetings Around the Clock.................................... 91
              At the Dining Table................................ 92
              Leaving Home and Coming Home 93
              At the End of the Day............................. 94
       Thanks, Sorry, and Excuse Me 94
       Good-Bye!.. 97
       The Magic Words 98
              Making a Request.................................. 98
              Giving and Receiving.............................. 98
              Survival Phrases.................................. 99

9   Meeting People 101
       My Name Is … 101
              X-wa Y-desu... 102
              Watashi-wa XYZ-desu................................. 102
              And You Are …?.................................... 103
       Beyond Exchanging Names..................................... 104
              Occupations....................................... 104
              Where Are You From?............................... 105
              Essential Party Greetings......................... 106

10   Talking About Yourself 111
       Purpose of Your Visit to Japan 111
       Talk About Your Background.................................. 113
              Where You Live.................................... 113
              Marital Status....................................114
              Occupation..114
       Talk About Your Hobbies.....................................117
       Talk About Your Family......................................119
              My Family Is … 120
              Counting People................................... 121
              Ages.. 122
       Putting Everything Together................................. 123
       Answers 125

11   Extending Invitations....................................127
       Polite Invitations 127
       "Let's …!" and "Shall We …?".................................. 130
              Let's!.. 130
              Shall We? 132
       Declining the Invitation 133
       Make Your Invitation Hard to Resist! 135
       Answers 136

Part 4:   The Essentials for Traveling 139

12   In the Airplane...141
Making Requests 141
XYZ-ni Shi-masu *142*
The TE-Form Request *143*
Making Requests of Your Fellow Passengers *145*
Polite Requests You Might Hear on the Airplane *148*
Answers 151

13   Is the Flight on Time? Time Expressions 153
Reading the Clock 153
Useful Time Expressions *155*
"From" and "Until" *157*
Duration *158*
Answers 161

14   At the Airport 163
At the Immigration Booth... 163
Oh, No! My Bag Is Missing! At Baggage Claim 168
At the Customs Counter 170
Answers 173

15   Getting to and Around Town............................... 175
Types of Transportation 175
Going by Train *176*
Going by Taxi.. *181*
Are You Sure You Want to Drive in Tokyo?........................... 185
Answers 187

16   At the Hotel..189
Making a Hotel Reservation... 189
Choosing the Hotel *190*
Check-In and Check-Out Dates *191*
Number of People and Types of Room *194*
Check-In and Check-Out 196
Staying in a *RyokaN*—a Japanese-Style Inn........................... 198
Answers 200

17   At the Bank 203
Bills and Coins..204
Currency Exchange.. 207
Opening a Bank Account.. 209
Answers 212

Part 5:   Japanese for Fun..**215**

18   Let's Go Shopping!.................................. **217**
Types of Shops...217
Shop Talk..219
Basic Counters... 220
I Want *This* One, Not *That* One!.................... 223
Don't You Have a Cheaper One?....................... 226
Answers... 229

19   More Than Just *Sushi*: Dining Out in Japan....... **233**
Likes and Dislikes 233
Making Comparisons..................................... 236
Ordering 238
Learning Eating Etiquette 241
Taste Words.. 243
Check, Please!... 244
Answers... 246

20   Touring a Japanese House **249**
A Typical Japanese Household 249
Entering the House—GeNkaN...................... 250
Japanese-Style Room—NihoNma 251
Family Room—Ima or Chanoma 252
"Bathroom"—Ofuro..................................... 253
Bedtime 255
Household Items... 257

21   Spending Leisure Time............................ **261**
Where Do You Wanna Go? 261
Make a Plan 263
Weather and Climate 265
Weather.. 266
Climates 267
Answers... 268

Part 6:   Troubleshooting **271**

22   Talking on the Phone **273**
Japanese Phone Facts... 273
Let's Call Home! 275
When You Must Call Someone's House.............. 277
Segment 1... 279
Segment 2... 279
Segments 3, 4, and 5 280
Important Numbers....................................... 281
Answers... 282

23   I'm Sick! Call 911? No, Call 119! 283

Health-Related Expressions...283

At a Doctor's Office 284

Parts of the Body...*285*

Symptoms *286*

Common Requests a Doctor Makes......................................*288*

At the Pharmacy 290

24   I Lost My Wallet! Nonmedical Emergencies 293

Safety Facts and Japanese Police 293

Lost and Found..295

If ... Then *297*

Theft! 297

What Were You Doing That Time?......................................*299*

Help! I Think I'm Lost!...300

Answers 302

25   Making Complaints......................................305

Staying at a Not-So-Great Hotel 305

Room-Related Problems *306*

Other Problems...*308*

Inconveniences at a Restaurant 309

Shopping-Related Problems 311

Damaged Items...*311*

This Is Not What I Bought!.. *312*

**26   Useful Signs and Symbols for Travelers
to Japan 315**

Essential Signs and Symbols...315

Emergency Exit: *316*

Entrance: *316*

Exit: *316*

Restroom: *317*

Push:...*317*

Pull:..*317*

Do Not Enter!:..*318*

Elevator OPEN/CLOSE Buttons: *318*

Telephone: *318*

Coin Locker: *319*

Police Box or Koban*:* *319*

Police Station: *319*

Shops and Facilities 320

    Pharmacy: *320*

    Bank: *321*

    Currency Exchange: *321*

    Post Office: *322*

    Bookstore: *322*

    Coffee Shop: *323*

    Cigarette Shop: *323*

    Smoking Area and No Smoking: *324*

    Cashier: *324*

Signs and Symbols Around Town 325

    Taxi Stand: *325*

    Taxi Vacancy: *325*

    Bus Stand: *326*

    Subway Sign: *326*

    Tokyo Metro Sign: *326*

    Subway Track: *327*

    Transfer: *327*

    Bullet Train (Shinkansen): *328*

    Ticket Vending Machine: *328*

    Ticket Reservation Center: *328*

Appendixes

    A   **Written Japanese: A Brief Introduction** **331**

    B   **English to Japanese Dictionary** **343**

    C   **Japanese to English Dictionary** **373**

           Index **401**

Introduction

Welcome to *The Complete Idiot's Guide to Conversational Japanese, Second Edition!* This book is neither an ordinary language textbook nor merely a phrasebook for travelers. It is a unique tool to help you get the most out of learning Japanese on your own in a fun way.

How is this book different from other books? Language textbooks are often designed for a classroom, and a teacher guides you through lessons over a long period of time. Because of this, such books tend to contain too much information for a self-study learner to absorb. On the other hand, phrasebooks for travelers are often designed to give you a minimally sufficient set of expressions. They tend to have too little information for a serious self-study learner who is eager to understand not only phrases and expressions, but also the *structure* of the language. This book was written to give you the most valuable information, as well as some insights into the structure of the language—and maybe make your life a little bit easier, too!

The Complete Idiot's Guide to Conversational Japanese, Second Edition, has three notable characteristics. First, the tone of the book is not overly academic, so it's easy to read through each chapter. There are many helpful tips and a lot of cultural information throughout the book so that you won't end up just memorizing dry sentence patterns.

Second, this book is not a plain list of unconnected phrases. Learning a language is like solving a jigsaw puzzle with lots of pieces. Once you find the core piece, completing the rest of the puzzle becomes easier! In language learning, the "core piece" is grammar. I introduce all the essential grammatical concepts first, with easy-to-understand explanations. This will enable you to understand sentence patterns that are newly introduced in subsequent chapters. I strongly encourage you to thoroughly read those chapters and come back to them if you need to. Don't miss the core piece of this puzzle!

Third, this book is designed to serve as a powerful survival tool. Ordinary phrasebooks can give you commonly used expressions that might suffice in many situations. However, life sometimes does not go as smoothly as you wish. If you merely memorize phrases without understanding the structure of the language, how can you survive in an unexpected situation? As a language teacher, I want you to be able to handle any situation you might come across. This is possible only if you have a grasp of the structure of the language—namely, the grammar. When you are comfortable with basic grammatical concepts, you can apply that knowledge to any situation using the necessary vocabulary. Between the main text and the English-Japanese and Japanese-English dictionaries in the appendixes, you will have the essential vocabulary you need.

I kept these three points in mind while preparing this book. Go through each chapter and learn patterns and expressions. Make sure that you speak aloud when memorizing them. That's the only way to achieve proficiency. In addition, do all the exercises to check your understanding of newly introduced items.

Japanese Sounds and Characters

Japanese is not a language relative to English or any of the Western languages. This means Japanese has a distinct sound system. Chapter 3 is devoted to the sound patterns of Japanese and the pronunciation of each sound. Don't overlook this chapter. With full understanding of all the sounds through repeated practice, you will be able to understand Japanese speakers, and they will understand your Japanese as well.

The Japanese writing system is also uniquely different from English or any Western language. Having taught Japanese for more than 15 years, I am fully aware that learning the Japanese writing system takes time. The main objective of this book is to help you learn conversational Japanese. Because I want you to focus on speaking and listening, all the vocabulary and examples are presented in *romanized* characters. However, in Appendix A, I provide a concise section on the writing system. This section explains what the writing system looks like and provides a list of basic Japanese alphabets.

If you're interested in learning the Japanese writing system along with conversation, I suggest that you start with an elementary writing textbook for non-native speakers. But even if you want to learn the writing system, you should begin to learn the sound system and basic conversation first. This way, you can identify each character more easily. Remember, the other way (writing first, speaking second) simply does not work.

In the English-Japanese and Japanese-English dictionaries (see Appendixes B and C), each entry accompanies words written in *kana* (native Japanese alphabets) and *kanji* (imported Chinese characters). You can use the dictionaries to become familiar with the writing system. In addition, when you need to show a certain word to a Japanese speaker, you can show him or her the Japanese characters in these dictionaries.

The Audio CD

This book comes with a supplementary CD. Look for the ![CD icon] icon in each chapter and listen to the corresponding segment on the CD. Make sure that you listen to the same segment and say it repeatedly until you internalize it. This way, you will significantly improve both your listening and speaking skills. After you study each chapter thoroughly using the CD, try listening to the CD alone and see how much you can pick up.

How This Book Is Organized

This book is divided into six parts, each of which focuses on a particular theme.

Part 1, Before You Get Started: The Basics, provides essential background information about the language. You will learn about Japanese people and their mentality, land, and language in detail. By knowing these facts, you can eliminate common myths and get yourself ready to learn the language. In Chapter 3, you are also introduced to the Japanese sound system, both its pronunciation and intonation. Don't overlook this chapter! Make sure that you go over each sound with the accompanying CD.

Part 2, The Survival Skills: Grammar, is the backbone of this book. These chapters provide the fundamental concepts of the grammar. You can skip other chapters as you wish, but I suggest that you don't skip these chapters because the mastery of subsequent chapters depends on how much you understand the material here.

Part 3, Getting to Know People, enables you to greet people, exchange self-introductions, talk about yourself, and ask people questions. Most of the expressions covered in these chapters are "fixed" or "ritualized" expressions. Learning these essential phrases will enable you to engage in conversation smoothly and comfortably to get to know people.

Part 4, The Essentials for Traveling, provides valuable tips for traveling and introduces a number of expressions useful at an airport, a hotel, and a bank, as well as for traveling around Japan. Specifically, you learn how to go through Immigration and Customs at the airport, give directions to a cab driver, make a hotel reservation, exchange currency, and so on.

Part 5, Japanese for Fun, enables you to have fun in Japan when shopping, dining, and spending leisure time. In particular, you learn how to buy things, order food at a restaurant, make a plan for various cultural events, and so on. For those who would like to do a home-stay in Japan, Chapter 20 prepares you to live in a Japanese house by taking you on a virtual house tour.

Part 6, Troubleshooting, focuses on possible inconveniences you might encounter in Japan and gives you solutions or tips for handling such situations. In particular, you learn how to deal with medical and other emergencies, how to make a phone call, how to make a complaint at places such as a hotel or restaurant, and so on. In addition, some essential signs and symbols, which you will encounter on the streets every day, are introduced with pictures.

If you read this book from beginning to end, doing the exercises and memorizing vocabulary, you will be able to travel in Japan and do most activities on your own with confidence. So believe in yourself! I know you can do it.

Sidebars

In addition to grammatical explanations, exercises, and newly introduced phrases and vocabulary, there are four types of useful information provided in sidebar format throughout the book. Look for the following:

HUH?

These sidebars provide definitions or explanations of unfamiliar or foreign words or concepts.

SHORTCUTS TO SUCCESS

Useful learning tips are provided in these sidebars. These tips will enable you to learn aspects of the language quickly and effectively.

LIFESAVERS

These sidebars provide cultural or learning tips that help you avoid making unnecessary mistakes.

GREEN TEA BREAK

These sidebars are for fun! Here you'll find interesting cultural remarks or notes on useful customs. These sidebars will help you become accustomed to Japanese society.

Acknowledgments

During the production of this second edition, I have benefited greatly from a number of people, especially Rebecca Forrey-Roofener, Melissa Bernhardt, Natsuko Alipio, Joyce Gabriel, Amanda Mobbs, Steven Caires, Paul Joyce, and Daniel Bial. My special thanks go to Copy Editor Megan Wade, Senior Production Editor Janette Lynn, Development Editor Mike Thomas, and Executive Editor Randy Ladenheim-Gil for their professionalism, and Nicole Cee (*The Language Lab*) for CD production. Finally, I would like to extend my special thanks to Technical Editor Andrew Scott (*and* my former student!) for this second edition, who did an excellent job carefully reviewing the entire book with thoughtful comments and input and providing the CD script. Thank you all!

Special Thanks to the Technical Reviewer

The Complete Idiot's Guide to Conversational Japanese, Second Edition, was reviewed by an expert who double-checked the accuracy of what you'll learn here, to help us ensure that this book gives you everything you need to know about learning conversational Japanese. Special thanks are extended to Andrew Scott.

Trademarks

All terms mentioned in this book that are known to be or are suspected of being trademarks or service marks have been appropriately capitalized. Alpha Books and Penguin Group (USA) Inc. cannot attest to the accuracy of this information. Use of a term in this book should not be regarded as affecting the validity of any trademark or service mark.

Before You Get Started: The Basics

Part

1

We start out with some background on the Japanese language, as well as the society and people. You don't have to worry about memorizing anything yet! Just read the chapters and familiarize yourself with Japan and Japanese because the knowledge will enable you to learn the language comfortably in the subsequent chapters.

In Chapter 3, I introduce the "sounds" of Japanese and show you how the sound inventory is organized. Spend some time learning Japanese sounds, and you will be able to listen to and understand people, as well as have them understand what you say. If you can't pronounce basic sounds correctly, you can't communicate with Japanese speakers, no matter how many words and phrases you memorize! So spend time on this chapter and become comfortable with the pronunciation. Also, don't forget to listen to the CD!

Can I *Really* Learn Japanese on My Own?

In This Chapter

- The Five Golden Rules for the successful mastery of Japanese
- Five guidelines for using this book
- The top ten reasons to learn Japanese

I am a Japanese teacher. I have seen thousands of students learn Japanese. But I am also a student—of English. I started learning English as an adult. Based on my experience as a language teacher and student, I believe that a "good" learner intuitively knows the Five Golden Rules for the successful mastery of Japanese.

The Five Golden Rules

Rule 1: Be confident! Believe in yourself. Believe that you will master the language in the near future.

Rule 2: Be brave! Don't be afraid of making mistakes.

Rule 3: Be persistent! Stick to one book or methodology from beginning to end. Make a habit of studying the material every day.

Rule 4: Be creative! Try to apply learned patterns to new, unexpected situations.

Rule 5: Be Japanese! Try to speak, behave, and think like a native Japanese speaker. In other words, "Japanize" yourself!

Let's go over each rule so that you will be fully prepared to learn Japanese.

Rule 1: Be Confident!

Okay, let's face reality. We all know that no one can master a foreign language overnight. People say that learning a foreign language is like walking through a long, dark tunnel. Besides appropriate guidance, what takes you to the end of the tunnel is *you*. Self-confidence is the most important key to success. To maintain self-confidence, you need to occasionally make sure you're on the right track. Here are some things you can do to increase your self-assurance:

- Repeat expressions you've learned to someone who knows Japanese. Start with simple greetings, and then advance to more complex expressions.

- Do occasional vocabulary checks. This task can be done more effectively if someone helps you in a question-answer format:

  Q: What is "How much"?

  A: *Ikura*.

- If you are a visually oriented learner, I suggest you learn the Japanese alphabet at an early stage. Write new words in Japanese. You will be amazed with how easy it is to learn words using Japanese characters. This method also helps you improve your pronunciation.

- Watch a relatively short Japanese video clip with English subtitles. Watch it repeatedly.

- When you begin to learn the Japanese writing system, try to follow children's short picture books in Japanese. Picture books are a great tool to help you understand the storyline and improve your "educated guess" skills.

- In each lesson in this textbook, be sure to do the exercises to self-evaluate your knowledge.

Rule 2: Be Brave!

Many people are afraid of foreign languages, especially seemingly difficult ones like Japanese. Some of the reasons you might fear learning Japanese are …

- You don't want people to make fun of you or your accent.

- You don't want to say the wrong words at the wrong times.

- You don't want to lose your self-esteem by making mistakes.

- You think you might look dumb if you can't understand what Japanese people say to you.

I can relate to these concerns. Nobody wants to be intimidated. But those embarrassing moments make you a better speaker. To illustrate, let me share with you a couple of my embarrassing moments.

As you might know, Japanese people have difficulty distinguishing between the *r* and the *l* sounds. In a college cafeteria, I was asked if I would like bread or rice. I replied aloud, *"Lice,* please!"

Here is another embarrassing moment. The Japanese language does not contain the *v* sound. I remember that my girlfriend laughed at me when I said "I love you!" because it sounded like "I rub you!"

These episodes were embarrassing enough for me, but they made me aware of my weaknesses and helped me to correct them.

 GREEN TEA BREAK

Your Japanese will significantly improve if you have a Japanese friend who can point out your mistakes. However, culturally speaking, many Japanese people find it extremely rude to correct someone. The ideal solution is to find a Japanese conversation partner whose English is not very good so that you can correct each other's mistakes without hesitation or intimidation.

If you don't speak, of course, you won't make mistakes. However, if you do speak, you might make mistakes and learn from them. After I realized this simple yet important fact, I no longer feared making mistakes. I knew I would not make the same mistakes again or that I would at least be aware of those possible pitfalls. So here is my motto:

> Better to be embarrassed now than sorry later!

When I speak English, I still make mistakes and occasionally experience embarrassing moments. People might laugh at me, but I always tell them, "Hey, I'm not a native speaker of English anyway. Given that, don't you think my English is pretty good?"

Rule 3: Be Persistent!

There is no mystery to mastering a foreign language. You have to make a habit of practicing it every day, just like brushing your teeth before going to bed. It can be any kind of practice—memorizing new vocabulary, reading a short passage, or watching a video. Only 30 minutes of exposure to the language every day leads to 183 hours of learning per year. That's 30 hours more than the total hours a college student is exposed in a language class. Needless to say, the more you are exposed to Japanese, the faster you can speak it. The key issue here, however, is consistency.

Consistency is important not only because of continual exposure to the language, but also because it encourages reinforcement of previously acquired skills. In this sense, learning a language is like learning to type. The more you practice typing, the faster and more accurately you will type.

The balance between *input* and *output* is important as well. Input is what you learn (knowledge) and output is what you produce based on your knowledge. Without output, your skills will easily become rusty. Make it a habit to use the language whenever you get the chance.

Rule 4: Be Creative!

How many English words do you know? You probably can't count all of them, but most likely you don't know them all. Yet you have no problem communicating with people in English. For instance, even if you don't know the word "sermonize," you can convey the same meaning by substituting the *synonym* "preach" for it.

HUH?

A **synonym** is a word that means the same or nearly the same as another word. A fluent speaker is often very good at using synonyms.

How about English grammar? The grammatical rules are finite. Yet you can say whatever you want using this finite set of rules. Isn't this amazing? No matter what language we speak, we are all equipped with an amazing skill to use grammar and vocabulary in a very creative fashion. Whether or not you become a fluent Japanese speaker depends on how creatively you can manipulate the language.

Here is an example to show the importance of creativity. One of my students went to Japan and stayed with a Japanese host family. One day her stereo broke, and she needed to have it repaired. She had just begun learning Japanese, so she could not say something like, "My stereo is broken. Could you take this to a radio shop and have them repair it for me?" Instead, what she said was

> *Stereo-ga byōki desu. Isha-ga irimasu.*

> "The stereo is sick. It needs a doctor."

Her host family immediately understood what she meant and took it to a shop for repair.

Imagine that you suddenly get ill in Japan and need immediate assistance. You probably would have to use the words you know and try to convey your needs to other people—perhaps together with body language. Life does not always go exactly as you learn it in a textbook. This is why I emphasize creativity as a great survival skill.

SHORTCUTS TO SUCCESS

When you start getting accustomed to basic Japanese vocabulary and grammar, try to imagine various unexpected situations and write them down, such as "At the New Tokyo International Airport, an immigration officer incorrectly identifies me as a drug smuggler. How can I convince him I am not a criminal?" Remember, you don't have to know all the words such as "criminal" or "smuggling." Explain things as much as possible by using limited vocabulary and grammar. You will find this task challenging, but you will also find it a lot of fun.

Rule 5: Be Japanese!

Last, but not least, keep in mind that you must try to be or act Japanese when you learn the language. Language learning begins with imitation. On TV, in movies, or in actual conversations, observe how Japanese people communicate, paying attention to the way they nod, argue, laugh, complain, show their anger, and so on. Try to imitate their intonation. Your friends might find you a little eccentric, but that's okay. This will help you build another personality within yourself—a personality suitable for speaking Japanese.

The title of this chapter is "Can I *Really* Learn Japanese on My Own?" As long as you carry out the Five Golden Rules, you really can learn Japanese on your own. However, keep in mind that you need to communicate with Japanese speakers as much as possible to improve your Japanese.

How to Use This Book

I hope you're starting to think that learning Japanese will be fun, not intimidating. I wrote this book in a specific way so that you will be able to accomplish the Five Golden Rules mentioned previously. Here are five guidelines you can use to accomplish the Five Golden Rules.

First, this book is organized in a step-by-step fashion, so you can grasp important grammatical and cultural concepts with confidence. Part 2 covers all the fundamental grammatical concepts. If you forget something in subsequent lessons, you can always go back to Part 2 to review these grammatical concepts.

Second, each chapter has a number of relatively easy, but extremely useful, expressions. I suggest you try out those expressions on someone who knows Japanese. By doing so, you will gain confidence, gradually erase inhibitions of using the language, and get rid of the fear of making mistakes.

Third, I included exercises in many chapters for you to use to self-evaluate your level of understanding and encourage your persistence. Remember, doing exercises over and over is a must for understanding the material. Make sure you answer *aloud*, in a clear voice—no mumbling! Answering aloud will significantly improve your speaking skills and pronunciation.

Fourth, I made sure each chapter contains new basic sentence patterns. Underline and memorize them. Mastery of these patterns is extremely important for you to improve your linguistic creativity. With this creativity, you will be able to survive in challenging situations.

Fifth, I included many sidebars. The sidebars (especially the "Green Tea Break" sidebars) give you brief, but useful, information about the Japanese culture and the behavioral psychology of Japanese people. They also help you "Japanize" yourself.

Because the main objective of this book is to improve your conversational skills as effectively as possible, emphasis on the writing system is kept to a minimum. Examples are written in *romaji*, or romanized characters, which is the way a Japanese word would look in English—for example, *karate* and *sushi*. However, those who are interested in learning the writing system are encouraged to look at Appendix A.

The Top Ten Reasons to Learn Japanese

Still not convinced you will conquer Japanese? Okay, then how about if I give you the top ten reasons you should learn Japanese?

10. You want to impress a grumpy *sushi* master by ordering *sushi* with a perfect Japanese accent.

9. You fell in love with someone from Japan, but he or she does not speak English.

8. You want to be called "King of Karaoke" at a local karaoke bar.

7. You want to be a bilingual business negotiator for your company.

6. You want to try out imported PlayStation games.

5. You want to travel to Japan and broaden your horizons.

4. You are thinking about becoming a Zen master.

3. You have Japanese in-laws.

2. You have a lot of Japanese friends, and you really want to know what they're talking about.

1. You don't know exactly *why*, but *why not?*

Whatever your reason, learning a foreign language is a rewarding experience. You can do many things using Japanese, whether in your business, your hobbies, or your personal life. Look at people around you. How many of them can speak Japanese? Not many. By having read this chapter, you're already a step ahead of the crowd. What are we waiting for? Let's get started.

The Least You Need to Know

- Learning Japanese will enrich your life in many ways.
- The keys to success in learning Japanese are confidence, courage, persistence, creativity, and imitation.
- Mistakes are positive experiences that can improve your Japanese.
- As long as your interest is there, Japanese is not a difficult language to conquer.

Behind the Language

In This Chapter

* Facts beyond the language make Japanese easy to learn
* What Japanese society is like
* The psychology of the Japanese people

If you are asked what Japan is known for, you might immediately think of cars, stereos, computers, *anime*, *sushi*, temples, and so on. Japan is certainly known for these. But when describing the country, these things suffice only superficially. Deeper knowledge of various aspects of Japan will help you learn Japanese with much more ease.

In this chapter, we explore Japan by looking at the land, people, society, culture, and mind. The more you know about Japan, the less of a culture shock you will experience if you visit. So let's forget about the mere "images" of Japan and learn the facts.

Geographic Facts About Japan

To Westerners in the nineteenth century, Japan was as far to the east of the prime meridian—0° longitude in Greenwich, England—as one could get and still be on dry land.

The Japanese people knew their nation was located in the Far East long before Westerners said so! In an official document that Japan sent to China in the seventh century C.E., the Japanese referred to their country as "the Land of the Rising Sun." In fact, the formal name of Japan, *Nippon* or *Nihon*, is written in *kanji* as a combination of the characters for "sun" and "origin."

Japan is an *archipelago* country—a country consisting of a chain of islands. Four main islands—Honshu, Hokkaido, Kyushu, and Shikoku—cover 95 percent of the total land area. Japan is approximately 150,000 square miles in size, slightly smaller than the state of California. Japan is not a big country, but it has 18,490 miles of coastline.

The population of Japan is roughly 127,000,000. Can you imagine 127,000,000 people squeezed into California? (For comparison, the population of California is 30,000,000.) Even more amazing, because more than 70 percent of Japan is mountainous, the population is concentrated in a few urban areas. There are 12 cities whose population exceeds 1,000,000. Tokyo, the capital of Japan, is the largest among those cities, with more than 8,000,000 people in its central district alone.

There are four distinct seasons almost everywhere in Japan. The winter in northern Japan is severe and snowy, but the summer is pleasantly cool. For example, in Hokkaido, the average temperature in summer is 71°F (21.7°C), and the average temperature in winter is 23°F (–4°C). On the other hand, in southern Japan, such as Kyushu, the average temperature in summer is 82°F (27.8°C), and in winter it is 50°F (10°C). If you go to Okinawa, farther south of Kyushu, you can even enjoy a Hawaiian-like vacation.

Japan also has a fifth, unofficial season called "Tsuyu." Tsuyu is the "rainy" season, which occurs usually from the middle of June to the middle of July. It brings higher temperatures, humidity, and rainfall to most of Japan.

Who Are the Japanese?

Japan is geographically isolated from the Asian continent. This factor made Japan's *national seclusion policy* easier from the early seventeenth century to the mid-nineteenth century, which kept Japan in peace for 215 years. In turn, however, Japan had very little contact with the rest of the world. There was almost no flow of people from outside Japan until the nineteenth century. Because of this, Japan is ethnically dense—98 percent of the residents of Japan are Japanese.

The majority of Japanese consider themselves "pure" Japanese. However, the Japanese race is actually a mixture of Pacific islanders and Continental Asian peoples (particularly peoples from areas such as northeastern China, the Korean Peninsula, and Mongolia). This mixture has made the Japanese language unique. The sounds of spoken Japanese resemble Pacific languages such as Hawaiian and Tahitian, whereas the grammar of Japanese resembles the grammar of languages such as Korean, Mongolian, Manchurian, and even Turkish.

Japanese Society

A society in which there are a variety of individuals and races tends to evolve into a diverse culture. The United States is a good example. Quite opposite of American society, Japanese society consists of an overwhelming majority of people from the same ethnic group—Japanese. As a result, Japanese society is very uniform and much less diverse than American society. Japanese society tends to be strongly dominated by social protocols and rituals. Getting accustomed to those protocols and rituals is crucial if you want to understand the society and its language.

Let's look at the Japanese culture in terms of interpersonal communication. When you meet a person for the first time, you must figure out who he is, what he does, what social status he has, and so on. This task is important for effective communication in Japanese: you have to adjust your greeting style and subsequent conversational style according to the social hierarchy established between you and him.

For example, there are a variety of ways to say "I'm going," depending on who you are talking to. Here are three versions of "I'm going," ranging from casual to very formal:

> *Iku.*
>
> *Ikimasu.*
>
> *Mairimasu.*

Many cultural rituals make communication smooth. You can compare this with conversation styles in American English. Casualness is typical in human interaction in a diverse society like America. You feel comfortable meeting with a stranger in a casual setting in which a conversation is carried out in an informal fashion. On the other hand, formality bears heavy weight on human interaction in a *homogeneous* society like Japan.

HUH?

By **homogeneous,** I mean "ethnically uniform." Japan is a homogeneous country because the majority of people living in Japan are from the same ethnic group. Note that I use this term loosely. As I mentioned earlier, there are minority groups of different ethnicities in Japan, too.

Living in a homogeneous society, Japanese people feel secure by being a loyal member of a rigid social structure. They feel extremely uncomfortable if placed outside their group. They try to remain in their "place" by obeying social obligations. This is illustrated by the famous old Japanese proverb, *Deru Kui-wa Utareru*—"A nail that sticks out is pounded down." This does not necessarily mean that Japanese people are exclusive or discriminating, however. Because of their group consciousness, they might not open the door to just anybody right away, but they will welcome those who respect their social values and culture.

In Chapter 1, I said it is extremely important to "Japanize" yourself if you want to master Japanese. By "Japanize," I mean that you need to become Japanese in thought. You probably know why by now. The most effective way to learn the language is to immerse yourself in the society. If you are resistant to adjusting your way of thinking, you probably will not be able to learn as much as you want to. Try not to compare the Japanese way of thinking to your own standards and be critical about it. Be open-minded to and accepting of the way Japanese people behave.

Communication for Peace and Harmony

The most important characteristic of the Japanese mind is "group consciousness." Having been isolated from the rest of the world for a long period of time, Japan still remains an almost perfectly homogeneous society. Wherever the Japanese go within their country, they see people who resemble them in looks as well as behavior. So to live in peace and harmony, the Japanese developed certain communication strategies. Here are three important principles you should keep in mind for better communication in Japanese.

SHORTCUTS TO SUCCESS

You might have noticed that Japanese people often say *eh* or *hai* during conversation. Besides "yes"—the common definition of these words—*eh* and *hai* also mean "I am listening to you." Try saying these words as you listen to people. It will make the conversation go more smoothly. Frequent use of these expressions does not mean you agree with whom you are speaking with, so don't worry!

Principle 1: No Matter Whom You Talk to, It's Safe to Be Polite

For people like you who want to learn Japanese, it's extremely important to give Japanese people the best possible first impression. With a good first impression, they are more likely to help you learn the language. Of course, the Japanese also have casual speech, which they use every day among friends and family members. In fact, because of its wide usage, some Japanese teachers teach their students very casual, informal Japanese. But I don't agree with this. If you were a kid who wanted to be immersed in school right away, sure, this would not be a bad idea.

However, I suspect most readers of this book are mature adults. Unlike kids whose first Japanese language encounter might be other kids who speak informal (and impolite) Japanese, chances are you will encounter a variety of people in Japan—businesspeople, teachers, home-stay families, immigration officers (!), and so on. If I were you, I wouldn't risk being mistaken for an obnoxious, impolite foreigner by picking up this informal form. Another reason I emphasize polite Japanese is because the conjugation of this form is far easier than that of casual speech.

Principle 2: Be Humble When Talking—a Good Listener Is a Better Communicator

Japanese people value humility. Remember the proverb "A nail that sticks out is pounded down"? The Japanese are extremely conscious of how they are perceived by other people and behave accordingly so that they will not stand out in a crowd. This characteristic is reflected in verbal communication as well. Japanese people tend to be receptive (and often passive) in communication to avoid confrontation.

In Western societies, verbal communication is active and people are trained to be good at argument and discussion. I remember my college experiences during my first couple of years in the States. I was very uncomfortable being in a discussion group or debate. As a result, I remained silent. My speech professor used to tell me that in America, if you don't speak up, people think you are dumb. It required a lot of courage for me to "speak up." Likewise, you might want to be conscious of your communication style when you speak Japanese. For Japanese, one needs to be less argumentative, even if you disagree with someone. Try to find agreeable points in your opponent's argument, admire them, and don't be afraid to accept his ideas. You might be amazed at how smoothly your conversations will follow.

Principle 3: Know the *TPO*

TPO stands for T(ime), P(lace), and O(ccasion):

T: A good speaker knows whether it is the *right time* to say something.

P: A good speaker knows whether he or she is in the *right place* with the right audience.

O: A good speaker knows whether it is the *right situation* to talk about something.

TPO is synonymous with "courteousness" or "good manners." TPO is the key to success in any language, but especially in Japanese. Japan is a group-conscious society, so speaking in front of the right audience is particularly important. Just make sure you look around before you speak. Is it the *right time* to say something? That is, are you speaking in turn, not surpassing anybody? Is it the *right place* to say something? That is, are you talking to the right audience? And, are you in the *right situation* to say something? That is, is the situation appropriate?

TPO is meant to help you become aware of the significance of relative social standing. It is *not* to discourage you from speaking up. Just by trying to be modest and paying attention to the situation surrounding you, and adhering to this principle, you can successfully converse in Japanese.

Merely learning Japanese grammar will make you an okay speaker, but knowing the rules of Japanese behavior will make you a better speaker. By being aware of the importance of behavior, your Japanese will sound more "Japanese."

The Least You Need to Know

- Deeper knowledge of Japan—including familiarity with Japanese geographical, demographical, and psychological facts—will make you a better speaker.
- Japan is an almost completely homogeneous society; group consciousness is woven throughout every aspect of social life.
- You will appear and sound natural if you conduct yourself and speak in harmony with the Japanese ways of thinking and behaving.
- What are the secrets of success in learning Japanese? Be polite! Be receptive! Be conscious of *TPO!*

Japanese Sounds: As Easy as *A, I, U, E, O*

In This Chapter

- Find out how simple Japanese sounds are
- Become accustomed to Japanese syllables
- Learn sounds that are commonly difficult for English speakers
- Keep *calm*

Unlike many commonly taught foreign languages, Japanese has a quite simple sound inventory. Japanese has only 14 *consonants* and 5 *vowels*; on the other hand, English has 24 consonants (including the semi-vowels, *y* and *w*) and although it, too, has 5 vowels, it has at least 12 vowel sounds. This is encouraging news for English-speaking students because most Japanese sounds are already in the English sound inventory. On the other hand, many Japanese speakers struggle with English pronunciation because they have to deal with many sounds that don't exist in their language.

Even though Japanese sounds are fairly simple, I don't think it's a good idea to underestimate them, especially when you've just started learning Japanese. Unfortunately, many Japanese textbooks don't tell readers how the Japanese sound system is organized. But without a clear understanding of it, how can you speak and understand Japanese properly?

HUH?

Consonants are speech sounds that are characterized by constriction or obstruction of airflow at varying points of the mouth or throat. For example, *t* is a consonant because to pronounce it you use the tongue to block airflow at the edge of the mouth between the upper teeth and the gum.

Vowels are speech sounds that are produced without any obstruction of airflow in the mouth. For example, *i* is a vowel because to pronounce it you push air forward and out smoothly, without using your tongue.

In this chapter, you will learn the basics of Japanese pronunciation, including the organization of the sound inventory, vowel lengthening, and accent patterns.

Keep Your Mouth Open, Please: Syllabication

Japanese *syllables* are almost always open-ended. What this means is that they always (with two exceptions—see the following "The Two Standalone Consonants" section) end in a vowel, not a consonant.

In Japanese, a possible syllable is composed of either a vowel alone, like *a, i, u, e, o,* or a consonant plus a vowel, as in *ka, ki, ku, ke, ko.* Each syllable has the same length. Because Japanese has such a restricted sound structure, only 102 syllables are possible in the entire Japanese sound inventory.

SHORTCUTS TO SUCCESS

As you read this book, make sure you articulate aloud all Japanese words, phrases, and sentences. Never read them silently. Clear articulation is the most effective way to make your brain recognize sounds as Japanese sounds. I emphasize this method from my own experience. My English learning was awful when I first started studying—because of my silent reading.

Keeping the Japanese style of syllabication in mind is important not only for learning vocabulary, but also for pronunciation. Because each syllable ends with a vowel, they are considered to have the same "weight"—that is, all Japanese syllables sound as though they have the same length.

HUH?

A **syllable** is a unit of spoken language that consists of a vowel or a vowel-like consonant alone, or a vowel or a vowel-like consonant pronounced with one or more consonant sounds before or after. For instance, the word *consonant* is divided into three syllables: *con-so-nant.*

Let's look at an example. The word *karaoke* has four syllables in Japanese (*ka-ra-o-ke*) and four syllables in English (*car-rie-oh-key*). In Japanese, each syllable sounds as though it has exactly the same length as the others. The syllables are short and open. If you have ever taken a music lesson, you must have seen a metronome—a device that assists a musician's timing by clicking in a perfectly uniform fashion: click, click, click. Japanese syllables are just like the clicks made by a metronome: *ka-ra-o-ke.* On the other hand, English syllables are not characterized by the same length. Listen to the English pronunciation: *car-rie-oh-key*. Perhaps you can hear the slight difference in length between "oh" and "key." Listen to the irregular length of the syllables in other examples like *Eng-lish* or *Jap-a-nese*. Do you hear the long "nese"?

If you want to sound like a Japanese person, keep your syllables short and even. You might practice Japanese syllables by clapping your hands or snapping your fingers to make sure each syllable is equal in length.

Remember that Japanese syllables are open-ended with vowels. This will help in your pronunciation because it means that your mouth remains open at the end of each sound. In other words, in Japanese your mouth is relaxed when speaking. If you watch Japanese people speak, pay attention to how they move their mouths. You will be surprised by how little their mouths move. This is because of open-ended syllables. To sound Japanese, just relax, try not to move your mouth too much, and keep it open.

All the Possible Japanese Sounds

 The following are tables of all possible Japanese syllables and sounds. (The five vowels *a, e, i, o, u* are traditionally listed in the order of *a, i, u, e, o* in Japanese.) Before we look at the tables, let's make sure you can pronounce each vowel correctly. The five Japanese vowels always make the same five sounds:

> [a] is pronounced *ah*, as in English "f<u>a</u>ther."
>
> [i] is pronounced *ee*, as in English "h<u>e</u>."
>
> [u] is pronounced *oo*, as in English "c<u>oo</u>l."
>
> [e] is pronounced *eh*, as in English "b<u>e</u>t."
>
> [o] is pronounced *oh*, as in English "b<u>o</u>re."

SHORTCUTS TO SUCCESS

When you pronounce Japanese vowels, try not to open your mouth too wide. By relaxing your mouth, you will be able to pronounce Japanese sounds naturally.

Each sound in the following tables is made by combining a consonant in the top column with a vowel in the leftmost row. For example, when the consonant *k* meets the vowel *i*, it is pronounced *ki*. (*ø* means that no consonant is attached; these are plain vowels.)

The Japanese Sounds

	ø	k	s	t	n	h	m	y	r	w
a	a	ka	sa	ta	na	ha	ma	ya	ra	wa
i	i	ki	shi	chi	ni	hi	mi		ri	
u	u	ku	su	tsu	nu	fu	mu	yu	ru	
e	e	ke	se	te	ne	he	me		re	
o	o	ko	so	to	no	ho	mo	yo	ro	

	g	z	d		b	p
a	ga	za	da		ba	pa
i	gi	ji			bi	pi
u	gu	zu			bu	pu
e	ge	ze	de		be	pe
o	go	zo	do		bo	po

	ky	sh	ch	ny	hy	my		ry
a	kya	sha	cha	nya	hya	mya		rya
u	kyu	shu	chu	nyu	hyu	myu		ryu
o	kyo	sho	cho	nyo	hyo	myo		ryo

	gy	j (= zy)		by	py
a	gya	ja		bya	pya
u	gyu	ju		byu	pyu
o	gyo	jo		byo	pyo

In traditional Japanese grammar, the Japanese sounds are divided into four separate tables, as seen previously. The sounds in the first table are considered "basic" sounds. The second table contains "relatives" of some of the sounds in the first table. *G* is a relative of *k*; *z* of *s*; *d* of *t*; and *b* and *p* are relatives of *h*. (In ancient Japanese, the *h* sounded similar to *p*, the "lip" sound.) The third table contains *y* on some of the basic sounds, and the fourth table contains *y* on the sounds in the second table.

Another reason why the Japanese sounds are represented in four separate tables is that Japanese *kana* characters are best illustrated this way (see Appendix A).

SHORTCUTS TO SUCCESS

There are some blanks in the tables, lacking sounds like *yi, ye, wi, wu, we, wo, di,* and *du*. These sounds do not exist in Japanese. For example, *yi* is pronounced the same as *i*, and *du* as *zu*.

> **SHORTCUTS TO SUCCESS**
>
> When *y* accompanies a consonant, as in *ky*, the only possible vowels that can be added after the *y* are *a, u,* and *o.*

The Two Standalone Consonants

In addition to the consonants discussed in the previous section, Japanese has two standalone consonants. A standalone consonant is a syllable that does not accompany a vowel. In Japanese, there are only two standalone consonants—the double consonant and *N.* Both are discussed in the following "Tricky Sounds" section.

Tricky Sounds

Although you can accurately pronounce most of the sounds just as they are spelled, there are some tricky sounds, such as the following:

tsu

Pronounce *tsu* just like the English *ts* in *ca̲t̲s̲.* Try the following word:

　　t̲s̲unami

fu

Unlike the English *f* sound, you don't bite your lower lip to make this sound in Japanese. To pronounce this sound, imagine you're blowing out a candle. This sound is pronounced somewhere between the English *h* and *f* sounds. Try the following word:

　　F̲u̲jita—the name of the author of this book

ra, ri, ru, re, ro

The Japanese *r* is by no means identical to the English *r.* When you make the *r* sound, try to lightly tap the back of your upper front teeth with the tip of your tongue. *Never* curl back the tip of your tongue as you do in English! For example, say "butter" very fast. This *tt* sound is very close to the Japanese *r.* Try the following words:

　　R̲a̲isu—"rice"　　　　　　　　*R̲e̲fute*—"left"

　　R̲i̲sa—"Lisa"　　　　　　　　*Pur̲o̲*—"pro(fessional)"

　　Hote̲r̲u̲—"hotel"

Position of the tongue for Japanese r (left) and English r (right).

wa

Unlike the English *w*, you don't round your lips when making this Japanese sound. Relax your mouth and keep it half open. Try the following word:

Watashi—"I; me"

y

In the preceding tables, you see a number of two-consonant sounds containing *y*, such as *kya* and *pyo*. Even though there are two consonants, this chunk of sounds is still considered one syllable. Try to pronounce them in one quick breath—"kya," "pyo"— instead of making two syllables, as in "ki-ya" and "pi-yo." Try the following words:

kyaNdoru (kya-N-do-ru) (four syllables)—"candle"

hyaku (hya-ku) (two syllables)—"hundred"

pyoNpyoN (pyo-N-pyo-N) (four syllables)—"hopping"

The Double Consonant

This standalone consonant is a silent sound. You might ask how Japanese can make a silent sound. English has this sound, too. Consider *Uh oh!* Between *Uh* and *oh*, there is a slight pause. The Japanese double consonant is like this slight pause. Look at the following words:

batto (ba-t-to) (three syllables)—"(baseball) bat"

poppu (po-p-pu) (three syllables)—"pop"

Both examples have three syllables, but the actual pronunciation can be described as follows:

bat-to   *pop-pu*

Again, the hyphen indicates a momentary break between the syllables.

Remember, this is a standalone consonant, so it carries the same length as a syllable. Make sure you are able to distinguish *ki<u>tt</u>e* ("stamp") from *kite* ("Come!"). The former word has three syllables, and the latter only two.

LIFESAVERS

When a vowel follows *N*, make sure the *N* is pronounced separately from the following vowel. For example, one of the common male names, *Shinichi*, is pronounced *Shi-N-i-chi*, not *Shi-ni-chi* (four syllables versus three syllables). In some cases, this might lead to miscommunication. For example, *shi-N-a-i* means "dear," but *shi-na-i* means "bamboo sword."

N

This is also a standalone consonant, which carries the same length as an ordinary syllable. The way you make this sound is quite different from the "regular" *n*. You know that to pronounce the regular *n*, the tip of your tongue touches the back of the upper teeth (actually, the edge between the teeth and the gum). On the other hand, pronunciation of this standalone *n* (represented in this book by a capital letter, *N*) requires that your tongue touch *nowhere* in the mouth. The sound is actually made in the throat. Try the following words:

ho<u>N</u>da (ho-N-da) (three syllables)—"Honda"

ko<u>N</u>nichiwa (ko-N-ni-chi-wa) (five syllables)—"hello; good afternoon"

ko<u>N</u>ba<u>N</u>wa (ko-N-ba-N-wa) (five syllables)—"good evening"

Please keep in mind that this standalone *N* never appears at the beginning of a word. If you see the uppercase *N* at the beginning of any word, it should be pronounced as the regular *n*, not the standalone *N*.

I strongly suggest that you read all the examples aloud in the subsequent chapters, paying attention to the preceding sounds (especially the *r* sound). Remember, silent reading is a waste of time in language learning. *Ga<u>N</u>batte (Ga-N-bat-te)*—"Good luck!"

My Husband Is a Prisoner? Importance of Long Vowels

 Japanese contains both short and long vowels. A long vowel should be clearly pronounced exactly twice as long as a short vowel.

The length of a vowel is very important. Compare the following pairs. (Note that the macron symbol ¯ indicates a long vowel.)

> *shujiN* (three syllables)—"husband"
> *shu-ji-N*
>
> *shūjiN* (four syllables)—"prisoner"
> *shu-u-ji-N*

The only difference between *shujin* and *sh—ujin* is the length of the vowel *u*, but the meaning is so different between the two! (What? No difference?) Here are a few more similar pairs:

> *obasaN* (four syllables)—"aunt"
> *o-ba-sa-N*
> *obāsaN* (five syllables)—"grandmother"
> *o-ba-a-sa-N*
>
> *nyūyoku* (four syllables)—"bathing"
> *nyu-u-yo-ku*
> *nyūyōku* (five syllables)—"New York"
> *nyu-u-yo-o-ku*

Remember, Japanese rhythm is uniform, just like a metronome. Practice these pairs by clapping your hands or snapping your fingers to maintain the same interval between syllables.

Japanizing English Words

 Japanese words do not have English cognates, but even as you begin to learn Japanese, you might find some words that are familiar to you. Those words are called *loanwords*. Japanese has a lot of Western loanwords called *gairaigo*, the majority of which have been borrowed from English.

HUH?

A **loanword** is a word imported from another language's word inventory. In Japanese, there are two types of loanwords—*gairaigo* (words that come from Western languages, especially English) and *kango* (words that come from Chinese). Most of *gairaigo* is relatively new to Japanese, whereas the history of *kango* is much longer. Some of the oldest *kango* are probably 1,600 years old.

This is good news for you because it increases your chances that Japanese people will understand common English nouns you say. However, when it comes to you hearing English-based loanwords in Japanese, it isn't always good news. Those words are so "Japanized" that they might not sound like English at all.

As Japanese has fewer sounds than English, many English sounds must be substituted with the closest-possible Japanese sounds. Here are those sounds with substitution examples:

- *L*—English *l* is replaced by *r* in Japanese. So both *blues* and *Bruce* are pronounced as *burūsu*.

- *TH*—English *th* is replaced by *s* or *z* in Japanese. The words *third* and *that* are pronounced as *sādo* and *zatto*, respectively. You might have heard the Japanese saying *saNkyū* for "Thank you."

- *V*—English *v* is replaced by *b* in Japanese. For example, *violin* is pronounced *baioriN*. Both *vest* and *best* are pronounced *besuto*.

- *F*—English *f* is replaced by the Japanese version of *f*. The Japanese *f* does not involve biting the lower lip. Instead, it's somewhere between an *f* and an *h*, very much like the light puff of breath used to blow out a candle. In certain English dialects (like the Southern accent in America), *wh* as in *what* or *which*, sounds like the Japanese *f*. Try to pronounce the following words without biting the lower lip: *faN* ("fan"), *fiNraNdo* ("Finland"), *kafe* ("café"), *fōku* ("fork" or "folk").

Because of the sound discrepancies between English and Japanese, when it comes to pronunciation, sometimes it's safer and less stressful to regard English-based loanwords *not* as English words. Actually, they're on permanent loan, and they're not going to be returned. Most important, when you pronounce English-based loanwords, make sure you obey the following rules:

- Use Japanese sounds.

- Attach a vowel to a consonant.

- Do not use English accents.

Keeping these rules in mind, try "Japanizing" the following common food-related loanwords.

English Words in Japanese Pronunciation

English Words	"Japanized" Pronunciation
beer	*bīru (bi-i-ru)*
hamburger	*haNbāgā (ha-N-ba-a-ga-a)*
steak	*sutēki (su-te-e-ki)*
soup	*supu (su-u-pu)*
salad	*sarada (sa-ra-da)*
juice	*jūsu (ju-u-su)*
coffee	*kōhī (ko-o-hi-i)*
cake	*kēki (ke-e-ki)*

Japanese Is a Calm Language

Every language has its unique intonation pattern, and this characteristic makes a language sound musical, strong, harsh, mellow, and so on. To me, English sounds very rhythmical. This rhythmic characteristic arises from the pattern of strong and weak accents. Even within a word like *television*, there are two accents:

> *tél-e-vì-sion*

In "television," *tel* has the primary accent, *vi* has the secondary accent, and the syllables *e* and *sion* carry no accents. This regular sequence between an accented syllable and a nonaccented syllable makes English very rhythmical.

What do you think about Japanese? How does Japanese sound to you? Does it sound as rhythmical as English? It probably doesn't. Japanese words don't carry as regular an accent/nonaccent sequence as heard in English. Instead, Japanese words are pronounced in a rather monotone, flat fashion. For example, take a look at the words *Yokohama* and *konnichiwa* ("hello"). English speakers tend to pronounce these words like this:

> *Yò-ko-há-ma (há = primary accent, Yò = secondary accent)*

> *kon-ní-chi-wà (ní = primary accent, wà = secondary accent)*

To Japanese ears, these pronunciations would sound heavily accented. If you want to speak Japanese like the Japanese, first try to forget the English accent pattern, and then *calmly* say the words while maintaining the same length on each syllable.

> *Yo-ko-ha-ma*
>
> *Ko-N-ni-chi-wa*

Some impersonators are amazingly good at sounding just like someone else. But this doesn't mean that they have special vocal cords. They first listen very carefully to people repeatedly, trying to figure out their intonation, pitch, and pronunciation. Then, they imitate those distinctive patterns.

SHORTCUTS TO SUCCESS

One of my students had a very strong accent when speaking Japanese. To help him fix this problem, I told him to "turn down the volume a little bit." The result was incredible. Even he could not believe himself! So if you're a loud speaker, try this method. Even if you aren't, it's worth giving it a try because toning down the volume results in less movement of the mouth, which is essential in articulating natural Japanese sounds.

Language learning is the same as what impersonators do. Listen carefully to how Japanese people talk. If there is no one who speaks Japanese around you, rent a Japanese video. You don't have to try to understand what they say. Close your eyes and concentrate on just listening. Listen to the CD included with this book, and keep listening until you're confident that you can say those phrases like a native Japanese speaker. This will not only improve your oral/aural skills, it will also give you confidence.

The Least You Need to Know

- Japanese syllables are uniform in length. Except for two special consonants, the *N* and the double consonant, all syllables are open-ended with a vowel.
- Among the 102 Japanese syllables, you should pay special attention to *tsu, fu, ra, ri, ru, re, ro, wa,* double consonants, and *N*.
- A long vowel should be clearly pronounced exactly twice as long as a short vowel.
- Avoid putting strong stresses on words and speak calmly.

The Survival Skills: Grammar

Language learning can be like mountain climbing. For a fun and safe experience, you must be prepared and fully equipped with all the necessities, such as food, warm clothing, a sturdy ice ax, rope, and so on.

Like mountain climbing, a new language is full of unexpected events. Besides greetings and idioms, people might not speak exactly the same way you do, nor use exactly the same phrases or words. So how can you be prepared for such unexpected events? The answer is simple: you must be fully equipped, and the most basic, necessary tool is grammar.

With an overview of the grammar, you will be able to not only construct sentences, but also understand newly introduced patterns. I guarantee that after carefully going through these chapters, you will find the rest of this book much easier. For those who think grammar is dry and unappealing, I have gone to great efforts to make these chapters as simple and informative as possible.

Speak Like Yoda: Basic Sentence Structure

In This Chapter

- Japanese as a "free word order" language
- Functions of particles
- The concept of topic
- Dropping phrases

"Do or do not, there is no try!"—Yoda

I'm a big fan of Yoda, a revered Jedi master in the *Star Wars* saga. When George Lucas created this character, he must have had an Asian hermit in mind. Yoda's word order is a little *different*. If Yoda were the author of this book, he would probably say something like, *"Today, something teach you I will. Grammar that is. Ready are you?"*

Was the language model for Yoda Chinese or Japanese? Chinese word order is similar to English word order; Yoda would not speak like that. I think that the language model for Yoda was Japanese. If I translate Japanese into English as literally as I can, it sounds like something Yoda would say.

A bizarre word order in one language might be a perfectly normal word order in another. In this chapter, let's see what Japanese sentences really "look" like. Ready are you? You will be!

Godzilla Ate John, or John Ate Godzilla?

The English language has what is known as a *fixed word order*. That is, every sentence is arranged in pretty much the same fashion, with the sequence of subject-verb-object. Let's look at the following English example to illustrate a fixed word order:

John gave *sushi* to Lisa.

If you're a native speaker of English, you probably don't say something like "To Lisa *sushi* John gave," even though it might make sense. How about using a different word order, such as "*Sushi* gave to Lisa John"? Does this mean "John gave *sushi* to Lisa"? No, this is just gibberish!

In Japanese, however, you can "scramble" words pretty much in any order you like, and this scrambled sentence still means "John gave *sushi* to Lisa." Let me translate this English sentence into Japanese (*age-mashita* = "gave"):

John-ga Lisa-ni sushi-o *age-mashita.*	"John to Lisa *sushi* gave."
John-ga sushi-o *Lisa-ni age-mashita.*	"John *sushi* to Lisa gave."
Lisa-ni John-ga sushi-o *age-mashita.*	"To Lisa John *sushi* gave."
Lisa-ni sushi-o *John-ga age-mashita.*	"To Lisa *sushi* John gave."
Sushi-o *John-ga Lisa-ni age-mashita.*	"*Sushi* John to Lisa gave."
Sushi-o *Lisa-ni John-ga age-mashita.*	"*Sushi* to Lisa John gave."

Wow! Isn't it amazing? As long as the *verb* stays at the end of the sentence, you can scramble all the other items, and they remain perfectly grammatical! The sentence structure of Japanese is characterized (very basically) by the following statement:

> In Japanese, the verb comes last.

A Quick Grammar Review

A quick grammar review might be in order before we talk more about Japanese sentence structure. Don't worry—we don't need to get into a lot of terminology here. We'll keep all definitions on the simplest level.

As you might recall from your grammar class, every sentence is made up of two main parts—a subject and a predicate. The subject is the person, idea, animal, or thing being described; the predicate is the explanation of the action of the subject. Subjects are usually nouns; predicates are usually verbs and the words that go with them to modify the noun. So in the sentence …

> John gave *sushi* to Lisa.

… the predicate is "gave *sushi* to Lisa." The verb (gave) modifies the subject (John). A good way to find the subject of a sentence, in fact, is to locate the verb and ask who or what is performing the verb's action. In this case, who or what "gave"? The answer is "John." Therefore, "John" is the subject of the sentence.

"John" is also the subject of the following three sentences. Notice that in addition to the verb, the predicate can contain adjectives and nouns as well:

John *ate pizza.*

John *is tall.*

John *is a student.*

The sentence "John gave *sushi* to Lisa" also provides a helpful refresher on the role of direct and indirect objects. The object of a sentence, in simplest terms (there are some exceptions), is the noun that is **directly** affected by the verb. "John gave," but what did he give? The answer is "*sushi*," so "*sushi*" is the direct object.

The indirect object (again, in simplest terms) is the person or thing to whom something is given, said, or shown. It is the noun that is **indirectly** affected by the verb. "John gave *sushi*," but to whom or what did he give it? The answer is "Lisa," so "Lisa" is the indirect object in this sentence.

Here's an easy way to tell direct and indirect objects apart in English: indirect objects usually have a **preposition** in front of them (as in "John gave *sushi* **to** Lisa"), whereas direct objects don't have one (for example, "John ate *pizza*").

HUH?

A **preposition** is a connecting word that shows the relationship of a noun or pronoun to some other word in a sentence.

Don't worry if you're a little rusty in this area. As you read through the exercises in this book, you'll get stronger at instinctively recognizing the relationship of the nouns to the verbs in a sentence. And, as you'll find out later in this chapter, you sometimes don't even have to include all the nouns in a sentence to be understood!

Particles

Did you notice in all of our "*John-ga Lisa-ni* sushi-o *age-mashita*" examples, that some tiny suffixes were attached to the nouns, such as *-o*, *-ga*, *-ni?* Thanks to these markers, we don't get confused no matter what order the nouns are used in a sentence. In a sentence with only two nouns, scrambling the words could be confusing in English:

John Godzilla ate.

Godzilla John ate.

In either case, it isn't clear who did the eating and who got eaten. But the tiny markers make any arrangement in Japanese perfectly clear:

Godzilla-ga John-o tabe-mashita.   "Godzilla ate John."

John-o Godzilla-ga tabe-mashita.   "Godzilla ate John."

The good news is that word order is flexible. The not-so-good news is that a sentence conveys a totally different meaning if you attach a wrong marker to a word, so you have to be diligent about learning particles. Who is the poor victim, John or Godzilla? Whoever it might be, one tiny particle makes a huge difference! Let's learn more about particles.

Particles: Tiny but Mighty!

Learning Japanese will be much easier if you familiarize yourself with those helpful markers called *particles*. (They're called *particles*, as in chemistry, because they're so tiny.) Bear in mind that every noun must accompany the appropriate particle in a Japanese sentence. In other words, particles are noun markers that reveal the relationship of the attached noun to the verb.

Here is a list of important particles. These are not all the particles, but the most basic.

Basic Particles

Particle	Function
-ga	subject marker
-o	object marker
-ni	"toward"; "in" (existence marker); "at" (time marker)
-mo	"also"
-kara	"from"
-made	"up to"; "until"
-de	"by means of"; "in; at" (activity marker)
-to	"together with"
-wa	topic marker

As I mentioned earlier, each of these particles is attached to a noun, and this noun with the particle indicates its grammatical relation to the verb. Let's look at each particle in depth.

-ga: Subject Marker

Subject, as I discussed previously, means someone or something of which something is said. The subject particle *-ga* is used in the following three cases:

- Identification of "doer"
- Someone/something that exists in a certain location
- Description of an unexpected or surprising event

Identification of "Doer"

By *doer*, I mean a person who causes something to happen. If John throws the ball to Tom, John is the doer (or "subject"), so "John" would get the subject marker *-ga*, as in *John-ga*. Let's consider a simpler sentence. The sentence "John cried" would be …

> *JoN-ga naki-mashita.*   "John cried."

Look at another example:

> *JoN-ga tabe-mashita.*   "John ate."

John is the doer of "crying" in the first example and of "eating" in the second example. Therefore, we attach *-ga* to it.

HUH?

Use *i-masu* when referring to the existence of something "animate" (for example, John, person, dog, and so on), and use *ari-masu* when referring to the existence of something "inanimate" (for example, pizza, pencil, and so on).

Someone/Something That Exists in a Certain Location

In English, when you describe someone or something as being in a certain location, you use the phrase *there is/are*, such as "There is a boy in the park," or "There are vases in the room." I will call these verbs "existence verbs." In Japanese, the equivalent existence verbs are *i-masu* and *ari-masu*. When you describe someone or something being in a certain place, the person or thing is marked by *-ga*.

> *JoN-**ga** i-masu.*   "John is there."
>
> *Piza-**ga** ari-masu.*   "There is pizza."

Description of an Unexpected or Surprising Event

When you want to describe something unexpected or surprising happening, attach -*ga* to the event noun. First, consider such events in English. When you see the bus coming earlier than the scheduled time, you alert your friend by saying, "Here comes the bus!" This is expressed in Japanese as follows:

> *Basu-**ga** ki-mashita!*   "(*Lit.*) The bus came!"

Consider another example. Suppose the lights go out. This unexpected event would be described as follows:

> *Raito-ga kie-mashita!*   "The lights went out!"
> (*kie-masu* = "go out")

HUH?

An **adjective** is a word that describes, or modifies, a noun. For example, in the phrase *a smart dog* and the sentence *My dog is smart*, "smart" is an adjective because it describes the noun "dog."

The preceding examples contain verbs ("come" and "go out"); however, an unexpected or surprising event can be described by an *adjective* as well. Suppose that you go to a pizza parlor in Tokyo and are surprised at its outrageous prices. This would be described in Japanese as follows:

> *Piza-ga taka-idesu!*   "Pizza is expensive!"
> (*taka-idesu* = "is expensive")

-*o:* Object Marker

Object, as discussed earlier, means someone or something that is affected by a certain action. So in "John ate pizza," "pizza" is the object of "ate," and in "John loves Lisa," "Lisa" is the object of "loves." An object noun is marked by -*o*, as in the following examples:

> *Piza-**o** tabe-te!*   "Eat pizza!"
>
> *JoN-ga Tomu-**o** shikari-mashita.*   "John scolded Tom."

-ni: "toward"; "in"

This particle has two major functions. One function is to show "destination," which is equivalent to *toward* in English.

> *JoN-ga Pari-**ni** iki-masu.*   "John will go to Paris."
>
> *JoN-**ni** piza-o age-te!*   "Give the pizza to John!"

Notice that in these examples, Paris is the destination of "going" and John is the destination of "giving (pizza)."

The other function is to specify the location in which someone/something exists. This is equivalent to the English *in*.

> *JoN-ga kicchiN-**ni** i-masu.*   "John is in the kitchen."
>
> *Piza-ga furīzā-**ni** ari-masu.*   "There is pizza in the freezer."

-mo: "also"

The particle *-mo* means "also." If you want to put "also" on the subject noun, as in "Tom also came," mark the subject noun with *-mo* instead of the subject marker *-ga*. This is illustrated as follows:

> *JoN-ga ki-mashita. Tomu-**mo** ki-mashita.*   "John came. Tom **also** came."

If you want to put "also" on the object noun, as in "Order fried chicken also," mark the object noun with *-mo* instead of the object marker *-o*. This is illustrated as follows:

> *Piza-o tanoN-de! Furaido chikiN-**mo** tanoN-de!*
> "Order pizza! Order fried chicken, **too**!"

HUH?

The particle *-mo* ("also") replaces the subject particle *-ga* and the object particle *-o*. However, for particles other than subject and object markers, *-mo* is simply added on to the particle:

JoN-ga Yokohama-ni iki-mashita. Hiroshima-ni-mo iki-mashita.
"John went to Yokohama. He also went to Hiroshima."

Notice that the particle *-ni* remains with *-mo*.

-kara: "from" / *-made:* "up to"; "until"

The particles *-kara* and *-made* are the same as the English prepositions "from" and "until," respectively. The only difference is, of course, that in Japanese these particles are not *pre*positions—they are *post*positions, and they are attached at the end of nouns, just like all Japanese particles:

> *JoN-ga Kurisumasu-**kara** BareNtaiNdē-**made** Hawai-ni i-masu.*
> "John will be in Hawaii from Christmas to Valentine's Day."

Note that *-made* also means "up to," referring to the destination of some action such as "going." It is similar to the particle *-ni*, but *-made* implies that you do not go beyond that point. *-Kara* and *-made* are often used in a pair, as seen in the next example:

> *JoN-ga Pari-**kara** Rōma-**made** iki-masu.*
> "John will go from Paris to Rome."

-de: "by means of"; "at"

This particle has two major functions. One is to state "by means of":

> *JoN-ga basu-**de** BosutoN-ni iki-masu.*   "John will go to Boston by bus."

The other function is to specify the location at which some activity takes place:

> *KicchiN-**de** beNkyō shi-te!*   "Study in the kitchen."

-to: "together with"

This is straightforward and easy! You simply add *-to* to a person to show the "with" relationship:

> *JoN-ga Tomu-**to** Pari-ni iki-masu.*   "John will go to Paris with Tom."

 LIFESAVERS

Note that the other location particle *-ni* specifies "existence," not an activity.

Some particles function the same as English prepositions, but remember again that in Japanese they are postpositions. You might need some time to get used to the subject and object markers because they are new concepts to English speakers.

We have quickly covered the basic particles. You might be wondering why I skipped one of the particles—*wa*, the "topic" particle. I left it out because it is a very important particle that requires a section of its own for explanation.

Before talking about the "topic" particle *-wa*, how about a short review? I will give you several sentences with blanks. Fill in the appropriate particles. With the translation, you should be able to understand each sentence.

1. "John ate *sushi* at the restaurant with Tom."
   JoN-____ resutoraN-____ Tomu-____ sushi-____ tabe-mashita.

2. "John came from Paris."
   JoN-____ Pari-____ ki-mashita.

3. "Please come by bus!"
   Basu-____ ki-te!

4. "Tom came. John also came."
   Tomu-____ ki-masita. JoN-____ ki-mashita.

How was it? Here are the answers:

1. *-ga, -de, -to, -o*

2. *-ga, -kara*

3. *-de*

4. *-ga, -mo*

For speakers whose native language has a strict word order, it will take some time to get used to the idea of attaching a particle to every noun. However, when you become accustomed, the rest is easy. You can say a sentence pretty much in "free" word order as long as you put the verb at the end.

In a sense, Japanese is an easy language because the word order is not rigid. Don't be afraid. Speak out! You will be amazed at how much Japanese you speak that will be understood by Japanese people.

GREEN TEA BREAK

The topic-comment structure is a manifestation of Japanese psychology. As explained in Chapter 2, Japanese people are conscious of their position in a given conversation. They do their best not to be considered egocentric by the listener, so they listen and speak carefully. The notion of "topic" makes doing the previously mentioned functions easy.

The Concept of "Topic"

Besides the extensive use of particles, perhaps the most significant feature Japanese has, but English doesn't, is the concept of "topic." When you talk with someone in Japanese, you provide the listener with the "topic" of the dialogue by marking it with *-wa*. Because of this characteristic, I call Japanese a "listener-friendly" language.

The "topic" has the following two functions:

- "Topic" lets the listener know that you are going to talk about X.
- "Topic" assures the listener that you and he are still talking about X.

"Topic" is a new concept to English speakers. It might be helpful to think of Japanese sentence structure in the following way:

Japanese Sentence = TOPIC + COMMENT

When you state a certain topic, the rest of the sentence is your "comment" about the topic.

Let's look at an example. With the particles you've learned so far, let's translate "John ate cake on Christmas." This sentence has three possible topics— "John," "on Christmas," and "cake." The one you want to talk about is the one you attach *-wa* to. If you want to let the listener know that you're going to talk about John, or if you want to assure the listener that you and he are still talking about John, you must mark John with the topic particle *-wa:*

*JoN-**wa** Kurisumasu-ni kēki-o tabe-mashita.*

This sentence means something like "As for John (*or* Speaking of John), he ate cake on Christmas."

Similarly, if you want to talk about "on Christmas," the sentence looks like this:

*Kurisumasu-ni-**wa** JoN-ga kēki-o tabe-mashita.*

This sentence means "Let me talk about a particular day, that is, Christmas. On Christmas, John ate cake."

If you want to talk about the "cake," you then should mark the word "cake" with the topic particle -*wa*:

> *Kēki-**wa** JoN-ga Kurisumasu-ni tabe-mashita.*

LIFESAVERS

When a subject or an object becomes a "topic," the topic particle -*wa* completely replaces -*ga* and -*o*. In the case of other particles, on the other hand, -*wa* is added on to the existing particle, as in *Kurisumasu-ni-wa*, "on Christmas."

This sentence means "Let me talk about a particular food, that is, cake. John ate it on Christmas."

In summary, anything can be made a topic by placing it with the topic particle -*wa* at the beginning of a sentence. Without a topic in Japanese, a sentence might sound unkind or unnatural.

At this point, just be aware of the function of -*wa*. In the rest of the book, you will see numerous examples with -*wa*, so you will eventually get used to it.

Simple Is Beautiful

Japanese sentences might sometimes appear incomplete because they lack a subject or an object. This is illustrated in the next example:

> *Tōkyō-ni iki-mashita.*   "I went to Tokyo."

The English translation shows that the subject is "I," but the Japanese sentence does not have "I" in it; it literally reads something like, "To Tokyo, went." You could add *watashi*, "I," as the topic of this sentence, as seen in the following, but it is not necessary:

> *(Watashi-wa) Tōkyō-ni iki-mashita.*   "I went to Tokyo."

In Japanese, if a phrase is understood between you and the listener in a given context, you can drop the phrase. In the previous example, you are sure that the listener knows you are talking about yourself, so "I" is omitted. Suppose that you and the listener are talking about "going to Tokyo." In this case, "to Tokyo" is also understood between the two of you, so you can drop it, too, as you can see in the following sentence:

Iki-mashita. "(I) went (to Tokyo)."

Wow! Amazing, isn't it? In English, you can't omit phrases even if they are understood. Instead of dropping them, you use pronouns, such as "it," "them," "he," and so on. In reply to a question like "Did you meet Lisa?" you don't say "Yes, I met" or "Yes, met" in English. For this reason, many students of Japanese first think that Japanese is a "broken" language. On the surface, it might appear so, but on the context level, it is not broken at all, just efficient.

Before closing this chapter, take a simple quiz. I will give you English sentences, and your task is to translate them into Japanese. The answers are at the end of the chapter. Don't worry about word order. Just check to see whether you've used the correct particles. The topic phrase is also indicated in each question.

Review Quiz

1. John (= topic) swam in the pool with Tom.
   (swam = *oyogi-mashita*)

   _____

2. As for the pizza (= topic), Lisa ate it.
   (ate = *tabe-mashita*)

   _____

3. I (= understood topic) went from Chicago to Boston.
   (went = *iki-mashita*)

   _____

4. John (= topic) was in the bar.
   (was = *i-mashita*)

   _____

Okay, that's it! As far as basic sentence structure is concerned, you've got it. After you have a good handle on this chapter, you should be able to follow all the sentences in this book.

Answers

1. John (= topic) swam in the pool with Tom.
   JoN-wa pūru-de Tomu-to oyogi-mashita.

2. As for the pizza (= topic), Lisa ate it.
   Piza-wa Risa-ga tabe-mashita.

3. I (= understood topic) went from Chicago to Boston.
   Shikago-kara BosutoN-made iki-mashita.

4. John (= topic) was in the bar.
   JoN-wa Bā-ni i-mashita.

The Least You Need to Know

- Particles are noun markers that show the relation of nouns to verbs.

- As long as you add the correct particle to each noun and put the verb at the end, you can say a Japanese sentence in any word order you want.

- The fastest way to master Japanese is to constantly pay attention to "topic." Know what is being discussed in a given dialogue and mark it with -*wa*.

- English has pronouns (it, them, and so on) to refer to already mentioned phrases, whereas Japanese often drops them.

Everything You Need to Know About Conjugation

In This Chapter

- The concept of conjugation
- Verb endings
- Adjective endings
- Noun endings

You've learned the sound system (see Chapter 3) and basic sentence structure (see Chapter 4). After you familiarize yourself with some more grammatical items in this and the following chapter, you'll be ready to start speaking Japanese!

Conjugation Is No Headache!

Those who have learned languages such as Spanish and French might suspect that Japanese conjugation is complicated and painful to master. Is it really? Let's consider Spanish. Although Spanish is known as being a relatively easy language to learn, you still have to deal with a complex conjugation system. The *conjugation* of a verb in Spanish depends on whether the subject is in first, second, or third person and whether the subject is singular or plural. Not to mention that this is just for a particular tense—you need to learn conjugations for multiple tenses.

HUH?

Conjugation is the transformation of a verb in a sentence based on such considerations as number, person, voice, mood, and tense. In English, for example, *walk* is conjugated as *walks* if its subject is third person singular and *walked* if it is in past tense.

English conjugation is also complicated, but in a different way. Hundreds of irregular verbs exist, such as *break, broke,* and *broken*. There is no easy way to systematically learn irregular verbs. You have to memorize each one of them—quite an ordeal!

Will the Japanese conjugation system haunt you like other languages? Not a chance! It's comparatively simple. Japanese grammar is not concerned with marking gender (masculine, feminine, or even neutral), number (singular or plural), or person (first, second, or third). For example, *tabe-masu* ("to eat") does not undergo any change whether the subject is *John, Mary, we, you, they,* or whomever!

All you need to know to conjugate words in Japanese is whether the *predicate* is (1) present or past tense, and (2) affirmative or negative. That's all!

HUH?

A **predicate** is the verb or phrase that modifies the subject of a sentence. See Chapter 4 for more information.

Basically, there are three types of predicates in Japanese—verb predicates, adjective predicates, and noun predicates. Here is an English example for each type:

John *ate* pizza.　　　[verb predicate]

John *is tall.*　　　　　[adjective predicate]

John *is a student.*　　[noun predicate]

In each example, the italicized phrase is the core of the sentence, the predicate. Because there are three types of predicates in Japanese, there are three types of conjugations. Let's look at each predicate in Japanese and its method of conjugation.

Verb Predicate Conjugation

Let's use the verb *watch* as an example and look at its conjugation in English. Keep in mind that two considerations affect conjugation: (1) present tense or past tense, and (2) whether the predicate is affirmative or negative. In English, the verb *watch* undergoes the following conjugation:

Conjugation of the Verb "Watch"

	Affirmative	Negative
Present	watch	do not watch
Past	watched	did not watch

Notice that the suffix -*ed* is attached to *watch* in the affirmative past tense. Japanese conjugation is similar to the way *watch-ed* is created. That is, you attach the appropriate suffix for any of the four forms a verb might be conjugated in. In other words, the affirmative present tense, affirmative past tense, negative present tense, and negative past tense each has its own distinctive suffix. The following table shows which suffix follows the verb in verb predicate conjugation:

Conjugation Suffixes for Verbs

	Affirmative	Negative
Present	VERB + *masu*	VERB + *maseN*
	(do)	(not)
Past	VERB + *mashita*	VERB + *maseN-deshita*
	(did)	(not-did)

Note that as indicated in the previous table, *masu* is equivalent to the English "do," *mashita* is equivalent to "did," *maseN* is equivalent to "not," and *maseN-deshita* is equivalent to "not-did." These English words are known as "helping verbs." In Japanese, the helping verbs are tacked onto the ending of a verb.

Let's go over each conjugation more thoroughly with an example verb, *mi* ("to watch").

When you use a verb in the affirmative present tense, such as *I watch TV*, the suffix *masu* is attached to the verb, as in:

> *mi-masu* ("watch" + "do")

When you use a verb in the affirmative past tense, such as *I watched TV*, the suffix *mashita* is attached to the verb, as in:

> *mi-mashita* ("watch" + "did")

When you use a verb in the negative present tense, such as *I don't watch TV*, the suffix *maseN* is attached to the verb, as in:

> *mi-maseN* ("watch" + "not")

Finally, when you use a verb in the negative past tense, such as *I did not watch TV*, the suffixes *maseN* and *deshita* are attached to the verb, as in:

> *mi-maseN-deshita* ("watch" + "not" + "did")

Verb conjugation is shown in the following table:

Verb Conjugation

	Affirmative	**Negative**
Present	*mi-masu* ("watch")	*mi-maseN* ("do not watch")
Past	*mi-mashita* ("watched")	*mi-maseN-deshita* ("didn't watch")

I want to emphasize again that Japanese does not have any grammatical markers for gender, number, or person. The preceding chart is "universal" for any verb.

For verb conjugation, all you have to remember is the ending of each function: *-masu*, *-mashita*, *-maseN*, and *-maseN-deshita*. The verb element that attaches to those endings, like *mi-*, is called the "verb stem."

This exercise shows a few verbs in various endings. Try to identify the stem of each example:

Exercise 1

1. *kakimashita* ("wrote")   _____

2. *hanashimaseN* ("does not speak")   _____

3. *ikimaseNdeshita* ("didn't go")   _____

4. *yomimasu* ("reads")   _____

How did you do? Check the answers at the end of this chapter. Here is another exercise. Conjugate each of the following verbs as instructed.

Exercise 2

1. *kaeri* ("to go home") (to negative present form)

_____

2. *oyogi* ("to swim") (to affirmative past form)

_____

3. *naki* ("to cry") (to negative past form)

_____

4. *iki* ("to go") (to affirmative present form)

_____

The order of conjugation for verbs is schematized as follows:

Verb Stem	+	(Negative)	+	Tense	Translation
mi				*masu*	"watch"
mi				*mashita*	"watched"
mi		*maseN*			"don't watch"
mi		*maseN*		*deshita*	"didn't watch"

Getting back to the original example, let's make actual sentences using "watch TV" (*terebi* = TV).

*JoN-wa terebi-o mi-**masu***.	"John watches (*or* will watch) TV."
*JoN-wa terebi-o mi-**mashita***.	"John watch**ed** TV."
*JoN-wa terebi-o mi-**maseN***.	"John does**n't** watch (*or* won't watch) TV."
*JoN-wa terebi-o mi-**maseN-deshita***.	"John **didn't** watch TV."

You might have noticed in the examples that *mi-masu* means both "watches" and "will watch" and *mi-maseN* means both "doesn't watch" and "won't watch." In Japanese, present tense takes care of present as well as future tense. In other words, Japanese tense is either "past" or "*non*past." This makes Japanese conjugation even easier, doesn't it?

In the next exercise, translate the English sentences into Japanese. This time you will need to find the words in the dictionary.

Exercise 3

1. "I ate *sushi*."

   _____

2. "John will not go to Japan." (The postposition for "to" is *-ni*.)

   _____

3. "John did not take a bath."

   _____

4. "I will buy a book."

   _____

Keep in mind that the most important point of verb conjugation in Japanese is that functions such as "past," "present," "negative," and "affirmative" are indicated by stacking these helping verbs onto a verb stem.

In the next sections, we look at the conjugations of adjective and noun predicates. You will see that the same concept applies to these conjugation systems.

Adjective Predicate Conjugation

A predicate can sometimes function as an adjective, as in *John is smart* and *It was expensive*. In English, the helping verb "be" is placed before an adjective to indicate tense and "not" is added if it is in negation—as in *is cheap*, *isn't cheap*, *was cheap*, *wasn't cheap*.

In Japanese, helping verbs appear after an adjective. In this way, adjective predicate conjugation is similar to verb conjugation.

Conjugation Suffixes for Adjectives

	Affirmative	**Negative**
Present	Adjective + *idesu*	Adjective + *kuna-idesu*
	(is)	(not-is)
Past	Adjective + *kattadesu*	Adjective + *kuna-kattadesu*
	(was)	(not-was)

As illustrated in the table, the helping verb *idesu* is equivalent to the English "is," *kattadesu* is equivalent to "was," and *kuna* is equivalent to "not." As with verbs, these helping verbs are tacked onto the ending of an adjective.

Let's go over each conjugation thoroughly with a sample adjective, *yasu*, "cheap."

When you use an adjective in the affirmative present tense, such as *It is cheap*, the suffix *idesu* is attached to the adjective stem, as in:

> *yasu-idesu* ("cheap" + "is")

When you use an adjective in the affirmative past tense, such as *It was cheap*, the suffix *kattadesu* is attached to the adjective, as in:

> *yasu-kattadesu* ("cheap" + "was")

When you use an adjective in the negative present tense, such as *It isn't cheap*, the suffixes *kuna* and *idesu* are attached to the adjective, as in:

yasu-kuna-idesu ("cheap" + "not" + "is")

Finally, when you use an adjective in the negative past tense, such as *It wasn't cheap*, the suffixes *kuna* and *kattadesu* are attached to the adjective, as in:

yasu-kuna-kattadesu ("cheap" + "not" + "was")

Adjective predicate conjugation is shown in the following table:

Adjective Conjugation

	Affirmative	Negative
Present	*yasu-**idesu***	*yasu-**kuna-idesu***
	"is cheap"	"isn't cheap"
Past	*yasu-**kattadesu***	*yasu-**kuna-kattadesu***
	"was cheap"	"wasn't cheap"

For adjective predicate conjugation, all you have to remember is the ending of each function: *-idesu*, *-kattadesu*, *-kuna-idesu*, and *-kuna-kattadesu*. The adjective element that attaches to those endings, like *yasu-*, is called the adjective stem. Following are a few adjectives in various endings. Try to identify the adjective stem of each example:

Exercise 4

1. *takakattadesu* ("was expensive")　　　　_____

2. *oishikunaidesu* ("isn't delicious")　　　　_____

3. *muzukashikunakattadesu* ("wasn't difficult")　_____

4. *omoidesu* ("is heavy")　　　　　　　　_____

Here is another exercise. Conjugate each of the following adjectives as directed.

Exercise 5

1. *waru* ("bad") (to negative present form)

_____

2. *tanoshi* ("enjoyable") (to affirmative past form)

_____

3. *samu* ("cold") (to negative past form)

_____

4. *hiku* ("low") (to affirmative present form)

_____

The order of conjugation for adjectives is schematized as follows.

Adjective Stem +	(Negative) +	Tense	Translation
yasu		*idesu*	"is cheap"
yasu		*kattadesu*	"was cheap"
yasu	*kuna*	*idesu*	"isn't cheap"
yasu	*kuna*	*kattadesu*	"wasn't cheap"

LIFESAVERS

Japanese has only one irregular adjective—*i-idesu* ("is good"). Its stem is simply *i*.

	Affirmative	**Negative**
Present	*i-idesu*	*yo-kuna-idesu*
	"is good"	"isn't good"
Past	*yo-kattadesu*	*yo-kuna-kattadesu*
	"was good"	"wasn't good"

Now, let's look at actual sample sentences using the adjective stem *yasu* ("cheap").

*Sono piza-wa yasu-**idesu**.*	"That pizza **is** cheap."
*Sono piza-wa yasu-**kattadesu**.*	"That pizza **was** cheap."
*Sono piza-wa yasu-**kuna-idesu**.*	"That pizza is**n't** cheap."
*Sono piza-wa yasu-**kuna-kattadesu**.*	"That pizza **wasn't** cheap."

In the next exercise, translate the English sentences into Japanese. As with Exercise 3 for verb conjugation, you need to find the words in the dictionary.

Exercise 6

1. "*Sushi* is delicious."

_____

2. "Japanese is not difficult!"

_____

3. "That pizza was not expensive."

_____

4. "(The) movie was interesting."

_____

Noun Conjugation

 A predicate can sometimes function as a noun, as in _John is a student_ and _John was a student_. Notice that in English, the helping verb "be" is placed before a noun to indicate tense and "not" is added if it is in negation—as in _is a student_, _isn't a student_, _was a student_, and _wasn't a student_.

In Japanese, as with verbs and adjective predicates, helping verbs appear after a noun. The following table shows how a noun conjugates:

Conjugation Suffixes for Nouns

	Affirmative	**Negative**
Present	NOUN + _desu_	NOUN + _jana-idesu_
	(is)	(not-is)
Past	NOUN + _deshita_	NOUN + _jana-kattadesu_
	(was)	(not-was)

You might have noticed that noun conjugation is similar to adjective conjugation, especially in negative forms.

Let's go over each conjugation thoroughly with a sample noun, _kyō_ ("today").

When you have a noun in the affirmative present tense, such as _It is today_, the suffix _desu_ is attached to the noun, as in:

kyō-desu ("today" + "is")

When you have a noun in the affirmative past tense, such as _It was today_, the suffix _deshita_ is attached to the noun, as in:

kyō-deshita ("today" + "was")

When you have a noun in the negative present tense, such as *It <u>isn't</u> today*, the suffixes *jana* and *idesu* are attached to the noun, as in:

> *kyō-jana-idesu* ("today" + "not" + "is")

Finally, when you have a noun in the negative past tense, such as *It <u>wasn't</u> today*, the suffixes *jana* and *kattadesu* are attached to the noun, as in:

> *kyō-jana-kattadesu* ("today" + "not" + "was")

For noun predicate conjugation, all you have to remember is the ending of each function: *desu, deshita, jana-idesu,* and *jana-kattadesu*. Because noun conjugation looks similar to adjective conjugation, be sure that you don't get confused between the two.

Noun Conjugation

	Affirmative	**Negative**
Present	*kyō-desu*	*kyō-jana-idesu*
	"is today"	"isn't today"
Past	*kyō-deshita*	*kyō-jana-kattadesu*
	"was today"	"wasn't today"

Do the following exercise, and conjugate each of the following noun predicates as directed.

Exercise 7

1. *NihoNjiN* "(be) Japanese" (to negative present form)

   _____

2. *seNsē* "(be a) teacher" (to affirmative past form)

   _____

3. *gakusē* "(be a) student" (to negative past form)

   _____

4. *AmerikajiN* "(be an) American" (to affirmative present form)

   _____

The order of negative conjugation for adjectives is schematized as follows:

Adjective Stem	+	(Negative)	+	Tense	Translation
Kyō				*desu*	"is today"
Kyō				*deshita*	"was today"
Kyō		*jana*		*idesu*	"isn't today"
Kyō		*jana*		*kattadesu*	"wasn't today"

Now, let's look at an example for each of the noun conjugations:

*Tesuto-wa kyō-**desu**.*	"The test **is** today."
*Tesuto-wa kyō-**deshita**.*	"The test **was** today."
*Tesuto-wa kyō-**jana-idesu**.*	"The test **isn't** today."
*Tesuto-wa kyō-**jana-kattadesu**.*	"The test **wasn't** today."

 LIFESAVERS

When you're used to the past tense affirmative form for nouns—NOUN + *deshita*, such as *kyō-deshita* ("was today")—it becomes tempting to do the same for adjectives, like *yasu-i-deshita* ("was cheap"). This is a common mistake. Remember that the adjective conjugation is ADJECTIVE + *kattadesu*—for example, *yasu-kattadesu*.

In the next exercise, translate the English sentences into Japanese. Just as with Exercises 3 and 6, you need to find the words in the dictionary.

Exercise 8

1. "I am a student."

   _____

2. "This is not my book." ("this (pronoun)" = *kore*; "my" = *watashi-no*)

   _____

3. "My car was not a Honda."

   _____

4. "This shop used to be a hospital." ("this" (adjective) = *kono*)

   _____

You have seen the conjugation of all the predicates, verbs, adjectives, and nouns. Let's summarize each conjugation in terms of the type of suffixes:

Conjugation: Summary

	Present Affirmative	**Examples**
Verbs	VERB STEM + *masu*	*mi-masu* ("watch")
Adjectives	ADJECTIVE STEM + *idesu*	*yasu-idesu* ("is cheap")
Nouns	NOUN STEM + *desu*	*kyō-desu* ("is today")
	Past Affirmative	**Examples**
Verbs	VERB STEM + *mashita*	*mi-mashita* ("watched")
Adjectives	ADJECTIVE STEM + *katta-desu*	*yasu-kattadesu* ("was cheap")
Nouns	NOUN STEM + *deshita*	*kyō-deshita* ("was today")
	Present Negative	**Examples**
Verbs	VERB STEM + *maseN*	*mi-maseN* ("don't watch")
Adjectives	ADJECTIVE STEM + *kuna-idesu*	*yasu-kuna-idesu* ("isn't cheap")
Nouns	NOUN STEM + *jana-idesu*	*kyō-jana-idesu* ("isn't today")
	Past Negative	**Examples**
Verbs	VERB STEM + *maseN-deshita*	*mi-maseN-deshita* ("didn't watch")
Adjectives	ADJECTIVE STEM + *kuna-kattadesu*	*yasu-kuna-kattadesu* ("wasn't cheap")
Nouns	NOUN STEM + jana-kattadesu	*kyō-jana-kattadesu* ("wasn't today")

Conjugation can be challenging no matter what language you learn. The good news with regard to learning Japanese is that you don't have to worry about issues such as number, person, and gender. Conjugation is the basic of basics. Make sure that you memorize all the forms correctly!

Answers

Exercise 1

1. *kaki* ("to write")

2. *hanashi* ("to speak")

3. *iki* ("to go")

4. *yomi* ("to read")

Exercise 2

1. *kaeri-maseN* ("do[es] not go home")

2. *oyogi-mashita* ("swam")

3. *naki-maseN-deshita* ("did not cry")

4. *iki-masu* ("went")

Exercise 3

1. "I ate *sushi*." *Watashi-wa* sushi-o *tabe-mashita*.

2. "John will not go to Japan." *JoN-wa NihoN-ni iki-maseN*.

3. "John did not take a bath." *JoN-wa ofuro-ni hairi-maseN-deshita*.

4. "I will buy a book." *Watashi-wa hoN-o kai-masu*.

Exercise 4

1. *taka* ("expensive")

2. *oishi* ("delicious")

3. *muzukashi* ("difficult")

4. *omo* ("heavy")

Exercise 5

1. *waru-kuna-idesu* ("is not bad")

2. *tanoshi-kattadesu* ("was enjoyable")

3. *samu-kuna-kattadesu* ("was not cold")

4. *hiku-idesu* ("is low")

Exercise 6

1. "*Sushi* is delicious." Sushi-wa *oishi-idesu*.

2. "Japanese is not difficult!" *NihoNgo-wa muzukashi-kuna-idesu*.

3. "That pizza was not expensive." *Sono piza-wa taka-kuna-kattadesu*.

4. "(The) movie was interesting." *Ēga-wa omoshiro-kattadesu*.

Exercise 7

1. *NihoNjiN-jana-idesu* ("is not Japanese")

2. *seNsē-deshita* ("was a teacher")

3. *gakusē-jana-kattadesu* ("was not a student")

4. *AmerikajiN-desu* ("is an American")

Exercise 8

1. "I am a student." *Watashi-wa gakusē-desu.*

2. "This is not my book." *Kore-wa watashi-no hoN-jana-idesu.*

3. "My car was not a Honda." *Watashi-no kuruma-wa HoNda-jana-kattadesu.*

4. "This shop used to be a hospital." *Kono mise-wa byōiN-deshita.*

The Least You Need to Know

- Predicate conjugations for verbs, adjectives, and nouns are the heart of grammar.
- In English, helping verbs appear before a verb. In Japanese, helping verbs are tacked onto the end of a verb.
- Verb conjugation is summarized by the following examples: *mi-masu* ("watch"), *mi-mashita* ("watched"), *mi-maseN* ("do not watch"), and *mi-maseN-deshita* ("did not watch").
- Adjective conjugation is summarized by the following examples: *yasu-idesu* ("is cheap"), *yasu-kattadesu* ("was cheap"), *yasu-kuna-idesu* ("is not cheap"), and *yasu-kuna-kattadesu* ("was not cheap").
- Noun conjugation is summarized by the following examples: *kyō-desu* ("is today"), *kyō-deshita* ("was today"), *kyō-jana-idesu* ("is not today"), and *kyō-jana-kattadesu* ("was not today").

Other Grammar Essentials

In This Chapter

- *TE*-form
- How to describe something
- How to ask questions

You learned the basic sentence structure and particles in Chapter 4 and conjugation in Chapter 5. There are a few more grammatical concepts that you should be familiar with before starting actual lessons. In this chapter, you first are introduced to another important conjugation called *TE*-form, which is used in many grammatical constructions. Second, you learn how to describe a thing or person. And third, you learn how to ask questions in Japanese.

TE-Form

English has a versatile verb ending —*ing*, as in *go* → *going*. This grammatical form is used in many sentence patterns:

> I am <u>studying</u>.
>
> <u>Seeing</u> is <u>believing</u>.
>
> No <u>smoking</u>!

In the first and second examples, the *-ing* form indicates ongoing actions—present progressive in the first example and past progressive in the second example. In the third and fourth examples, the *-ing* form makes verbs function like nouns (called "gerunds"). The *-ing* form is required by the preceding sentence patterns. Because of this requirement, it is not grammatical to say, for example, *I am <u>study</u>* or *<u>See</u> is <u>believe</u>*.

Japanese has a special form known as the *TE*-form, whose function is similar to the -*ing* form. Like the -*ing* form, the *TE*-form is a bare form that is neutral to number, person, and tense. It is also used to indicate continuous action. And just as the last two English sentences in the preceding exercise require the use of -*ing*, certain special Japanese sentence structures (such as expression of a request, asking permission, or indicating a prohibition) require the use of the *TE*-form.

Let's explore some of the uses of the *TE*-form.

Continuous Action

In Chapter 5, you learned to conjugate verb, noun, and adjective predicates. This type of conjugation might be thought of as the "simple" conjugation of present, past, or future. We say that something happens, happened, or will happen. In English, we might say "Bob ate" or "Lisa writes."

But what if you want to suggest continuous actions—that is, "Bob was eating" or "Lisa is writing"? In English, you would just add the -*ing*. In Japanese, you would switch to the *TE*-form.

The *TE*-form is so called because you generally add -*te* to the verb if you want to indicate a continuous action. (There are some exceptions, such as when you add -*de* instead to indicate a slightly different pronunciation.) You also need to add the conjugation suffixes you learned in Chapter 5.

Let's compare the use of the verb "watch," *mi (-masu)*, in simple present and continuous present forms.

Suppose you want to say, "John watches TV." As you learned in Chapter 5, you would say:

> *JoN-wa terebi-o mi-masu.* "John watches TV."

If you want to say that John <u>is watching</u> TV, you would say:

> *JoN-wa terebi-o <u>mi-te</u> i-masu.* "John is watching TV."

Note that *mi-te* is translated as "watching" and *i-masu* as "is" (*Lit.* "be-present").

That is, you add -*te* to the verb stem *mi* and the verb *i-masu*. This indicates the continuous action of John watching television.

The order of conjugation for the verb "is watching," *mi-te i-masu*, is schematized as follows:

Verb Stem	+	*TE*	+	"Be"	+	Present Tense	Translation
mi		*te*		*i*		*masu*	"is watching"

The *TE*-form can get a little complicated because the shape of the *TE*-form changes depending on the ending of a verb. In order to come up with the right conjugation, you need a verb stem. The verb stem is a bare form without -*masu*. For example, the stem of the verb *tabe-masu* ("eat") is *tabe*.

There are two types of verb stem endings, one ending with an [-e] sound and the other ending with an [-i] sound. I list a few common verbs here as examples.

Two Types of Verb Endings

[e]-Ending	Verb Stems	[i]-Ending	Verb Stems
ne	"sleep"	*mi*	"see"
tabe	"eat"	*ki*	"come"
oboe	"memorize"	*shi*	"do"
oshie	"teach"	*ai*	"meet"
mise	"show"	*machi*	"wait"
tate	"build"	*kaeri*	"return home"
yame	"quit"	*nomi*	"drink"
		yobi	"invite"
		shini	"die"
		kaki	"write"
		oyogi	"swim"
		hanashi	"speak"

There are four different conjugations of the *TE*-form, depending on the kinds of stems you have. I call them Type 1, Type 2, Type 3, and Type 4.

Type 1

If the stem (1) is an [e]-ending stem, (2) contains only one syllable, or (3) ends with -*shi*, all you have to do is to add -*te* to the stem:

ta*be*	"eat"	→	*tabe-te*
ne	"sleep"	→	*ne-te*
mi	"see"	→	*mi-te*
hana*shi*	"speak"	→	*hanashi-te*

Type 2

If the stem ends with -*i*, -*chi*, or -*ri*, replace those syllables with the double consonant and add -*te*:

a*i*	"meet"	→	*at-te*
ma*chi*	"wait"	→	*mat-te*
kae*ri*	"return home"	→	*kaet-te*

Type 3

If the stem ends with -*mi*, -*bi*, or -*ni*, replace those syllables with -*N* and add -*de*:

no*mi*	"drink"	→	*noN-de*
yo*bi*	"invite"	→	*yoN-de*
shi*ni*	"die"	→	*shiN-de*

Type 4

If the stem ends with -*ki*, replace that syllable with -*i* and add -*te*. If the stem ends with -*gi*, replace that syllable with -*i* and add -*de*.

ka*ki*	"write"	→	*kai-te*
oyo*gi*	"swim"	→	*oyoi-de*

Type 1 of the *TE*-form is relatively easy, but you might find Types 2, 3, and 4 a bit challenging. Here is a way to make learning Types 2, 3, and 4 of the *TE*-form a little easier and more enjoyable. I am sure you know the song "Clementine" (a.k.a. "Oh My Darling"). With this music, replace the original lyrics with the following *TE*-forms. Ready? Here we go.

*i-chi-ri **tte***	*mi-bi-ni **Nde***	*ki **ite***	*gi **ide***
Oh my darling	*Oh my darling*	*Oh my darling*	*Clementine*
[Type 2]	[Type 3]	[Type 4]	[Type 4]

LIFESAVERS

The only irregular *TE*-form-verb is *iki-masu* ("go"). Its stem ends with *-ki*, but its *TE*-form is *it-te*, not *ii-te*.

How did you do? In each phrase you sing the verb-ending syllables together with the appropriate *TE*-forms. Try this simple memory trick to help you learn all the types of the *TE*-form.

Exercise 1

Provide the *TE*-form of each of the following verbs:

1. *hashiri-masu*   "run"
2. *aruki-masu*   "walk"
3. *tachi-masu*   "stand up"
4. *ake-masu*   "open"
5. *oshi-masu*   "push"

Connecting Predicates

I mentioned earlier that, aside from indicating ongoing/continuous actions, the *TE*-form is required by a number of grammatical structures, such as the connection of predicates. If you wanted to knit two sentences into one—for example, "John is a student" and "John is an American"—you would use the *TE*-form to do it. There are two important steps to remember:

1. You first need to determine whether your predicates are verb, adjective, or noun.

2. To combine the two, you only need to turn the first predicate into its *TE*-form. The second predicate remains as it is.

Let's connect the following two sentences ending with verb predicates:

> *JoN-wa tabe-mashita.*   "John ate."
>
> *JoN-wa ne-mashita.*   "John slept."

To connect the two predicates, *tabe-mashita* and *ne-mashita*, you need to turn the first predicate *tabe-mashita* into the *TE*-form, as in *tabe-te*. The result is shown here:

TE-Form Connecting Verb Predicates

> *JoN-wa tabe-**te**, ne-mashita.*   "John ate and (then) slept."

Just like verb predicates, noun and adjective predicates also have their own *TE*-forms. Let's start with the simpler form—a noun *TE*-form.

TE-Form for Noun Predicates

Let's learn how to convert a noun predicate to its *TE*-form for the purpose of combining two noun predicates.

The Japanese translation of "John is a student" would be …

> *JoN-wa gakusē-desu.*   "John is a student."

The noun predicate is *gakusē-desu*. To make the *TE*-form of this predicate, you only need to attach *-de* to the noun, as shown here:

TE-Form for Noun Predicate (for example, *gakusē-desu*, "to be a student")

> *JoN-wa gakusē-**de** …*   "John being a student …"

HUH?

In some cases of the *TE*-form, *-te* is pronounced *-de*, as seen in the *TE*-form for a noun predicate.

To connect predicates, you must turn the first predicate into the *TE*-form. To illustrate this point, look at the following two noun predicates:

> *JoN-wa gakusē-desu.*   "John is a student."
>
> *JoN-wa AmerikajiN-desu.*   "John is an American."

To connect the two predicates, *gakusē-desu* and *AmerikajiN-desu*, you need to turn the first predicate *gakusei-desu* into the *TE*-form, as in *gakusē-de*. The result is shown here:

TE-Form Connecting Noun Predicates

JoN-wa gakusē-de, AmerikajiN-desu.   "John is a student and (is) an American."

Note that in a combined sentence, the first and second predicates do not have to be the same type. The *TE*-form can connect a noun predicate and verb predicate, as shown here:

JoN-wa gakusē-desu.   "John is a student."

JoN-wa okane-ga ari-maseN.   "John has no money."

JoN-wa gakusē-de, okane-ga ari-maseN.   "John is a student and he has no money."

Make sure that the *TE*-form for a noun predicate follows this formula:

Noun Stem + -*de* (for example, *gakusē-de*, "being a student")

Now, do the next exercise.

Exercise 2

Connect two noun predicate sentences using the *TE*-form.

1. *Watashi-wa NihoNjiN-desu.*   "I am Japanese."
   Watashi-wa kyōshi-desu.   "I am a teacher."

   _____

2. *Risa-wa KanadajiN-desu.*   "Lisa is a Canadian."
   JoN-wa AmerikajiN-desu.   "John is an American."

   _____

TE-Form for Adjective Predicates

Now let's look at the *TE*-form for adjective predicates, for the purpose of combining two adjective predicates. First, here's a regular sentence containing an adjective predicate:

Sono piza-wa yasu-idesu. "That pizza is cheap."

The adjective predicate is *yasu-idesu.* To make the *TE*-form of this predicate, change *-idesu* to *-kute*, as seen here:

TE-Form for Adjective Predicate (for example, *yasu-idesu*, "to be cheap")

Sono piza-wa yasu-kute … (*Lit.*) "That pizza being cheap …"

I showed in the previous section that the *TE*-form connects two noun predicates. Let's connect two adjective predicates:

Sono piza-wa yasu-idesu. "That pizza is cheap."

Sono piza-wa oishi-idesu. "That pizza is delicious."

The *TE*-form connects these two sentences as follows:

TE-Form Connecting Adjective Predicates

Sono piza-wa yasu-kute, oishi-idesu. "That pizza is cheap and (is) delicious."

Make sure you remember the formula for converting an adjective predicate to the *TE*-form:

Adjective Stem + *kute* (for example, *yasu-kute*, "being cheap")

Now, do the next exercise.

Exercise 3

Connect two sentences using the *TE*-form:

1. *John-wa yasashi-idesu.* "John is kind."
   John-wa atama-ga i-idesu. "John is smart."

   _____

2. *NihoNgo-wa omoshiro-idesu.* "Japanese language is fun."
   NihoNgo-wa yakuni tachi-masu. "Japanese is useful."

   _____

Other Instances When You Want to Use the TE-Form

The *TE*-form is useful for situations other than connecting predicates and indicating ongoing action. Without this form, you won't be able to express a lot of basic concepts. The following is a list of three useful patterns that require the *TE*-form:

- Making a request
- Expressing permission
- Expressing prohibition

Let's look at an example of each:

Making a Request

*Tabe-**te**! or Tabe-**te** kudasai!*   "Eat!" *or* "Please eat!"
(tabe-te < tabe-masu)

Expressing Permission

*Kaet-**te** mo i-idesu ka?*   "May I go home?"
(kaet-te < kaeri-masu)

Expressing Prohibition

*Koko de noN-**de** wa, ike-maseN!*   "You cannot drink here."
(noN-de < nomi-masu) (koko de = "here")

Let's sum up what we have learned about the *TE*-form:

- The *TE*-form is comparable to the English *-ing* in that it expresses an "ongoing/continuous action."

- The *TE*-form is used in various grammatical patterns such as in "requests," "permission," and "prohibition," among others.

- Each predicate type (verb predicate, noun predicate, and adjective predicate) has its own *TE*-form.

- The conjugation of the *TE*-form for verb predicates is slightly complicated. I suggest that you review the section on verb predicates thoroughly. Remember, the song "Clementine" is helpful for remembering the three most difficult endings of the *TE*-form for verbs.

How to Describe Something or Someone

Life would be dull if you could not describe a person or thing in detail. Suppose you want your friend to hand you a particular book from the bookshelf. You might have to say something like, "the yellow book," "the expensive-looking book," "the old book," or "the book written in Japanese."

There are three basic ways to describe a thing or person:

- By an adjective

- By a noun

- By a *na*-adjective

No matter which type of describer you use, remember that a describer always comes *before* a thing/person to be described, as in the following diagram:

<u>Describer</u> (adjective, and so on) + <u>Thing/Person</u>

Adjectives

You have already seen adjective predicates like *oishi-idesu* ("delicious"), *yasu-idesu* ("inexpensive"), and *i-idesu* ("good"). When you use an adjective as a noun describer, delete **desu** from the adjective predicate:

oishi-idesu	→	*oishi-i*	"delicious"
yasu-idesu	→	*yasu-i*	"cheap"
i-idesu	→	*i-i*	"good"

To describe a noun, simply place an adjective before the noun.

See the following examples using these adjectives:

*oishi-**i*** sushi	"delicious *sushi*"
*yasu-**i*** *peN*	"cheap pen"
*i-**i*** *hoN*	"good book"

Make sure that an adjective ends with *-i* when describing a noun.

Exercise 4

Using the English to Japanese dictionary in Appendix B, describe the following nouns using adjectives. All the adjectives are listed with the *-i* ending.

1. "big bag" _____

2. "small clothes" _____

3. "dirty room" _____

Nouns

When you describe a noun using another noun, the describer is marked by *-no*. Let's describe the nouns *sushi*, *peN*, and *hoN* (book) using noun describers.

*JoN-**no** sushi*	"John's *sushi*"
*NihoN-**no** peN*	"pen made in Japan"
*Kanada-**no** hoN*	"book about Canada"; "book printed in Canada"

Noun describers are basically the same as adjective describers: they appear before the thing/person to be described. The only difference is that noun describers are marked by *-no*.

Exercise 5

Just like in Exercise 4, describe the following nouns by using nouns, using the English to Japanese dictionary in Appendix B. The core noun that is to be described is underlined in the questions.

1. "<u>student</u> of the Japanese language"

    _____

2. "<u>shop</u> in Tokyo"

    _____

3. "<u>John</u> from Toyota"

    _____

Na-Adjectives

I said previously that there are three types of describers and that the third one is called "*na*-adjectives." *Na*-adjectives are hybrids that function as adjectives but conjugate exactly like nouns.

Look at the following examples:

JoN-wa <u>heN-desu</u>.	"John is strange."
KoNpyūtā-wa <u>beNri-desu</u>.	"Computers are convenient."
JoN-wa <u>haNsamu-desu</u>.	"John is handsome."

"Strange," "convenient," and "handsome" are all adjectives, but the words *heN*, *beNri*, and *haNsamu* do not look like the familiar adjectives. They look different because they don't end with *idesu*.

When these "adjectives" describe a noun, they are marked by *-na*, just as their names suggest. Let's see how *na*-adjectives describe nouns:

*heN-**na** sushi*	"strange-looking *sushi*"
*beNri-**na** peN*	"handy pen"
*haNsamu-**na** hito*	"handsome person"

GREEN TEA BREAK

By now, you know that there are several Western loanwords in Japanese. Most loanwords are nouns. However, quite a few are adjectives, as shown here:

haNsamu(-na)	"handsome"
ricchi(-na)	"rich"
eregaNto(-na)	"elegant"
karafuru(-na)	"colorful"
gōjasu(-na)	"gorgeous"

"Colorful pens" would be translated as *karafuru-na peN*.

Exercise 6

Again, using the English to Japanese dictionary in Appendix B, describe the following nouns using *na*-adjectives:

1. "inconvenient telephone"

2. "favorite book"

_____

3. "quiet person"

_____

In short, Japanese has two types of adjectives—*i*-adjectives and *na*-adjectives. For describing a noun, the only difference is the ending (*-i* or *-na*). However, when it comes to conjugation, *na*-adjectives look quite different from *i*-adjectives. They behave just like noun predicates.

NA-Adjective Predicate Conjugation

	Affirmative	Negative
Present	*heN-desu*	*heN-jana-idesu*
	"is strange"	"isn't strange"
Past	*heN-deshita*	*heN-jana-kattadesu*
	"was strange"	"wasn't strange"

I-Adjective Predicate Conjugation

	Affirmative	Negative
Present	*yasu-idesu*	*yasu-kuna-idesu*
	"is cheap"	"isn't cheap"
Past	*yasu-kattadesu*	*yasu-kuna-kattadesu*
	"was cheap"	"wasn't cheap"

Noun Predicate Conjugation

	Affirmative	Negative
Present	*kyō-desu*	*kyō-jana-idesu*
	"is today"	"isn't today"
Past	*kyō-deshita*	*kyō-jana-kattadesu*
	"was today"	"wasn't today"

Na-adjectives are bizarre, but once in a while you see bizarre grammar in any language!

Asking a Question

 Let's learn how to ask a question. As in English, Japanese has two types of questions:

- *Yes-no* questions

- *Wh*-questions (questions containing words like *who, what, where, when,* and so on)

> **HUH?**
>
> I have stated elsewhere in this book that a Japanese sentence ends with a verb. However, in the case of questions, *-ka* follows the verb. This marker is just like the question mark (?).

Compared to other languages, asking a question in Japanese is extremely easy because you don't have to shuffle words. If you want to make a question out of "John is a student" in English, you have to bring "is" to the beginning, as in "Is John a student?" *Wh*-questions are even more complex in English. When you make a question out of "John ate an apple," asking what he ate, you have to insert a question word and add the helping verb "did," as in "What did John eat?"

ka

In Japanese, forming a question sentence is easy. For *yes-no* questions, all you have to do is add the question word *ka?* at the end of a sentence.

Yes-No **Questions**

Q: *JoN-wa AmerikajiN-desu **ka**?*	"Is John an American?"
A: *Hai, AmerikajiN-desu.*	"Yes, he is an American."
Q: *Pari-ni iki-masu **ka**?*	"Will you go to Paris?"
A: *Īe, iki-maseN.*	"No, I will not go to Paris."

> **LIFESAVERS**
>
> *Hai* means "What you've said is correct," and *īe* means "What you've said is *not* correct." In a negative *yes-no* question, this causes *hai* to mean "no" and *īe* to mean "yes." Suppose you are asked if you *don't* eat pizza:
>
> Q: *Piza-wa tabe-maseN ka?* "You don't eat pizza?"
>
> If you indeed *do not* eat pizza, you should say *Hai, tabe-maseN* because what the speaker said is correct. On the other hand, if you *do* eat pizza, you should say *Īe, tabe-masu* because what the speaker said is *not* correct.

Exercise 7

Make question sentences based on the following information. Pay attention to the tense.

1. "Did you eat?" ("eat" = *tabe-masu*)

   _____

2. "Is Japanese difficult?" ("difficult" = *muzukashi-idesu*)

   _____

3. "Was the movie interesting?" ("movie" = *ēga*; "interesting" = *omoshiro-idesu*)

   _____

4. "Are you returning home?" ("return home" = *kaeri-masu*)

   _____

5. "Is John a student?" ("student" = *gakusē*)

   _____

Wh-Questions

 For *wh*-questions, you just need to put an appropriate question word where its answer normally appears. Let's look at a couple of examples:

> ### *Wh*-Questions
>
> Q: ***Nani-o*** *tabe-mashita* **ka?**   "What did you eat?"
>
> A: ***Piza-o*** *tabe-mashita.*   "I ate pizza."
>
> Q: ***JoN-wa*** **doko-ni** *iki-masu* **ka?**   "Where will John go?"
>
> A: ***Pari-ni*** *iki-masu.*   "He will go to Paris."

Basically, when you answer a *wh*-question, all you need to do is listen to the question carefully and replace the question word with your answer. That's it! You don't have to worry about word order or a helping verb! Isn't that great?

Although you will see a number of questions in the rest of the book, I think it's a good idea to list frequently used question words.

Question Words

what	*nani* or *naN*
who	*dare*
where	*doko*
when	*itsu*
which one	*dore*
which X	*dono* X
which direction	*dochira*
why	*dōshite* or *naze*
how	*dōyatte*
how much (money)	*ikura*
how much (quantity)	*donogurai*

Exercise 8

Answer the following questions:

1. *Nani-jiN-desu ka?* (American)

   _____

2. *Namae-wa naN-desu ka?* (*namae* = "name")

   _____

3. *AmazoN-wa doko-ni ari-masu ka?* (*AmazoN* = "Amazon") (Brazil)

   _____

Review

Before we leave this chapter, let's do a short review to check your grammatical under-standing. I've given you the answers at the end of the chapter. I don't expect you to have completely memorized all the things covered in this chapter. Refer to the discussions in Chapters 5 and 6 to answer the questions.

Review Quiz

1. How would you say the following in Japanese?

   a. John is not an American. (American = *AmerikajiN*)

   _____

   b. Japan was fun! (fun = *tanoshi-idesu*)

   _____

   c. I didn't drink sake. (drink = *nomi-masu*)

   _____

2. Write the *TE*-form for each verb:

   a. *yomi-masu*   "read"   _____

   b. *shi-masu*   "do"   _____

   c. *tsukuri-masu* "make"   _____

   d. *tame-masu*   "save (money, etc.)"   _____

3. Describe the pizza:

   a. healthy pizza   (healthy = *herushī*)

   _____

   b. John's pizza

   _____

   c. small pizza   (small = *chīsa-i*)

   _____

Answers

Exercise 1

1. *hashit-te*   ←   *hashiri-masu*   "run"
2. *arui-te*   ←   *aruki-masu*   "walk"
3. *tat-te*   ←   *tachi-masu*   "stand up"
4. *ake-te*   ←   *ake-masu*   "open"
5. *oshi-te*   ←   *oshi-masu*   "push"

Exercise 2

1. *Watashi-wa NihoNjiN-**de** kyōshi-desu.*
   "I am Japanese and (am a) teacher."

2. *Risa-wa KanadajiN-**de** JoN-wa AmerikajiN-desu.*
   "Lisa is a Canadian, and John is an American."

Exercise 3

1. *John-wa yasashi-**kute** atama-ga i-idesu.*
   "John is kind and (is) smart."

2. *NihoNgo-wa omoshiro-**kute** yakuni tachi-masu.*
   "Japanese is fun and (is) useful."

Exercise 4

1. *ōki-i baggu* or *ōki-i kabaN*   "big bag"

2. *chīsa-i fuku*   "small clothes"

3. *kitana-i heya*   "dirty room"

Exercise 5

1. *NihoNgo-no gakusē*   "student of the Japanese language"

2. *Tōkyō-no mise*   "shop in Tokyo"

3. *Toyota-no JoN*   "John from Toyota"

Exercise 6

1. *fubeN-na deNwa*   "inconvenient telephone"

2. *daisuki-na hoN*   "favorite book"

3. *shizuka-na hito*   "quiet person"

Exercise 7

1. *(Anata-wa) taba-mashita ka?*   "Did you eat?"

2. *NihoNgo-wa muzukashi-idesu ka?*   "Is Japanese difficult?"

3. *Ēga-wa omoshiro-kattadesu ka?*   "Was the movie interesting?"

4. *(Anata-wa) kaeri-masu ka?*   "Are you returning home?"

5. *JoN-wa gakusē-desu ka?*   "Is John a student?"

Exercise 8

1. *Nani-jiN-desu ka?* "What nationality are you?"

   Amerika-jiN-desu. "I'm an American."

2. *Namae-wa naN-desu ka?* "What is your name?"

   Namae-wa XYZ-*desu.* "My name is XYZ."

3. *AmazoN-wa doko-ni ari-masu ka?* "Where is the Amazon?"

   AmazoN-wa Burajiru-ni ari-masu. "The Amazon is in Brazil."

Review Quiz

1. a. *JoN-wa AmerikajiN-jana-idesu.*

   b. *NihoN-wa tanoshi-kattadesu!*

   c. *(Watashi-wa) sake-o nomi-maseN-deshita.*

2. a. *yoN-de*

   b. *shi-te*

   c. *tsukut-te*

   d. *tame-te*

3. a. *herushī-na piza*

   b. *JoN-no piza*

   c. *chīsa-i piza*

The Least You Need to Know

- The *TE*-form is essential because so many expressions require it.
- A noun can be described by (1) an *i*-adjective (ending with -*i*), (2) a *na*-adjective (ending with -*na*), or (3) a noun (ending with -*no*).
- To make a *yes-no* question, simply add *ka?* at the end of a sentence. To make a *wh*-question, simply insert an appropriate question word in the sentence where its answer normally appears.

Numbers

In This Chapter

- Basic numbers
- Really big numbers
- Counters

Numbers are an indispensable tool for everyday life. Without numbers, you cannot count objects, tell your age, check prices when shopping, and so on. In this chapter, you will be introduced to basic numbers and the concept of "counters."

Basic Numbers

 The following is a table of basic Japanese numbers.

Basic Numbers 1 Through 10

0	*zero* or *rē*
1	*ichi*
2	*ni*
3	*saN*
4	*yoN* or *shi*
5	*go*
6	*roku*
7	*shichi* or *nana*
8	*hachi*
9	*kyū* or *ku*
10	*jū*

These numbers are certainly different from the English numbers, but not extremely difficult to learn. When you are comfortable with these basic numbers, the numbers beyond 10 are relatively easy.

GREEN TEA BREAK

In Japan, 4 is the unlucky number (not 13) because the reading *shi* is identical to the pronunciation of the word for "death." For this reason, some people prefer saying *yoN*, not *shi*.

10 to 99

Japanese numbers beyond *jū* (10) are simple. For example, 11 is *ten one* in Japanese. First, look at how to count from 11 to 20.

Numbers 11 Through 20

11	*jū ichi*
12	*jū ni*
13	*jū saN*
14	*jū yoN* or *jū shi*
15	*jū go*
16	*jū roku*
17	*jū shichi* or *jū nana*
18	*jū hachi*
19	*jū kyū* or *jū ku*
20	*ni-jū*

Simple, aren't they? Notice that 20 is said as *two ten*. Likewise, 20 to 90 are pronounced as follows:

Numbers 20 Through 90

20	*ni-jū*
30	*saN-jū*
40	*yoN-j̄ū*
50	*go-jū*
60	*roku-jū*

70	*nana-jū*
80	*hachi-jū*
90	*kyū-jū*

Now, how would you say the following numbers in Japanese?

1. 72 _____

2. 48 _____

3. 36 _____

How did you do? Here are the answers:

1. 72: *nana-jū ni*

2. 48: *yoN-jū hachi*

3. 36: *saN-jū roku*

SHORTCUTS TO SUCCESS

You don't have to be in a classroom to learn a language. There are a lot of places where you can practice Japanese numbers. For example, practice counting to 100 in Japanese while taking a shower or driving to work. If you go to a gym, count weight-lifting reps in Japanese. In an elevator, count floors in Japanese. Consistent practice makes perfect.

100 to 9,999

Wow, numbers are getting bigger and bigger! We have covered up to 99 so far. Let's first look at the unit of "hundred." Unlike the previous numbers, you will notice that there are three irregular pronunciations, which are boldfaced in the following list.

Numbers 100 Through 900

100	*hyaku*
200	*ni-hyaku*
300	***saN-byaku***
400	*yoN-hyaku*
500	*go-hyaku*
600	***rop-pyaku***

700	*nana-hyaku*
800	***hap-pyaku***
900	*kyū-hyaku*

HUH?

The irregular versions of *hyaku* ("hundred") aid in the pronunciation of some numbers. For example, pronouncing 600 as *roku-hyaku* would be a tongue twister for Japanese speakers, so it is pronounced as *rop-pyaku*.

Let's do a short practice activity again. How would you say the following?

1. 172 _____

2. 348 _____

3. 936 _____

How did you do? Here are the answers:

1. 172: *hyaku nana-jū ni*

2. 348: *saN-byaku yoN-jū hachi*

3. 936: *kyū-hyaku saN-jū roku*

Let's move on to the unit of "thousand." Again, there are a couple of irregular pronunciations (3,000 and 8,000):

Numbers 1,000 Through 9,000

1,000	*seN*
2,000	*ni-seN*
3,000	***saN-zeN***
4,000	*yoN-seN*
5,000	*go-seN*
6,000	*roku-seN*
7,000	*nana-seN*
8,000	***has-seN***
9,000	*kyū-seN*

With the numbers introduced so far, you can say up to 9,999. How would you say the following in Japanese?

1. 7,380 _____

2. 3,075 _____

3. 2,601 _____

 LIFESAVERS

Japanese people usually write "big" numbers like "year" or "price" in Arabic numbers rather than Japanese characters.

How did you do? Here are the answers:

1. 7,380: *nana-seN saN-byaku hachi-jū*

2. 3,075: *saN-zeN nana-jū go*

3. 2,601: *ni-seN rop-pyaku ichi*

As an example of practical application of these numbers, you can talk about "years," which use the unit of "thousand." All you need to do is attach the word for "year" (*-neN*) to the end of the number. For example, the year 2002 would be …

> *ni-seN ni-neN*   "year 2002"

Now I will ask you the following question:

> *Anata-wa naN-neN-ni umare-mashita ka?*   "In what year were you born?"
> (*umare-masu* = "be born")

The word *naN-neN* is the question word for "what year." If you were born in 1971, the answer would be …

> *SeN kyū-hyaku nana-jū ichi-neN-ni umare-mashita.*
> "I was born in 1971."

 SHORTCUTS TO SUCCESS

Notice that the topic phrase for "I" is missing in the answer of the dialogue. As explained in Chapter 4, you can omit any item in a sentence if it is understood by both the speaker and listener.

Beyond 10,000

You will find the expression *ichi-maN* (10,000) to be particularly useful because it is the denomination of the largest bill in Japanese money. As we did previously, you count by saying "two 10,000"; "three 10,000"; and so on.

Numbers 10,000 Through 100,000			
10,000	(= 1,0000)	*ichi-maN*	1 × 10,000
20,000	(= 2,0000)	*ni-maN*	2 × 10,000
30,000	(= 3,0000)	*saN-maN*	3 × 10,000
40,000	(= 4,0000)	*yoN-maN*	4 × 10,000
50,000	(= 5,0000)	*go-maN*	5 × 10,000
60,000	(= 6,0000)	*roku-maN*	6 × 10,000
70,000	(= 7,0000)	*nana-maN*	7 × 10,000
80,000	(= 8,0000)	*hachi-maN*	8 × 10,000
90,000	(= 9,0000)	*kyū-maN*	9 × 10,000
100,000	(= 10,0000)	*jū-maN*	10 × 10,000

How would you say the following "big" numbers in Japanese?

1. 24,720 _____

2. 98,254 _____

3. 70,541 _____

GREEN TEA BREAK

The idea that a counting unit changes every four digits (as opposed to every three digits as is common in Western countries) originated in China. Japan's adoption of this system was a result of the country's aggressive importation of Chinese civilization about 1,600 years ago.

How did you do? Here are the answers:

1. 24,720: *ni-maN yoN-seN nana-hyaku ni-jū*

2. 98,254: *kyū-maN has-seN ni-hyaku go-jū yoN*

3. 70,541: *nana-maN go-hyaku yoN-jū ichi*

Because a new unit appears every four digits, "one million," or 1,000,000, is 100,0000 in Japanese:

> *hyaku-maN*   "1,000,000" (= 100,0000 in Japanese)

Big Numbers

The most likely setting in which you might have to deal with very big numbers is counting money when you are shopping. As of December 2010, U.S. $1 is about 84 *yen*. This means that if you exchange U.S. $100 for Japanese currency, you will have only 8,400 *yen* in hand. U.S. $150 would yield approximately …

> *ichi-maN ni-seN rop-pyaku eN*   "12,600 *yen*"
> (Literally: 1 ten-thousand and 2 thousand 6 hundred *yen*)

Note that the Japanese monetary unit is pronounced *eN*, not *yen*. Its international symbol is ¥.

What Is a "Counter"?

In English, when you count "uncountable" substances such as paper, rice, and coffee, you use words such as "one <u>sheet</u> of paper," "two <u>scoops</u> of rice," or "three <u>cups</u> of coffee." These underlined words are called "counters." When you count objects in Japanese, the appropriate counter must accompany them. Just as English has a number of counters such as *sheets*, *scoops*, and *cups*, Japanese has numerous counters that refer to particular types of objects.

You will learn several basic counters in this book; however, to illustrate the concept in this chapter, I will explain one such counter now.

When you count objects that are "thin and flat," you use the counter *-mai*. Can you think of any "thin and flat" objects? Paper, CDs, postcards, stamps, mouse pads, windowpanes, pizza, plates, T-shirts—all are examples of thin, flat objects.

If you want to say, "I ate two sheets (not slices!) of pizza," the sentence should look like this:

> *Watashi-wa piza-o ni-mai tabe-mashita.*   "I ate two sheets of pizza."

Here is the complete list of this "thin and flat" counter for numbers from 1 to 10:

Counter for Thin and Flat Objects

1	*ichi-mai*
2	*ni-mai*
3	*saN-mai*
4	*yoN-mai*
5	*go-mai*
6	*roku-mai*
7	*nana-mai*
8	*hachi-mai*
9	*kyū-mai*
10	*jū-mai*
How many?	*naN-mai*

Suppose that you want to buy 10 stamps at the post office. You might expect the following dialogue to take place:

You: *Kitte-o kudasai.*   "Stamps, please."

Clerk: *NaN-mai-desu ka?* "How many?"

You: *Jū-mai kudasai.*   "Ten, please."

Here are some commonly used counters.

Common Counters

Objects	Counter	Examples
Bound objects	*-satsu*	Books, magazines
Long objects	*-hoN*	Pens, carrots, sticks
Small objects	*-ko*	Fruits, erasers, marbles
Machinery	*-dai*	Cars, computers
Small animals	*-hiki*	Dogs, cats, rabbits
Large animals	*-tō*	Lions, elephants, horses
People	*-niN*	

Memorizing numbers might take time, but what you can do with numbers is unlimited—you can shop without going over your budget, read the calendar, count things, and so on.

Before concluding this chapter, let's do some review exercises. How would you say the following in Japanese?

Review

1. 98 _____

2. 276 _____

3. 3,476 _____

4. 28,505 _____

5. 110,000 _____

6. Year 1986 (with the appropriate counter) _____

7. 25,048 *yen* _____

Answers

1. 98 *kyū-jū hachi*

2. 276 *ni-hyaku nana-jū roku*

3. 3,476 *saN-zeN yon-hyaku nana-jū roku*

4. 28,505 *ni-maN has-seN go-hyaku go*

5. 110,000 *jū ichi-maN*

6. Year 1986 *seN kyū-hyaku hachi-jū roku-neN*

7. 25,048 *yen ni-maN go-seN yoN-jū hachi-eN*

The Least You Need to Know

* Master the basic numbers so that you can count objects, tell your age, check prices when shopping, and so on.
* In Japanese, counting units change every four digits, not three digits as is common in Western countries.
* When you count objects, you must use the appropriate "counter" for the noun being counted.

Getting to Know People

Even if you are a shy person, getting to know people is not a difficult task at all if you learn the expressions for greetings and self-introductions. These phrases are "fixed," or "ritualized"—mechanical and simple, yet very effective. Take a close look at the next few chapters and learn those expressions as conversation starters.

After you master greetings and self-introductions, you will want to know more personalized expressions so you can talk more about yourself and ask other people more questions. Politeness is important in Japanese, and I will show you how to carry out these conversations without being perceived as rude or nosy.

At the end of these chapters, you also learn how to invite people to various activities and are given a few tips that can make your invitations hard to resist. Don't miss them!

Greetings

In This Chapter

- Greeting expressions
- How to express thanks and apologies
- Other useful expressions

Don't take this chapter on greetings too lightly. Greetings are very effective and can give people a good first impression of you. In this chapter, you learn how to use the proper greetings in the appropriate situations. Try them as you learn them. Even though you can't speak much Japanese at this point, greetings are powerful enough to draw people's attention and start a conversation, so don't be shy!

The expressions in this chapter are all "ritualized" or "fixed" expressions. When you say *hello*, you don't think about what this word means, do you? Likewise, don't worry about the meanings behind Japanese *ritualized expressions*. Instead, accept them as they are and pay attention to which expression you need to say in a given situation. With the proper use of fixed expressions, your Japanese will sound more natural.

HUH?

Ritualized expressions are expressions of social protocol. Most such expressions have been used for daily greetings, and the original meanings were lost over time.

Greetings Around the Clock

English has handy greeting words such as *hi* and *hello*. You can say these to pretty much anyone at any time, be it friends, acquaintances, or strangers. These greetings can also be used whether it is morning, afternoon, or night.

I wish I could say that Japanese has a handy word like *Hi!* Japanese people are particular about greetings. You must remember to use the right greeting at the appropriate time:

Good morning!	*Ohayō gozaimasu!*
Good afternoon!	*KoNnichiwa!*
Good evening!	*KoNbaNwa!*

Did you actually move your mouth and say these words aloud rather than read them silently? Remember, silent reading does not improve your speaking skill.

Let's imagine that you're staying with a Japanese family. You'll hear a lot of ritualized or fixed expressions at home. Let's learn those expressions as they are used in specific situations.

At the Dining Table

Eating is an important part of Japanese daily life. Food is considered a gift from God (or gods, in Japan), and, therefore, we express our thanks not only before we begin eating, but when we finish:

Before you eat:	*Itadakimasu.*
After you eat:	*Gochisōsama deshita.*

The French say *Bon appétit!* before eating. *Bon appétit!* means "good appetite," whereas *itadakimasu* literally means "I will humbly accept (the food)." *Itadakimasu* was originally a very religious expression, although most Japanese probably have never thought about its origin because it's so ritualized. *Gochisōsama deshita* means "That was a feast!" Again, it is a ritualized expression, so you say this even if what you've just eaten was not a "feast."

 GREEN TEA BREAK

Bowing is essential for greetings in Japan, but a big bow is not necessary. A slight bow will do. I occasionally notice foreign people putting their hands together as they bow. This is not a Japanese custom.

What if your host offers you food, but you can't eat any more? You can say either of the following:

No, thank you.	*Īe, kekkō-desu.*
I am full.	*Onaka-ga ippai-desu.*

If you're still hungry, you can accept the offer by saying the by-now-familiar *itadaki-masu* because you are "humbly accepting" the food.

And remember, it's always nice to give the host a compliment for her or his cooking:

That was delicious!   *Oishi-kattadesu!*

SHORTCUTS TO SUCCESS

Dining is one of the most desirable opportunities to learn new words. If you're dining with a Japanese speaker, point to the food and ask:

Kore-wa naN-desu ka? "What is this?"

There is no doubt that the best way to learn a new word is by association, and tasting delicious food is a wonderful way of association! So don't be afraid to try exotic foods.

Leaving Home and Coming Home

When you leave for work in the morning, what do you say to your family and what does your family say to you in English? You probably say something like *See you, Later,* or *I love you!* The expression varies from person to person.

In Japanese, on the other hand, no matter what circumstances you're in, the following dialogue is exchanged between the one leaving and the one seeing her or him off:

Person leaving: *Itte kimasu.*   "I am going." (*Lit.* "I am going and coming back.")

Person seeing her or him off: *Itte rasshai.*   "See you." (*Lit.* "Please go and come back.")

The bottom line is that, without saying a word, it would be extremely rude to leave home or to see someone off.

After long hours of work, you get home. What do you say to your family then? In English, perhaps you say *Hi* or maybe *Honey, I'm home!* Again, in Japanese, the expressions are fixed, and 99 percent of people—if not 100 percent—say the following:

Person getting home: *Tadaima.*   "I'm home." (*Lit.* "I am here right now.")

Family, welcoming you home: *Okaeri nasai.*   "Welcome back." (*Lit.* "Please come home.")

Notice that the literal translations are somewhat bizarre, but that's what "ritualized" expressions are all about.

These four phrases are musts if you don't want to be perceived as being a rude person!

At the End of the Day

Your long day with your host family is nearing its end, and it's time to say *good night*. But before you say *good night*, it would be a good idea to indicate or imply to the family that you're sleepy. This kind of "communication buffer" is really important in Japanese. Without an extra *buffer expression*—a little hint before you say something directly—you will appear blunt and self-centered.

HUH?

By **buffer expressions,** I mean "filler" expressions uttered before making a point. This is to avoid direct statements and subsequently portray yourself as being self-centered. For example, if you are hungry, you would utter a seemingly unrelated expression before saying "I'm hungry," like "What time is it?" This way, you can give the listener a "hint" as to what you are going to say afterward. This is a very important communication strategy in Japanese.

Here are some "buffer" expressions suitable for this particular situation:

> *Chotto tsukare-mashita.*   "I am a bit tired."
>
> *Ashita-wa haya-idesu.*   "I must wake up early tomorrow."

Then, you can finally say this:

> *Oyasumi nasai.*   "Good night."

These around-the-clock expressions are all daily essentials. Practice and use them. If you have a Japanese-speaking friend near you, that's great! Even if you don't, say these words to a friend anyway. You will gain more this way rather than mumbling to yourself!

Thanks, Sorry, and Excuse Me

When I was a child, my mother used to tell me that you could never say *thanks* too much, even for a tiny favor. She was absolutely right. Whether you speak English or Japanese, thanking doesn't hurt a person's feelings. Here is the Japanese way of saying *thanks:*

| *Arigatō!* | "Thanks!" |
| *Dōmo arigatō!* | "Thank you!" |

In a formal setting, or if you want to sound polite, say the following:

Dōmo arigatō gozaimasu!   "Thank you very much!"

In a very casual setting, simply saying *dōmo* is also acceptable. You might also hear *saNkyū* among young people—the Japanized loanword for *thank you*.

LIFESAVERS

Dōmo, which literally means "indeed" or "truly," is a handy word. In a casual setting, you can say *dōmo* when meeting people, excusing yourself, entering a room, and so on. Because it's a context-sensitive word, pay attention to when Japanese people use *dōmo*.

If someone says *arigatō* to you, reply to him or her by saying …

Dō itashi mashite.   "You're welcome!"

When I was learning English in Japan, my English teacher taught me that I should not say *sorry* unless I was acknowledging my fault. I was shocked at that comment because in Japanese, "sorry" is used in a much broader sense. The word for "sorry" in Japanese is …

(Dōmo) SumimaseN.

It might not be a good idea for me to simply translate *sumimaseN* as "sorry" because it can sometimes mean "thank you" as well. For example, when someone works very hard on your behalf, you should thank her or him by saying *sumimaseN* rather than *arigatō*.

Japanese people use *sumimaseN* when they think they are causing the other party some kind of trouble or inconvenience. Suppose that your friend spent hours fixing your kitchen sink. You think that you caused him trouble, even though he volunteered to do so. This feeling makes you say *sumimaseN*.

If someone says *sumimaseN* to you in order to apologize, reply by saying either of the following:

Ie ie or *Īe!*   "No problem!"

GREEN TEA BREAK

When you say *ie* or *ie ie* as the reply to a person's apology, you should shake your head from side to side.

On the other hand, if she or he says *sumimaseN* to "thank" you, reply by saying:

Dō itashi mashite!   "You're welcome!"

The borderline between "sorry" and "excuse me" is also vague in Japanese. For instance, when you must walk in a hurry through a crowd of people, you would say "excuse me" in English. In Japanese, you would use *sumimaseN*. Then, when should you use "excuse me"?

Here are some clear situations in which you should use "excuse me" in Japanese:

- When entering a room
- When leaving a room
- When excusing yourself (for going to the bathroom, for example)
- When saying good-bye (in a formal setting)

In these cases, you should say …

Shitsurē shimasu.   "Excuse me."

Here are typical replies to someone saying *shitsurē shimasu*. When someone (1) enters your room or (2) asks for permission to temporarily excuse her- or himself saying *shitsurē shimasu*, you should say …

Dōzo.   "Please (come in/go ahead)."

When someone at work says *shitsurē shimasu* for "good-bye" at the end of the day, you should reply as follows:

Otsukaresama-deshita.   "Good-bye." (*Lit.* "You must be exhausted [due to hard work].")

SHORTCUTS TO SUCCESS

Because of the *shi* and *tsu* sounds combined, you might find it difficult to pronounce *shitsurē shimasu*. You might want to say the word slowly, by dividing it into syllables: *shi-tsu-re-e shi-ma-su*. Even if you do so, you would not sound awkward to Japanese ears at all.

We quickly went through the words for "thanks," "sorry," and "excuse me." Among these words, pay special attention to *sumimaseN* because the usage of this phrase is so wide.

Good-Bye!

There are many ways to say "good-bye" in Japanese, and each use depends on the degree of formality and the type of parting. If parting is short and you expect to see that person soon, you could say any of the following, ranging from a formal to a casual style:

Shitsurē shimasu.	[formal]
Soredewa.	
Sorejā.	
Jā! or *Jāne!*	[casual]

If you are going to see this person tomorrow, you can attach *mata ashita* ("again tomorrow") to some of the preceding expressions:

Soredewa mata ashita.

Sorejā mata ashita.

Jā mata ashita!

If you part from someone for a longer period of time, the following would be appropriate:

Mata oai shimashō.	"I will see you again."
Sayōnara or *Sayonara.*	"So long."

You might know *sayonara*, but once you arrive in Japan, you will notice that it isn't used as often as you might expect. It's a rather formal and "heavy" word for parting. In a formal parting, you might want to add the following phrase to *sayōnara*:

Sayōnara, ogeNkide!	"So long, I wish you the best!"

In daily conversation, probably the most common expression for good-bye is *sorejā*. It's neither too casual nor too polite—a neutral expression that can be used on any occasion.

The Magic Words

The beauty of ritualized expressions is that even one tiny phrase can easily and effectively convey your feelings to the listener. Those magic words literally work "magic" in that they make conversation run smoothly. Let's learn some more useful expressions.

Making a Request

There are a number of ways to ask for a favor, but they boil down to one simple expression. The magic phrase is …

> *Onegai shimasu.* "Please."

This is an extremely powerful phrase. Even in the worst-case scenario, when you can't remember any appropriate Japanese sentences, body language and using this expression might save you (just like I survived in Paris with only *s'il vous plaît*—"Please!").

Situations in which this phrase can be used are countless. Here are some examples for when to use *onegai shimasu*:

> **Situation 1:** When you buy something, you can point to it and say, *Onegai shimasu.*

> **Situation 2:** When you submit a document to someone (such as an immigration officer at the airport), say *Onegai shimasu.* You will give him or her a much better impression.

> **Situation 3:** When you want someone to pass the salt, you can point to it and simply say, *Onegai shimasu.*

Think about any suitable situations and practice this phrase in preparation.

In a situation in which you must ask for a big favor, or simply when you want to make a request politely, you can add the by-now-familiar magic word *sumimaseN* to *onegai shimasu*:

> *SumimaseN. Onegai shimasu.* "Excuse me. Please (do it)."

You'll learn more about making a request in Chapter 12.

Giving and Receiving

If you plan to visit someone in Japan, you might be thinking about taking a gift with you. Here is an easy dialogue that you can practice in such a situation:

Giver:	*Dōzo.*	"Here you are."
Receiver:	*Dōmo (arigatō).*	"Thank you."

You can use this handy *dōzo/dōmo* dialogue in any giving/receiving situation—not just for gift-giving.

You can also use *dōzo* whenever you offer some kind of service to someone. Suppose that you're sitting in a crowded train and see an elderly woman standing near you. You can offer her your seat by saying *dōzo.* Similarly, when you're in line and kindly let someone go ahead of you, you can use *dōzo,* meaning "After you, please."

Survival Phrases

What if you didn't catch what the other party said and you want her or him to repeat it? Here is a list of useful phrases:

Mō ichido onegai shimasu.	"One more time, please."
Mō ichido it-te kudasai.	"Please say one more time."
Yukkuri it-te kudasai.	"Please say it slowly."
Wakari-maseN.	"I don't understand."
Ēgo-de i-idesu ka?	"Is English okay?"
Ēgo-de onegai shimasu.	"In English, please."

You can make these requests more polite by adding *SumimaseN* at the beginning of each phrase.

You might think the last two phrases are kind of "cheating" because this is a book about Japanese. However, in a really urgent situation, you might desperately need to communicate in English. You will be pleasantly surprised that many Japanese do understand English. Make sure that you speak English slowly and clearly.

 GREEN TEA BREAK

When you give a gift to someone in Japan, always hand it to him or her *with both hands.* Likewise, when you receive a gift, never receive it with one hand because you will be considered rude. This principle also applies when you exchange business cards (*mēshi*).

LIFESAVERS

If you need assistance from Japanese people in English, you have a better chance of success by asking in writing rather than speaking. Make sure to use plain English when you write. When you ask someone to write something down, say the following:

Kai-te kudasai.   *"Please write it down."*

The Least You Need to Know

- Greetings are a great way to start a conversation—if you're careful to make a good first impression.
- Use buffer expressions—little hints before you say something directly—or you will appear blunt and self-centered.
- Be comfortable with magic words such as *sumimaseN* (excuse me), *onegai shimasu* (please), and *dōzo* (here you are).
- Don't be afraid to use ritualized expressions. Practice makes proficient!

Meeting People

In This Chapter

- Meeting people for the first time
- Exchanging names
- Useful conversation starters

With the greetings you learned in Chapter 8, you will have more success with first meetings. However, you don't want your conversation to stop there just because you lack something to talk about. You should get to know more about the person you're talking to, and subsequently you need her or him to learn more about you. In this chapter, you learn a number of sentences and questions that are useful when meeting people for the first time.

My Name Is ...

Suppose you're meeting someone for the first time. Because you don't know who he or she is, it's safe to start a conversation by exchanging formal greetings.

> *Hajime mashite.* "How do you do?"

The phrase *Hajime mashite* literally means "for the first time." At this point, if this is a business setting, you might encounter the ritual of a business card exchange. If that's the case, as I pointed out in Chapter 8, make sure that you give your card (*mēshi*) as well as receive the other person's business card with both hands.

GREEN TEA BREAK

Unless they are familiar with Western customs, Japanese people do not shake hands when greeting, nor do they hug or kiss. Polite bowing is all you need to do. Also, an overly big smile on your face might cause some degree of discomfort among the Japanese, especially on the first meeting.

Naturally, the next step is to introduce yourself. Let's suppose that your name is Brown.

BurauN-desu. "I am Brown."

This sentence is a shorter version of the following:

Watashi-wa BurauN-desu. "I am Brown."

Because you are introducing yourself, it is obvious that the "topic" of the sentence—"I"—is understood by the listener. So you can omit *watashi*, as seen in the first example.

Alternatively, you can introduce yourself using a more formal pattern, *[Your Name Here] to mōshi-masu*, as shown in the following example:

BurauN to mōshi-masu. "I am Brown."

X-*wa* Y-*desu*

In the sentence *Watashi-wa BurauN-desu*, I start the dialogue with "I," (*watashi*) as the topic. What follows the topic is the speaker's comment on the topic—that is, "Brown," (*BurauN*). This "X is Y" kind of equationlike sentence is common, and you should be familiar with its structure, as shown here:

X-*wa* Y-*desu*. "X is Y."

Let's look at a few examples of the X-*wa* Y-*desu* pattern:

Amerika-wa ōki-idesu. "America is big."

Toyota-wa nihoN-no kaisha-desu. "Toyota is a Japanese company."

Sushi-wa *oishi-idesu*. "*Sushi* is delicious."

In all these examples, -*wa* serves as the bridge between the topic and the comment. For instance, in the first example, the equation [America = big] is established by -*wa*.

Watashi-*wa* XYZ-*desu*

Another helpful sentence pattern to be learned here is *Watashi-wa* XYZ-*desu*. With the sentence pattern *Watashi-wa* XYZ-*desu*, not only can you identify your name, but you can also talk about anything concerning "you," as in the following examples:

Watashi-wa [AmerikajiN/KanadajiN/IgirisujiN]-desu.
"I am a(n) [American/Canadian/British]."

Watashi-wa jānarisuto-desu.   "I am a journalist."

And You Are ...?

After you have identified your name, the next step is to ask the listener what her or his name is:

> *SumimaseN ga, o-namae-wa naN to osshai-masu ka?*
> "Excuse me. What is your name?"

Because this is a question sentence, the question marker *ka* is attached at the end, as explained in Chapter 6. Note that to sound even more natural, you can omit *naN to osshai-masu ka*:

> *SumimaseN ga, o-namae-wa?*   "Excuse me. Your name is?"

HUH?

The Japanese word for "name" or "given name" is **namae**. If you refer to someone else's name, you should attach the polite marker *o-* to *namae*, as in *o-namae*, to show your respect to that person. Don't attach *o-* when you refer to your own name because you don't have to and should not show respect to yourself.

By the way, the word for "family name" (or "last name") is *myōji*.

In Chapter 6, you learned how to ask a question. Remember, in Japanese, you don't move a question word to the beginning of a sentence, as in **What** *is your name?* in English. Instead, its Japanese counterpart is more like *Your name is* **what**? This is what you see in the preceding example: The question word for "what," *naN*, does not appear at the beginning of the sentence, but toward the end.

Now, let's practice asking each other's names. My name is Fujita. Suppose that your family name is *Brown*:

> Me: *SumimaseN ga, o-namae-wa?*   "Excuse me. What is your name?"
>
> You: *BurauN to mōshi-masu.*   "My name is Brown. And your
> *O-namae-wa?*   name is?"
>
> Me: *Fujita to mōshi-masu.*   "(My name is) Fujita."

GREEN TEA BREAK

In English, you usually introduce yourself by your first name. In Japanese, on the other hand, you go by your last name first. When Japanese people refer to their full names, they say their family name first and then their given name, as in:

Watashi-wa Fujita Naoya-desu.   *"I am Naoya Fujita."*

However, if you have a Western name, either order is acceptable. Japanese people will honor your custom.

Notice that in your part of the dialogue, when you ask me what my name is, you simply say *O-namae-wa?* It's an incomplete sentence when translated into English, but a perfect sentence in Japanese. This is because in Japanese, you can omit whatever is understood in the context, as explained in Chapter 4. For the same reason, in response to the question *O-namae-wa?* I said *Fujita to mōshi-masu* instead of answering with a full sentence.

Beyond Exchanging Names

I believe that the most important factor for successful language learning is curiosity. Curiosity makes you ask people questions. A willingness to know something makes you listen to people more carefully. Even if you consider yourself a quiet person when speaking English, don't despair! I know many quiet or shy people who are learning a foreign language. Interestingly, many of them turn out to be quite talkative when speaking a foreign language. In language learning, there is nothing to lose, so don't be shy.

In the rest of this chapter, I introduce you to useful questions that serve as appropriate and effective ice-breakers for meeting someone for the first time. Most of the questions fall into the X-*wa* + predicate + *ka?* pattern, such as *O-namae-wa naN to osshai-masu ka?* ("What is your name?"). Ask these questions repeatedly. Repetition is the fastest way to become fluent in Japanese.

In the following section, just pay attention to question patterns and don't worry about answering the questions. I don't want to keep you too busy here. We'll get into answering questions in Chapter 10.

Occupations

The Japanese word for "job" is *shigoto*. If you refer to someone else's job, you should make the word sound polite by attaching *o-*, as in *o-shigoto*. Now, let's ask what the other party's occupation is. Because it's a somewhat personal question, it's a wise idea to first say *SumimaseN ga* ("Sorry for my rudeness").

SumimaseN ga, o-shigoto-wa nani-o sarete i-masu ka?
"Sorry for my rudeness. What do you do?"

For businesspeople, *kaisha* ("company") is an important word. If you're curious where she or he works, ask the following question:

Dochira-no kaisha-ni otsutome-desu ka?   "Where do you work?"

HUH?

The question word *dochira* ("where") is the polite version of *doko*.

Suppose that the person mentioned the name of the company she or he works for, but you don't know what kind of business that company engages in. You can ask a question by combining the question word *naN* ("what") and the noun *kaisha* ("company"):

NaN-no kaisha-desu ka?   "What company is it?"

Notice that this sentence does not have the topic "your company" because it is mutually understood between you and the listener. In other words, it is not there because it would be redundant if it were included.

HUH?

When the question word *naN* ("what") precedes a noun such as *kaisha* ("company"), the noun connector particle *-no* is attached to the question word, as in *naN-no*. For the explanation of *-no*, see the section "How to Describe Something or Someone" in Chapter 6.

Where Are You From?

It might be rude to ask the age or marital status of the person, but asking where she or he is from is certainly safe. You have just learned *dochira* ("where"). Using this question word, ask the following:

XYZ-saN-no goshusshiN-wa dochira-desu ka?   "Where do you come
(*goshusshiN* = birth place)   from?"

Notice that this question contains XYZ-*saN*. It is common practice to use *-saN* with the person's name instead of using the second-person pronoun *anata*, "you." In fact, you hardly hear personal pronouns in Japanese. The Japanese prefer calling or being called by their names rather than by "you." Likewise, you can omit the topic XYZ-*saN* in the preceding example.

LIFESAVERS

Remember, when you introduce yourself, do not add -*saN* to your own name. This is a big no-no! You would sound very eccentric because you would be showing respect to yourself.

At a private setting such as a party, asking where someone lives might be acceptable. Again, you can use the same question word, *dochira*. The new word you should know is *o-sumai* ("residence"):

> *O-sumai-wa dochira-desu ka?*   "Where do you live?"

Essential Party Greetings

If the first encounter with a person takes place where eating is involved, such as at a party or restaurant, there are a lot of things you can talk about and use as conversation starters. You can give a compliment on the food served or ask whether she or he likes a certain food. Let's first learn how to give a compliment on the food:

> *Kore-wa oishi-idesu **ne**!*   "This is delicious, **isn't it**?"

Oishi-i means "delicious." Did you notice the tiny particle at the end of the sentence, *ne?* This particle functions as a kind of exclamation. Use *ne* when you expect an agreement from the listener. I call *ne* the "agreement-seeking particle."

Let me introduce another useful sentence-final particle, *yo*. I call *yo* the "information-giving particle." By attaching *yo*, you are giving the listener new information. So if you want to tell the listener that the food is delicious, say the following:

> *Kore-wa oishi-idesu yo!*   "**I tell you** this is delicious!"

Sometimes, a conversation begins when you show interest in the food that the listener is eating. Here is how to ask what something is in reference to what the listener has:

> *Sore-wa naN-desu ka?*   "What is that?"

So far, we have seen *kore* ("this one") and *sore* ("that one"). Let me list all the "pointing" words. Please note that there are two kinds of "that one" in Japanese, as seen in the following table.

"Pointing" Words		
Object in speaker's domain	*kore*	"this one"
Object in listener's domain	*sore*	"that one"
Object away from speaker and listener	*are*	"that one over there"
Question word	*dore?*	"which one?"

Notice that I use the term "domain," such as "listener's domain." This does *not* necessarily mean that an object is in the listener's possession. As long as it is *near* the listener, you can refer to that object by using *sore*.

If you want to know what something is that is away from you and the listener, point to it and say:

    Are-wa naN-desu ka?   "What is that over there?"

If she or he does not know which one of several things you're referring to, she or he would say:

    Dore-desu ka?   "Which one?"

Pointing words are all nouns. When you want to use a pointing word together with another noun, such as *that person (over there)*, you need to use a different form, as shown in the following table.

"Pointing" Adjectives		
In speaker's domain	*kono* X	"this X"
In listener's domain	*sono* X	"that X"
Away from speaker and listener	*ano* X	"that X over there"
Question word	*dono* X	"which X?"

Here are examples of each expression:

Kono hoN-wa yasu-idesu.	"This book is cheap."
Sono hoN-wa dare-no-desu ka?	"Whose book is that (near you)?"
Ano hito-wa dare-desu ka?	"Who is that person over there?"
Dono hoN-o kai-masu ka?	"Which book are you going to buy?" (*kai-masu* = "buy")

HUH?

To remember all the "pointing" words, remember "*ko-so-a-do*." All four pointing words start with one of these syllables, as in the following examples based on "place":

koko	"this place; here; where I am"
soko	"that place; there; where you are"
asoko	"that place away from us; over there"
doko?	"which place? where?"

Oops! Let's get back to the dining table. Let's imagine that a girl sitting next to you at the table keeps eating *sushi*. Let's ask if she likes it:

O-sushi-ga *o-suki-desu ka?* "Do you like *sushi*?"

SHORTCUTS TO SUCCESS

For *suki-desu* ("like"), its object (such as *sushi*) must be marked by *-ga*, not the object marker *-o*. This is an exception.

If her answer is *hai* or *ē* ("yes") and you also like *sushi*, great! You have something in common to talk about. Without a doubt, *o-suki-desu ka* is one of the most frequently used phrases. Note that *o-*, which is attached to *suki-desu*, is an honorific prefix. Attach *o-* when you are addressing someone. However, when you refer to yourself, as in "*I* like *X*," simply say X-*ga suki-desu*, without *o-*.

Even if the answer is *Ie* ("no"), you might still continue the conversation, perhaps by asking, "Then, what kind of food do you like?" Important words here are *doNna* ("what kind of") and *tabemono* ("food"):

Jā, doNna tabemono-ga o-suki-desu ka?	"Then, what kind of food do you like?"

If it's a beverage, the word is *nomimono*:

Jā, doNna nomimono-ga o-suki-desu ka?	"Then, what kind of drink do you like?"

In this chapter, we have looked at useful conversation expressions. As in Western societies, it isn't a good idea to ask overtly personal questions, such as the person's age or marital status, especially when meeting someone for the first time. The rule of thumb is before asking any personal questions of someone, talk about yourself first. In Chapter 10, I introduce a number of useful patterns to use when talking about yourself.

The Least You Need to Know

- Japanese people usually do not shake hands when greeting, nor do they hug, kiss, or sport big smiles. Polite bowing is all you need to do.
- The X-*wa* Y-*desu* pattern is useful for making "X is Y" statements.
- Never add -*saN* to your own name when introducing yourself.
- Some basic questions such as *Hajime mashite* ("How do you do?") can be used as effective ice-breakers.
- Use the *ne* particle when you expect an agreement from the listener and *yo* when imparting information to him.

Talking About Yourself

In This Chapter

- Sharing personal information
- Talking about your hobbies
- Talking about your family

There is no doubt that you will master Japanese much more quickly if you consistently participate in actual conversation. You can't just wait for an opportunity to try out your Japanese. You need to make an opportunity! In Chapter 9, you learned how to make such an opportunity by using conversation starters. In this chapter, you learn how to elaborate on the conversation by talking about yourself.

Purpose of Your Visit to Japan

Again, let's assume that you're visiting Japan. Perhaps the person you're talking with is curious to know the purpose of your visit. She or he might ask you the following question:

NaN-de nihoN-ni ki-mashita ka?   "What made you come to Japan?"

The question word *naN-de* means "for what (purpose)." There could be many possible reasons; here are some common ones:

business	*shigoto*	fun/pleasure	*asobi*
business trip	*shucchō*	study abroad	*ryūgaku*
sightseeing	*kaNkō*	traveling	*ryokō*
sightseeing trip	*kaNkō ryokō*		

Do you remember how to answer a question (see Chapter 6)? In Japanese, it's important to listen to the question carefully and simply replace the question word, such as *naN* ("what"), with your answer word without changing the word order. So in reply to the previous question, *NaN-de nihoN-ni ki-mashita ka?* if your answer is "for sightseeing" (*kaNkō*), you would say the following:

> *KaNkō-de ki-mashita.*   "I came for sightseeing."

SHORTCUTS TO SUCCESS

Remember that any element that is understood by speakers within the context of the conversation can be omitted in Japanese. You can even omit the verb by replacing it with *-desu:*

> *KaNk ō(-de) desu.*   "For sightseeing."

The words *ryokō* ("traveling"), *kaNkō* ("sightseeing"), and *shigoto* ("business") are all nouns. What if you want to answer with a verb such as "to study Japanese" or "to meet friends" instead? All you need to do is attach the particle *-ni* to the stem of that verb. The stem is always the verb without *-masu* (see Chapter 5 for details). Let's find stems of these verbs:

> *nihoNgo-o beNkyō shi-masu*   "study Japanese"
>
> *nihoNgo-o beNkyō **shi***
>
> *tomodachi-ni ai-masu*   "meet friends"
>
> *tomodachi-ni **ai***

Using these stems, your answers should look like the following:

> *NihoNgo-o beNkyō **shi-ni** ki-mashita.*   "I came to study Japanese."
>
> *Tomodachi-ni **ai-ni** ki-mashita.*   "I came to see my friends."

The use of the stem for "purpose" is handy with motion verbs like *ki-masu* ("to come"). You can also use other motion verbs such as *iki-masu* ("to go"):

> Q: *Kyōto-ni nani-o **shi-ni** iki-masu ka?*   "For what purpose will you go to Kyoto?"
>
> A: *Tomodachi-ni **ai-ni** iki-masu.*   "To see my friends."

Let's practice this pattern. Answer the following question using the helpful tips provided. The answers are at the end of this chapter.

Exercise 1

Q: *NihoN-ni nani-o **shi-ni** iki-masu ka?*
"For what purpose will you go to Japan?"

A1: _____

"To eat delicious *sushi*." ("eat" = *tabe-masu*; "delicious" = *oishi-i*)

A2: _____

"To buy a Nikon camera." ("buy" = *kai-masu*; "camera" = *kamera*)

Talk About Your Background

Although it might be rude to ask the listener a personal question, it is okay to discuss something personal about yourself. In this section, you learn how to talk about:

- Where you live
- Your marital status
- Your job

Where You Live

The verb "to live" is *suNde i-masu* in Japanese. Look at an example:

*Tōkyō-**ni** suNde i-masu.*   "I live in Tokyo."

Make sure that you attach the "existence" particle *-ni* to the place name. By the way, if you want to ask where the listener lives, use *doko* ("where"):

*Doko-**ni** suNde i-masu ka?*   "Where do you live?"

On a related note, here is how you mention your birthplace:

*Kanada-**de** umare-mashita.*   "I was born in Canada."

ShusshiN-wa Kanada-desu.   "My birthplace is Canada."

Marital Status

Now let's move on to your marital status. The verb "married" is *kekkoN shite i-masu* in Japanese. If you are married, say …

KekkoN shite i-masu.   "I am married."

If you are not, then say …

KekkoN shite i-maseN.   "I am not married."

These two forms refer to your current status. If you want to refer to the future—as in "I will marry"—you must use a slightly different form, *kekkoN shi-masu:*

(Watashi-wa) raineN kekkoN shi-masu.   "I will marry next year."

Occupation

In Chapter 9, you learned how to ask the listener what her or his job is …

O-shigoto-wa nani-o sarete i-masu ka?   "What do you do?"

Now it's your turn to say what you do. The pattern is simply …

[Your Occupation Here]-desu.   "I'm XYZ."

For example, if you are a journalist, say:

Jānarisuto-desu.   "I'm a journalist."

Here is a list of some occupations.

Occupations

English	Japanese
company worker	*kaishaiN*
designer	*dezainā*
homemaker	*shufu*
journalist	*jānarisuto*
lawyer	*beNgoshi*
medical doctor	*isha*
missionary	*seNkyoshi*

English	Japanese
musician	*myūjishaN*
pastor	*bokushi*
priest	*shiNpu*
professor	*kyōju*
salesperson	*ēgyō*
self-employed	*jiēgyō*
student	*gakusē* (general term) *daigakusē* (university) *daigakuiNsē* (graduate school) *kōkōsē* (high school)
teacher	*kyōshi*

Using this list, let's practice a couple of basic dialogues. Suppose that you're an English teacher but the person you're talking with mistakenly believes that you're a student. The following dialogues make use of noun predicate conjugation. Before looking at the dialogues, let's quickly review noun predicate conjugation.

Noun Predicate Conjugation

	Affirmative	Negative
Present	*gakusē-desu*	*gakusē-jana-idesu*
	"is a student"	"isn't a student"
Past	*gakusē-deshita*	*gakusē-jana-kattadesu*
	"was a student"	"wasn't a student"

Okay, here is the dialogue:

Q: *Gakusē-desu ka?*   "Are you a student?"

A: *Īe, gakusē-jana-idesu.*   "No, I'm not a student."

Ego-no kyōshi-desu.   "I'm an English teacher."
(*Ēgo* = "English")

What if you're asked whether you *were* a teacher back in your home country? Let's answer that you were not a teacher but *were* a college student. Pay attention to the tense.

Q: *Amerika-de-wa kyōshi-deshita ka?*   "Were you a teacher in America?"

A: *Īe, kyōshi-jana-kattadesu.*   "No, I was not a teacher."

Daigakusē-deshita.   "I was a college student."

If you're learning Japanese with a partner, practice these dialogues with her or him. For an even better result, if there is a Japanese speaker around you, ask her or him to take one of the parts in the dialogue!

 LIFESAVERS

Sensē also means "teacher." The word *sensē* is an honorific (or polite) version of the general term *ky -oshi,* so don't use *sensē* when referring to yourself.

Do you want to tell people exactly where you work, rather than what type of job you do? The word for "to be employed" is *tsutomete i-masu.* Suppose that you work for Sony:

Watashi-wa Sony-ni tsutomete i-masu.   "I work for Sony."

Of course, using this pattern, you can ask the question "Where do you work?"

Doko-ni tsutomete i-masu ka?   "Where do you work?"

Suppose that you're asked where your company is located. The question you're most likely to hear takes the following pattern (note that your name is indicated as *XYZ*). The key word in this sentence pattern is *ari-masu,* which literally means "exist."

XYZ-saN-no kaisha-wa doko-ni ari-masu ka?
"Where is your company located?"

Let's answer this question. It should be easy by now, right? Keep the verb, omit what is understood, drop *ka*, and replace the question word *doko* with your answer:

Shikago-ni ari-masu.   "It is in Chicago."

I omitted the topic "my company" in the example because it is understood. You could keep it, of course.

Talk About Your Hobbies

 If you're looking for a good conversation topic, try talking about each other's hobbies, *shumi*. How would you say "What is your hobby?" in Japanese? Using the by-now-familiar question pattern X-*wa naN-desu ka?*, it looks like this:

> *Shumi-wa naN-desu ka?*   "What is your hobby?"

In reply to this question, all you need to do is insert your answer where *XYZ* appears in the following sentence pattern:

> *Watashi-no shumi-wa* XYZ-*desu.*   "My hobby is *XYZ*."

Here is a list of some common hobbies.

Hobbies

English	Japanese	English	Japanese
anime (animation)	*anime*	sports	*supōtsu*
art	*āto*	movies	*ēga*
coin collecting	*koiN shūshū*	music	*oNgaku*
comics	*maNga*	reading	*dokusho*
computer games	*koNpyūtā gēmu*	sewing/knitting	*shugē*
computers	*koNpyūtā*	shopping	*kaimono*
cooking	*ryōri*	stamp collecting	*kitte shūshū*
gardening	*gādeniNgu*	studying Japanese	*nihoNgo-no beNkyō*
Internet	*iNtānetto*	traveling	*ryokō*
karaoke	*karaoke*		

If I say to you "My hobby is sports," what would be the next question you might ask me?

> *DoNna supōtsu-ga suki-desu ka?*   "What kind of sports do you like?"

Or:

> *DoNna supōtsu-o shi-masu ka?*   "What kind of sports do you play?"

If you have a particular sport you're crazy about—for example, skating (*sukēto*)—and you want to find out if the listener also likes it, here's how you ask the question using *suki-desu* ("like"):

Sukēto-wa o-suki-desu ka? "Do you like skating?"

If she likes skating, she will say:

Hai, suki-desu. "Yes, I do."

If she doesn't like it, the answer will be:

Īe, (amari) suki-jana-idesu ga ... "No, (not much)."

In a negative answer like this, I suggest that you use *amari*, "not much; not very." By adding this word, your answer becomes softened and doesn't sound rude. The addition of *ga ...* at the end of the sentence softens the tone, too.

 HUH?

For any sport-related words, the verb for "play" is **shi-masu**, which literally means "to do."

As most sports are of Western origin, you can just treat the English words as being loanwords. Here is a list of some common sports. Notice that some sports names are not loanwords.

Sports

English	Japanese	English	Japanese
baseball	*yakyū*	rugby	*ragubī*
basketball	*basuketto*	skateboarding	*sukēto bōdo*
bicycling	*saikuriNgu*	skiing	*sukī*
dancing	*daNsu*	soccer	*sakkā*
golf	*gorufu*	swimming	*suiē*
(scuba) diving	*daibiNgu*	surfing	*sāfiN*
exercise in general	*uNdō*	tennis	*tenisu*
hiking	*haikiNgu*	volleyball	*barē*
jogging	*jogiNgu*		
mountain climbing	*tozaN*		

As you probably already know, some sports originated in Japan:

jūdō	judo	*keNdō*	kendo
karate	karate	*aikidō*	aikido
sumō	sumo		

Perhaps you practice or once practiced a Japanese sport such as *judo* or *karate* (probably not *sumo*). If so, try stopping by a local *dojo* ("exercise hall") when you visit Japan. It's nice to meet comrades in the same discipline, and this would be a great opportunity to get to know people.

Talk About Your Family

Family-related topics also facilitate conversation. These topics allow you to expand conversation simply because you have more people to talk about and the listener can relate to the topics easily.

Before we take a look at frequently used family terms, understand that there are two types of family terms. In Japanese, many nouns have polite counterparts. For example, the polite versions of *doko* ("where") and *kyōshi* ("teacher") are *dochira* and *sensē*, respectively. The same rule applies to family terms. The word for "family" is *kazoku*, and its polite version is *go-kazoku*. When you talk about your own family, you use the plain form, but when you talk about someone else's family, you use the polite form.

 Family Members

English	Your Family (Plain)	Someone's Family (Polite)
grandfather	*sofu*	*ojīsaN*
grandmother	*sobo*	*obāsaN*
father	*chichi*	*otōsaN*
mother	*haha*	*okāsaN*
uncle	*oji*	*ojisaN*
aunt	*oba*	*obasaN*
older brother	*ani*	*onīsaN*
older sister	*ane*	*onēsaN*
husband	*shujiN* or *otto*	*goshujiN*
wife	*kanai* or *tsuma*	*okusaN*

continues

Family Members   (continued)

English	Your Family (Plain)	Someone's Family (Polite)
younger brother	*otōto*	*otōtosaN*
younger sister	*imōto*	*imōtosaN*
sibling	*kyōdai*	*gokyōdai*
child	*kodomo*	*okosaN*
son	*musuko*	*musukosaN*
daughter	*musume*	*musumesaN*
grandchild	*mago*	*omagosaN*
cousin	*itoko*	*oitokosaN*
nephew	*oi*	*oigosaN*
niece	*mei*	*meigosa*

LIFESAVERS

Remember that syllable length is important in Japanese. The four-syllable *ojisaN* means "uncle," but the five-syllable *ojīsaN* means "grandfather."

In the rest of this chapter, you learn the following tasks:

- Telling people what your family is like
- Counting family members
- Counting the age of your family members
- Talking about your family members in detail

My Family Is ...

First, let's tell the listener whether your family is big or small:

> *Watashi-no kazoku-wa dai-kazoku-desu.*   "My family is big."

Dai-kazoku is a compound word, literally meaning "big family." If you want to say "My family is *not* big," you need to use the negative form of the noun "big family." Do you remember noun conjugation from Chapter 5? Here is the table.

	Affirmative	**Negative**
Present	*dai-kazoku-desu*	*dai-kazoku-jana-idesu*
	"is a big family"	"isn't a big family"
Past	*dai-kazoku-deshita*	*dai-kazoku-jana-kattadesu*
	"was a big family"	"wasn't a big family"

The sentence should look like this:

> *Watashi-no kazoku-wa dai-kazoku-jana-idesu.*   "My family is not big."

Now, let's learn how to say, "I have a such-and-such family member." In Japanese, when you refer to "having" family members as in "I have children," you use the verb *i-masu* ("exist"). For example, if you have a son (*musuko*), you say:

> *Watashi-wa musuko-ga i-masu.*   "I have a son."

Counting People

 Japanese does not have a plural marker like the English -*s* in "sons." In the previous example, there is no way for the listener to find out if I have one son or more. Let's learn how to ask "how many people" there are. The question word for "how many people" is *naN-niN*.

> *MusukosaN-ga **naN-niN** i-masu ka?*   "How many sons do you have?"

The question word *naN-niN* consists of two parts, *naN* ("how many") and *niN* ("people"). In Japanese, when you count someone or something, you must use the appropriate "counter." In this case, the counter is for "human beings"—*niN*. (Refer to Chapter 7 for a review of the basic number words.) There are two exceptions, as you can see in the following table. Notice that "one person" and "two people" are *hitori* and *futari*, respectively.

Counting People

1	***hitori***	7	*shichi-niN* or *nana-niN*
2	***futari***	8	*hachi-niN*
3	*saN-niN*	9	*kyū-niN* or *ku-niN*
4	*yo-niN*	10	*jū-niN*
5	*go-niN*	11	*jū ichi-niN*
6	*roku-niN*	How many?	*naN-niN*

If you have three sons, answer in the following way:

> *(Watashi-wa)* ***musuko-ga saN-niN*** *i-masu.*   "I have three sons."

This sentence illustrates the basic pattern used when including a number in a sentence:

> Noun-Particle + Number-Counter + Predicate

In this example, the noun-particle is *musuko-ga*, then comes the number-counter *saN-niN*, and then the verb *i-masu*.

Let's look at a slightly more complicated case. What if you have three sons *and* four daughters? You'll need the noun connector *to* ("and"):

> *Musuko-ga saN-niN* **to** *musume-ga yo-niN i-masu.*
> "I have three sons and four daughters."

Now, how about a mini-test? How would you say the following? It's perfectly okay to go back to the preceding tables. The answers are at the end of this chapter.

Exercise 2

1. I have five siblings.

   _____

2. I have two uncles and one aunt.

   _____

Ages

You've learned how to count people. Now, let's learn how to say the age of a person. The counter for "age" is *-sai*. I list the ages between 1 and 11 in the following table. As usual, for numbers above 10, we repeat the same counting system. Again, there are some irregularities in pronunciation, which are indicated in bold.

Counting Ages

1	*is-sai*	7	*nana-sai*
2	*ni-sai*	8	*has-sai*
3	*saN-sai*	9	*kyū-sai*
4	*yoN-sai*	10	*jus-sai*
5	*go-sai*	11	*jū is-sai*
6	*roku-sai*	How old?	*NaN-sai?* or *Ikutsu?*

Asking the listener's age might be rude, but it's okay for you to tell her or him *your* age! Suppose that you're 36 years old. Here is how you tell your age:

> *Watashi-wa saN-jū roku-sai-desu.*   "I'm 36 years old."

For the sake of practice, may I ask your age?

> *NaN-sai-desu-ka?*   "How old are you?"

Or even more politely:

> *SumimaseN ga, o-ikutsu-desu ka?*   "Excuse me, but how old are you?"

Notice that I'm trying to make my question polite by using *sumimaseN ga*. Now, tell me your age:

> *Watashi-wa _____-sai desu.*

Putting Everything Together

We've covered a lot of topics in this chapter: residence, marital status, occupations, hobbies, family members, and ages. You could, of course, give these information bits separately, sentence by sentence, but you might be tempted to put them together in one sentence. This task can be done by using the conjugation form called the *TE*-form, explained in Chapter 6.

First, let's review some of the useful verbs covered in this chapter, along with their *TE*-forms.

	Regular Form	*TE*-Form
"to live"	*suNde i-masu*	*suNde i-te*
"to be married"	*kekkoN shite i-masu*	*kekkoN shite i-te*
"to work"	*tsutomete i-masu*	*tsutomete i-te*
"my hobby is *XYZ*"	*shumi-wa* XYZ-*desu*	*shumi-wa* XYZ-*de*
"is *XYZ* years old"	XYZ-*sai-desu*	XYZ-*sai-de*

Suppose that you want to put together the following bits of information:

> I live in Tokyo. And I work for IBM.

All you need to do is change the first verb, "live," into the *TE*-form:

> *Watashi-wa Tōkyō-ni <u>suNde i-te</u>, IBM-ni tsutomete i-masu.*
> "I live in Tokyo and work for IBM."

LIFESAVERS

You might have been tempted to use the connector -*to* ("and"). But remember, this is a noun connector and never connects sentences. For example, you can say *JoN-to Risa* ("John and Lisa"), but you can *never* say:

Watashi-wa Tōky ō-ni <u>suNde i-masu</u> to, IBM-ni tsutomete i-masu.
"I live in Tokyo and work for IBM."

Connecting sentences using the *TE*-form is useful, as shown previously. Most importantly, with this connector, your Japanese will sound more sophisticated!

Before closing this chapter, do the following exercise for sentence connection. Because this is not a memorization test, it's perfectly okay to refer to the rest of the chapter to find the correct words. As usual, the answers are given at the end of the chapter.

Exercise 3

1. My father is 62 years old, and his hobby is golf.

   _____

2. I am John and (I) have four children.

   _____

3. My older brother works for Sony and is not married.

   _____

This chapter might have seemed intensive. Although there are many new words, the grammatical structures introduced here are pretty simple. I suggest that you first become familiar with the grammatical patterns and then gradually increase your vocabulary.

Answers

Exercise 1

A1: *Oishi-i* sushi-o *tabe-ni iki-masu.*

A2: *NikoN-no kamera-o kai-ni iki-masu.*

Exercise 2

1. *Watashi-wa kyōdai-ga go-niN i-masu.*

2. *Watashi-wa oji-ga futari to oba-ga hitori i-masu.*

Exercise 3

1. *Chichi-wa roku-jū ni-sai -**de**, shumi-wa gorufu-desu.*

2. *Watashi-wa JoN-**de**, kodomo-ga yo-niN i-masu.*

3. *Ani-wa Sony-ni tsutomete i-**te**, kekkoN shite i-maseN.*

The Least You Need to Know

- Don't be afraid to talk about your personal background, such as hobbies and family, using the patterns and vocabulary in this chapter.
- Use the question word *naN-de* when you want to ask someone "for what (purpose)?"
- Use the polite counterparts of nouns when you talk about someone else's family, but use the plain form when you talk about your own family.
- Use negatives when you can't remember a certain word. For example, if you can't come up with the adjective for "big," as long as you know the adjective for "small" (*chīsa-i*), you can convey the message by saying "not small" (*chīsa-ku na-i*).
- Count people and talk about age using the appropriate "counters." The counter for "human beings" is *-niN* (except for *hitori* and *futari*, "one" and "two"). The counter for "age" is *-sai*.
- Use the *TE*-form to connect sentences.

Extending Invitations

In This Chapter

- Two ways to ask people out
- Making your invitation tempting
- How to turn down invitations

As I emphasized in Chapter 10, it's extremely important to create opportunities to practice Japanese with native speakers. You learned in Chapter 10 how to initiate conversations in Japanese. In this chapter, you learn how to ask people to dinner, a movie, and so on, so that you can create a language learning opportunity.

Polite Invitations

If you want to ask the listener to do something together, such as go to dinner or a movie, use the following pattern:

Verb Stem + *maseN ka?* "Won't you …?"

As you can see, the invitation pattern uses the negative form of a verb. Here's an example using this pattern:

ResutoraN-ni iki-maseN ka? "Won't you go to the restaurant (with me)?"

SHORTCUTS TO SUCCESS

To make the *-maseN ka* pattern sound natural, add a slight rising intonation toward the end of the sentence.

Of course, you can use verbs other than *iki-masu* in this pattern, but let's stick to *iki-masu* for the time being because this is probably the most common verb to use when asking people out.

Here is a list of place names you might find common when inviting your friend to go somewhere with you:

Places to Go

English	Japanese	English	Japanese
art museum	*bijutsukaN*	mall (shopping)	*mōru*
bar	*bā*	mountain	*yama*
beach	*bīchi*	movie	*ēga*
bookstore	*hoNya*	movie theater	*ēgakaN*
club	*kurabu*	museum	*hakubutsukaN*
concert	*koNsāto*	park	*kōeN*
department store	*depāto*	party	*pāti*
dining/meal	*shokuji*	picnic	*pikunikku*
driving	*doraibu*	play (theater)	*eNgeki*
fishing	*tsuri*	pub/tavern (Japanese style)	*izakaya*
for a walk	*saNpo*	restaurant	*resutoraN*
hiking	*haikiNgu*	shopping	*kaimono*
karaoke	*karaoke*	sports game/match	*shiai*
lake	*mizūmi*	swimming pool	*pūru*
live house (for music)	*raibu hausu*	traveling	*ryokō*

GREEN TEA BREAK

In the previous table, you find *izakaya*. An *izakaya* is a casual-style pub or tavern where beverages and delicious Japanese food are served at reasonable prices. It's worth checking out.

Now let's practice this pattern. Please invite your friend to the following places.

Exercise 1

1. Movie (*ēga*)

   _____

2. Shopping (*kaimono*)

   _____

3. Dining (*shokuji*)

Instead of putting a "destination" phrase into the pattern XYZ-*ni iki-maseN ka?* you could put a "purpose" phrase in the pattern, meaning "Won't you go out *for doing XYZ?*" You learned this pattern in Chapter 10. Simply replace *XYZ* with a verb stem, as seen in the following example:

*Ēga-o **mi**-ni iki-maseN ka?*   "Won't you go out to watch a movie?"

This pattern is useful because, by using an activity verb, you can make your invitation more specific. Here are some more verbs you can use in this pattern.

 LIFESAVERS

The verb *shi-masu* is handy. By adding *shi-masu* to a western loanword, you can turn it into one of the verbs you see here:

doraibu	*shi-masu*	"to drive (for fun)"
ekusasaizu	*shi-masu*	"to exercise (for fitness)"
jogiNgu	*shi-masu*	"to jog"

Activity Verbs

English	Verb Stem	English	Verb Stem
buy	*kai*	have fun	*asobi*
dance	*odori*	listen	*kiki*
do, play (sports)	*shi; yari*	swim	*oyogi*
drink	*nomi*	sing	*utai*
eat	*tabe*	watch	*mi*

Now with a place name and an activity verb combined, you can ask a more elaborate question. Suppose that you want to go to the beach (*bīchi*) to swim (*oyogi-masu*):

Bīchi-ni oyogi-ni iki-maseN ka?   "Won't you go to the beach to swim with me?"

Remember that Japanese word order is flexible. In addition to the previous sentence, you could also say the following:

Oyogi-ni bīchi-ni iki-maseN ka?

Let's do a short exercise here. For each of the following questions, ask the listener out to do the indicated activity. The answers are given at the end of this chapter.

Exercise 2

1. to the art museum to see the *Mona Lisa*

   _____

2. to the *sushi* bar to eat delicious *sushi* ("*sushi* bar" = *sushiya;* "delicious" = *oishi-i*)

   _____

3. to the live house to listen to jazz

   _____

So far, we have focused on *iki-masu* ("to go") for the *-maseN ka* pattern. Here are some examples with other commonly used invitational verbs:

Uchi-ni ki-maseN ka?	"Won't you come to my house?"
XYZ-o tabe-maseN ka?	"Won't you eat *XYZ*?"
XYZ-o nomi-maseN ka?	"Won't you drink *XYZ*?"
Isshoni kaeri-maseN ka?	"Won't you go home (with me)?"
Notte iki-maseN ka?	"Need a ride?"
Isshoni XYZ-o mi-maseN ka?	"Won't you watch *XYZ* (with me)?"

"Let's …!" and "Shall We …?"

The pattern you have just learned, *-maseN ka*, is a modest way to ask people out to do something. Let's look at a couple of other ways.

Let's!

If you're pretty sure that the listener would accept your invitation, you could use a different pattern, which is equivalent to the English "Let's …!" The pattern looks like this:

Verb Stem + *mashō!*   "Let's …!"

Here is an example:

Ēga-ni iki-mashō!   "Let's go to a movie!"

As you can see, we combined the verb stem *iki* with *mashō*.

To make sure that you are comfortable with this pattern, do the following exercise.

Exercise 3

1. Let's go home! ("go home" = *kaeri-masu*)

   _____

2. Let's eat! ("eat" = *tabe-masu*)

   _____

3. Let's take a rest here! ("take a rest" = *yasumi-masu*; "here" = *koko-de*)

   _____

Just as with the *-maseN ka* pattern, you can combine a destination phrase (like *egakaN*) with an activity verb (like *ēga-o mi-masu*):

ShiNjuku-no ēgakaN-ni ēga-o mi-ni iki-mashō!
"Let's go to the movie theater in Shinjuku to watch a movie!"

What if you feel like making a suggestion, but you aren't sure exactly what to do? Useful words you can count on are "something (to do)," *nanika*, and "some place (to go to)," *dokoka*. For example, when your friends all look bored, you can make a suggestion by saying the following:

Nanika shi-mashō!   "Let's do something!"

Dokoka iki-mashō!   "Let's go somewhere!"

If your friends look hungry, what suggestion would you make?

Nanika tabe-mashō!   "Let's eat something!"

Or in an even more sophisticated way:

Nanika tabe-ni iki-mashō!   "Let's go eat something!" (*iki-masu* = "go")

HUH?

The word *nanika* ("something") is made of *nani* ("what") and *ka* (question particle). *Dokoka* ("somewhere") is made of *doko* ("where") and *ka*. You can make a "some-" word by attaching *ka* to a question word:

dare ("who") + *ka dareka*	"someone"
itsu ("when") + *ka itsuka*	"someday"
ikura ("how much") + *ka ikuraka*	"some amount"
naze ("why") + *ka nazeka*	"for some reason"

Shall We?

With the *-mashō* pattern, you make a strong suggestion. However, by attaching the question marker *ka* at the end of this pattern, you make it sound less forceful:

> Verb Stem + *mashō ka?*   "Shall we …?"

Let's look at one example. Imagine a situation in which you and your friends are wondering what kind of food you should eat for dinner (*ryōri* = "cuisine"):

> *NihoN ryōri-o tabe-mashō ka?*   "Shall we eat Japanese food?"

Unlike other question sentences, the *-mashō ka?* pattern has falling intonation toward the end of a sentence.

The *mashō ka?* pattern is used with a question word as well. This way, instead of making a suggestion, you can ask for a suggestion from your listener(s). Here are some frequently used suggestion-seeking questions:

Nani-o shi-mashō ka? (*nani* = "what")	"What shall we do?"
Nani-o chūmoN shi-mashō ka? (*chūmoN shi-masu* = "order food")	"What shall we order?" (at a restaurant)
Doko-ni iki-mashō ka? (*doko* = "where")	"Where shall we go?"
Doko-de ai-mashō ka? (*ai-masu* = "meet")	"Where shall we meet?"
NaN-ji-ni VERB STEM-mashō ka? (*naN-ji-ni* = "at what time")	"What time shall we …?"

Wow, we've seen lots of examples! If you're feeling a little overwhelmed, try memorizing a core dialogue. When you become comfortable with the core dialogue, you can try to apply it to other verbs. Let's look at a core dialogue involving the -*mashō ka?* pattern.

Q: *Nani-o tabe-mashō ka?*   "What shall we eat?"

A1: Sushi-o *tabe-mashō!*   "Let's eat *sushi!*"

Or:

A2: Sushi-o *tabe-mashō ka?*   "Shall we eat *sushi*?"

Declining the Invitation

So far, you have learned invitational questions. When you hear these question patterns, you can easily recognize them and answer properly. Suppose that your friend asks you the following question. Can you figure out what she is saying?

Sushi-o *tabe-ni iki-maseN ka?*

You got it! This means "Wanna go out to eat *sushi*?" If you want to go, your answer looks like this:

Hai, iki-mashō!   "Yes, let's go!"

Or:

I-idesu ne! Iki-mashō!   "Sounds good! Let's go!"
(*i-idesu* = "good")

What if, for some reason, you must turn down the invitation? Here is the easiest way to decline the invitation:

SumimaseN, kyō-wa chotto …   "Sorry, I cannot make it today …"

Here are some more useful expressions of declination, in case you want to make your answer more specific:

SumimaseN, chotto tsugō-ga warukute …   "Sorry, I have some conflict …"

SumimaseN, chotto yōji-ga arimashite …   "Sorry, there is something I have to take care of …"

Chotto can mean many things; I can't give you the exact definition of the word. In this case, *chotto* functions as a "hesitation" marker. *Chotto*, in this case, keeps your answer ambiguous and lets the listener make assumptions about your feelings, rather than you bluntly expressing these feelings.

 GREEN TEA BREAK

Here are other functions of *chotto*:

- Getting someone's attention, equivalent to "Hey!" Example: *Chotto mi-te!* ("Hey! Look!")
- Asking people to wait for you. Example: *Chotto mat-te!* ("Wait!")
- Meaning "a little." Example: Q: *Samu-idesu ka?* ("Are you cold?") A: *Ē, chotto.* ("Yes, a little.")

Perhaps you think that the *chotto* expressions are not sufficient to decline the offer, and you feel like adding a more specific excusable reason. Then I suggest that you use *kara*, which means "therefore; so." Here is the sentence pattern when *kara* connects the reason sentence with the main sentence:

[REASON *kara* RESULT]

Suppose that you want to decline the listener's invitation because you have another appointment (*yakusoku*):

Yakusoku-ga ari-masu kara chotto ...   "I have an appointment, so I cannot ..."
(*ari-masu* = "have")

What other excuses can you think of? Here are a few:

"I have some more work to do."   *Shigoto-ga ari-masu kara chotto ...*

"I am busy."   *Isogashi-idesu kara chotto ...*

"I don't feel well."   *Guai-ga waru-idesu kara chotto ...*
(*guai* = "feeling," *waru-i* = "bad")

"I'm allergic to *XYZ*."   *XYZ arerugī-desu kara chotto ...*

"I must wake up early tomorrow."   *Ashita haya-idesu kara chotto ...*
(*ashita* = "tomorrow," *haya-i* = "early")

If you must decline the invitation, it would be nice to thank her for the kindness:

> *Arigatō gozaimasu. Mata koNdo onegai shimasu.*
> "Thank you. Please let me know next time."

Make Your Invitation Hard to Resist!

When you ask the listener out to do something, just saying *Iki-maseN ka?* might not be appealing enough. In this section, let's learn how to make your invitation harder to resist.

You have just learned the "reason" marker *kara*. You can use *kara* to make your question tempting. Let's consider an example. Suppose that there is a restaurant where food is inexpensive (*yasu-idesu*). Let's ask the listener out to that restaurant to eat:

> *Ano resutoraN-wa yasu-idesu **kara** tabe-ni iki-maseN ka?*
> "That restaurant is cheap, **so** won't you go out to eat with me?"

Let's do some exercises using this pattern. Write convincing invitations based on the following information. Make sure that you include *kara*.

Exercise 4

1. It's fun, so won't you come to the party? ("fun" = *tanoshi-idesu*)

   _____

2. It's interesting, so won't you go to the movie theater to watch *XYZ* (with me)? ("interesting" = *omoshiro-idesu*)

   _____

3. It's hot today, so won't you go to the beach to swim? ("hot" = *atsu-idesu,* "today" = *kyō*; "swim" = *oyogi-masu*)

   _____

How did you do? Compare your answers with the answer keys at the end of this chapter. Remember that word order is flexible, so even if your answers look different from mine, as long as you use the same words and particles and the verb predicate stays at the end of the sentence, your answers should be perfectly fine.

There is another way to make your invitation more convincing. In Chapter 9, I introduced *yo*, the sentence-final particle. This particle functions as an "assertion" marker. Let's see an example involving *yo*:

> *Nomi-maseN ka? Totemo oishi-idesu* **yo!**
> "Won't you drink (this)? It's *very* delicious, **you know**!"

HUH?

The adverb ***totemo*** means "very," and it modifies an adjective.

Let's take a mini-quiz again. Using the preceding example sentence as a guide, write (or say) sentences based on the following information.

Exercise 5

1. Won't you buy this pen? It's cheap! ("buy" = *kai-masu*)

   _____

2. Won't you listen to this CD? It's good! ("listen" = *kiki-masu*)

   _____

3. Won't you watch this *anime?* It's funny! ("funny" = *okashi-i*)

   _____

Answers

Exercise 1

1. *Ēga-ni iki-maseN ka?*

2. *Kaimono-ni iki-maseN ka?*

3. *Shokuji-ni iki-maseN ka?*

Exercise 2

1. *BijutsukaN-ni Mona Riza-o mi-ni iki-maseN ka?*

2. *Sushiya-ni oishi-i* sushi-o *tabe-ni iki-maseN ka?*

3. *Raibu hausu-ni jazu-o kiki-ni iki-maseN ka?*

Exercise 3

1. *Kaeri-mashō!*

2. *Tabe-mashō!*

3. *Koko-de yasumi-mashō!*

Exercise 4

1. *Tanoshi-idesu kara, pāti-ni ki-maseN ka?*

2. *Omoshiro-idesu kara, ēgakaN-ni XYZ-o mi-ni iki-maseN ka?*

3. *Kyō-wa atsu-idesu kara, bīchi-ni oyogi-ni iki-maseN ka?*

Exercise 5

1. *Kono peN-o kai-maseN ka? Yasu-idesu yo!*

2. *Kono CD-o kiki-maseN ka? I-idesu yo!*

3. *Kono anime-o mi-maseN ka? Okashi-idesu yo!*

The Least You Need to Know

- Learn as many activity verbs and location words as possible. They are essential for extending invitations.
- Use "Shall we …?" (-*mashō ka?*), "Let's …!" (-*mashō!*), and "Won't you …?" (-*maseN ka?*) patterns properly.
- Make your invitation tempting by using *kara* ("therefore").
- When you must decline someone's invitation, use the *[REASON] kara chotto …* pattern.

The Essentials for Traveling

The following chapters prepare you to travel on your own to Japan and within the country. You learn how to go through Immigration and Customs at the airport and find out how ground transportation works in Japan. With the phrases you learn in these chapters, you will be able to tell a cab driver, for example, to take you to the hotel of your choice. These chapters provide step-by-step instructions for check-in and check-out at the hotel. Bank-related phrases and expressions are also covered, in case you want to exchange money.

As in the previous chapters, the number of must-memorize expressions is minimal. However, with additional vocabulary of your choice, these basic expressions will enable you to say what you need in most travel-related situations.

In the Airplane

In This Chapter

- How to make requests
- Helpful in-flight expressions

In Chapters 12 through 21, you learn important travel-related expressions for activities such as checking into a hotel, getting around town, dining, and so on. However, you don't have to wait until the plane lands in Japan to practice Japanese. Chances are, on a flight to Japan, the people surrounding you are Japanese speakers. Some of the flight attendants might also be Japanese natives or be fluent in Japanese. Don't waste time; talk to them! By the time you arrive in Japan, you will become more confident about your communication skills.

Making Requests

In Chapter 8, you learned a basic expression to use when making a request. Do you remember it? Here it is:

> *Onegai shimasu.* "Please (do it)."

If you want to make your request more polite, add *sumimaseN* at the beginning:

> *SumimaseN, onegai shimasu.* "Excuse me, please (do it)."

Onegai shimasu is a multipurpose request expression. If you have a dinner tray in front of you and you want a flight attendant to take it away, you can point to it and gently say *Onegai shimasu*. Simple, isn't it? Using body language and pointing at an object, *onegai shimasu* is a powerful tool for expressing what you want.

XYZ-*ni Shi-masu*

What would you do in the following situation? As a meal is being served, you are asked which one you would prefer, Japanese tea (*ocha*) or coffee (*kōhī*):

> *Ocha-ni shi-masu ka, kōhī-ni shi-masu ka?*   "Japanese tea, or coffee?"

HUH?

XYZ-*ni shi-masu* means "to decide on *XYZ*." You will often hear this pattern at a restaurant or coffee shop.

GREEN TEA BREAK

Ocha usually refers to green tea. It is green because it is not roasted like British tea. British tea, or "black tea," is called *k ōcha* (literally, "red tea").

Suppose that you want to drink Japanese tea, *ocha*. Using *onegai shimasu*, you can make a request as follows:

> *Ocha-o onegai shimasu.*   "Japanese tea, please."

By just adding XYZ-*o* to the expression as shown previously, the range of a request can be expanded. You no longer have to point to an object or use body language. With XYZ-*o*, you can even ask an attendant to bring something to you. Suppose that you dropped your fork and want another one:

> *SumimaseN, fōku-o onegai shimasu.*   "Excuse me, would you get me a fork?"

When you get what you requested, don't forget to say thank you!

> *Dōmo (arigatō).*   "Thank you."

GREEN TEA BREAK

You might recall that as an alternative to *dōmo (arigatō)*, you can use *sumimaseN* to show your appreciation. *SumimaseN* would be more appropriate, especially if you are thanking the listener for the extra work that your request has caused.

Instead of *onegai shimasu*, you can use the verb XYZ-*o kudasai*, "Please give me *XYZ*." For example:

Kōhī-o kudasai.   "Please give me some coffee."

Let's look at some realistic situations in which you can use this pattern. When you travel to Japan, you will need to fill out an *Embarkation card* and submit it to an immigration officer at the airport upon arrival. Flight attendants hand these forms out to passengers. Suppose that you were asleep when they came with the form, and did not get one. Ask for an Embarkation card (*nyūkoku kādo*) as follows:

Nyūkoku kādo-o kudasai.   "Please give me an Embarkation card."

 GREEN TEA BREAK

The immigration officer will keep one portion of the Embarkation card and staple the smaller portion to your passport. Don't lose the smaller portion because you will need it to leave the country. For visa or related information, please visit the official website of the Japanese Ministry of Foreign Affairs at www.mofa.go.jp.

The *TE*-Form Request

Now, let's learn a slightly more sophisticated request expression. Do you remember the *TE*-form, the multipurpose conjugation introduced in Chapter 6? If you've forgotten this conjugation, this is a good time to go back to Chapter 6 and review it. The new request pattern you're about to learn makes extensive use of the *TE*-form, as seen here:

TE-form + *kudasai.*   "Please do so-and-so."

With this pattern, you will be able to make a variety of requests. For example, let's ask your friend to come. The verb is *ki-masu* and its *TE*-form is *ki-te*. So the request sentence looks like this:

(SumimaseN,) ki-te kudasai.   "(Excuse me,) please come."

Now, try taking a mini-test. How would you make a request in each of the following situations? Be prepared, because I've made the exercise a little challenging. I have provided question words in English; look for these words in Appendix B. Additionally, you will need to convert the verb to the *TE*-form. If you aren't sure about how to do that, refer to Chapter 6. The answers are at the end of this chapter.

Exercise 1

1. Please call (= telephone).

   _____

2. Please speak in English. (Hint: The postposition for "in" is -*de*.)

   _____

3. Please wait!

   _____

How did you do? Look at the following list of verbs that can be used while in flight:

In-Flight Request Verbs

English	*MASU*-form	*TE*-form
bring	*motte ki-masu*	*motte ki-te*
take *X* away	*motte iki-masu*	*motte it-te*
clear the tray	*torē-o sage-masu*	*torē-o sage-te*
throw away	*sute-masu*	*sute-te*
take; grab; pick up	*tori-masu*	*tot-te*
open	*ake-masu*	*ake-te*
close; shut	*shime-masu*	*shime-te*

Let me give you realistic examples of some requests using each of the preceding verbs. They could be used to request something from both a nearby passenger or a flight attendant.

You can probably think of several things that you want a flight attendant to bring to you. Let's ask her to bring water (*mizu*) because you're thirsty:

> *SumimaseN, mizu-o motte ki-te kudasai.*   "Excuse me, please bring water."

HUH?

Motte ki-masu is the verb for "bring" and ***motte iki-masu*** for "take (away)." These are called "compound" verbs:

motte ki-masu ("bring") = *mochi-masu* ("hold") + *ki-masu* ("come")

motte iki-masu ("take away") = *mochi-masu* ("hold") + *iki-masu* ("go")

The first half of such a compound is in the *TE*-form. In the rest of this book, you will see additional compound verbs in this category.

You finish eating the meal. Suppose that the flight attendants forgot to take your tray away. Using a pointing word, *kore* ("this thing"), say the following:

(Pointing at the tray) *Kore-o motte it-te kudasai.*   "Please take this away."

You can also use *torē-o sage-masu*, "clear the tray":

Torē-o sage-te kudasai.   "Please clear the tray."

Yes, *torē* is a loanword for "tray."

Suppose that your seat pocket is full of trash (*gomi*). How would you ask an attendant to throw it away for you? You're causing the attendant to do extra work for you, so be sure you add the magic word, *sumimaseN*:

SumimaseN, gomi-o sute-te kudasai.
"Excuse me, please throw away the trash."

You can make your request even politer by adding an extra phrase at the end of the *-te kudasai* pattern:

TE-form + *kudasai maseN ka?*   "Could you please do so-and-so?"

Let's change the previous examples to the politer versions:

SumimaseN, mizu-o motte ki-te kudasai maseN ka?
"Excuse me, could you please bring (me) water?"

Torē-o sage-te kudasai maseN ka?
"Could you please clear the tray?"

SumimaseN, gomi-o sute-te kudasai maseN ka?
"Excuse me, could you please throw away the trash?"

Making Requests of Your Fellow Passengers

Flight attendants aren't the only people you might have to ask for help. Sometimes, it could be passengers sitting near you. What if you sit in a window seat, and you have something in the overhead bin that you want a nearby passenger to hand to you? You would ask the following question:

SumimaseN, XYZ-o tot-te kudasai.   "Excuse me, please hand *XYZ* to me."

XYZ could be anything, but in this particular situation, here are things you might put in the overhead bin:

bag	*kabaN* or *baggu*
suitcase	*sūtsu kēsu*
briefcase/attaché case	*atasshu kēsu*

Chances are, there are many bags in the bin and you will have to describe your bag. In such a case, the other passenger will ask you *which one* is yours:

Dore-desu ka?   "Which one is it?"

SHORTCUTS TO SUCCESS

When you memorize an adjective, try to pair it with another adjective that is opposite in meaning (antonym), such as:

ōki-i ("big") vs. *chīsa-i* ("small")

kuro-i ("black") vs. *shiro-i* ("white")

taka-i ("expensive") vs. *yasu-i* ("cheap")

omo-i ("heavy") vs. *karu-i* ("light")

This kind of association method makes vocabulary learning easy and meaningful.

Here are helpful description words:

big	*ōki-i*	blue	*ao-i*
small	*chīsa-i*	red	*aka-i*
black	*kuro-i*	brown	*chairo-i*
white	*shiro-i*	yellow	*kīro-i*

LIFESAVERS

No matter what their origins are, all loanwords are nouns. So *bēju* ("beige"), even though it functions as an adjective, must be attached to the noun connection marker *–no*—as in *bēju-no atasshu kēsu*, "a beige attaché case." If you've forgotten noun description, go back to Chapter 6 and review the section, "How to Describe Something or Someone."

If you can't remember color words in Japanese, you can use loanwords, as long as they are common colors:

gray	*grē (-no)*
orange	*oreNji (-no)*
beige	*bēju (-no)*
green	*gurīN (-no)*

In response to *Dore-desu ka?* let's suppose that yours is a small black bag:

Chīsa-i kuro-i kabaN-desu.　　　"It's the small black bag."

How about a big beige attaché case?

Ōki-i bēju-no atasshu kēsu-desu.　　"It's the big beige attaché case."

If you and the neighbor can see your bag, instead of describing it, you can simply say the following using the appropriate pointing word:

Are-desu.　　　"That one."

HUH?

Remember the four pointing words?

are	"that one away from you and me"
kore	"this one near me" (= speaker's domain)
sore	"that one near you" (= listener's domain)
dore	"which one?"

The neighboring passenger has finally grabbed your bag and asks you for confirmation:

Kore-desu ka?　　　"This one (in my hand)?"

In reply to this question, answer with the following handy expression:

Hai, sō-desu.　　　"Yes, that's right."

This expression can be used whenever you agree with the listener's statement.

GREEN TEA BREAK

You might have heard Japanese speakers saying *Sō! Sō! Sō!* Now you know what it means: "Right, right, right!" Similarly, *Ā sō-desu ka!* means "Oh, really?!"

If you're in a window seat, it isn't fun to disturb your neighbors when you need to go to the bathroom—especially when they're asleep. But that's life, and you need to know the phrase for this kind of occasion:

SumimaseN, chotto tōshi-te kudasai. "Excuse me, please let me through."

Notice the handy *chotto* here as well. As an alternative to the preceding expression, you can say:

SumimaseN, shitsurē shimasu. "Excuse me, coming through."

When you sit in an aisle seat, on the other hand, *ake-te* ("open") and *shime-te* ("close") might be handy request verbs, too. Suppose that an in-flight movie is on and you want your neighbor in the window seat to close the blind (*buraiNdo*):

BuraiNdo-o shime-te kudasai. "Please close the blind."

If you want him to open it, then say:

BuraiNdo-o ake-te kudasai. "Please open the blind."

Wow! You've learned a series of request patterns. Remember, the sentence formation is [*TE*-form + *kudasai*], and it is a polite request form. In a very casual situation, you can use a *TE*-form verb by itself as a request expression, as in:

Sore-o tot-te! "Get me that one!"

Please note that this is an extremely casual expression. Obviously, in situations in which you are surrounded by strangers, such as in the airplane, the polite version is always preferred.

Polite Requests You Might Hear on the Airplane

Politeness is important in Japanese, especially in a situation in which service is rendered. You, a passenger, are an important customer, so flight attendants will speak to you very politely, especially when they ask a favor of you. You won't have to say the following expressions; just be familiar with them in case you use a Japanese airline, especially a domestic flight in which Japanese is the primary language.

Shīto beruto-o o-shime kudasai. "Please fasten your seatbelt."
(*shime-masu* = "fasten")

Zaseki-o moto-no ichi-ni o-modoshi kudasai.
"Please set the seat back to the original position."
(*zaseki* = "seat"; *moto-no ichi-ni* "to the original position";
modoshi-masu = "set back")

Torē-o moto-no ichi-ni o-modoshi kudasai.
"Please set the tray back to the original position."

Tenimotsu-wa zaseki-no shita-ni o-oki kudasai.
"Please put your carry-on item under the seat."
(*tenimotsu* = "carry-on item"; *oki-masu* = "put; place")

You might have noticed that the preceding request patterns are different from the one you've learned. The form of this more polite request is …

O + Verb Stem + *kudasai*   "Please do so-and-so." (polite request)

Some requests made by a flight attendant are in negation, as in "Please do not do so-and-so."

Tabako-wa goeNryo kudasai.	"Please refrain from smoking."
Toire-no go-shiyō-wa goeNryo kudasai. (*go-shiyō* = "use")	"Please refrain from using the bathroom."
DeNshi kiki-no go-shiyō-wa goeNryo kudasai. (*deNshi* = "electronic"; *kiki* = "device")	"Please refrain from using electronic devices."
XYZ-wa + *goeNryo kudasai*	"Please refrain from *XYZ*." (polite request)

Before closing this chapter, try a mini-dialogue. The dialogue is between you and a flight attendant (abbreviated as *FA*). Note that some expressions are from previous chapters.

Exercise 2

FA   *Shīto beruto-o o-shime kudasai.*
     "Please fasten your seatbelt."

YOU 1 _____
     "Ah, excuse me."

FA 1 _____
"Yes."

YOU 2 _____
"Excuse me, but could you please get my bag for me?" (Ask politely.)

FA 2 _____
"Which one?"

YOU 3 _____
"It's a red bag."

FA 3 _____
"This one?"

YOU 4 _____
"Yes, that's it!"

_____
"Thank you very much."

(The flight attendant is handing out something.)

YOU 5 _____
"What is that (in your hand)?"

FA 5 _____
"(This is) an Embarkation card. Please fill it in." ("fill in" = *kaki-masu*)

YOU 6 _____
"Yes. Oh, there isn't a pen."   ("there is" = *ari-masu*)

_____
"Excuse me, please lend me a pen." (Ask politely.)
("lend" = *kashi-masu*)

FA 6 _____
"Sure. Here you are."

YOU 7 _____
"Thank you very much."

FA 7 _____
"You're welcome."

Answers

Exercise 1

1. Please call (telephone). *DeNwa shi-te kudasai.* (*deNwa shi-masu* → *deNwa shi-te*)

2. Please speak in English. *Ēgo-de hanashi-te kudasai.* (*hanashi-masu* → *hanashi-te*)

3. Please wait! *Mat-te kudasai.* (*machi-masu* → *mat-te*)

Exercise 2

FA　*Shīto beruto-o o-shime kudasai.* "Please fasten your seatbelt."

YOU 1　*SumimaseN.* "Excuse me."

FA 1　*Hai.* "Yes."

YOU 2　*SumimaseN ga, kabaN-o tot-te kudasai maseN ka?* "Excuse me, but could you please get my bag for me?"

FA 2　*Dore-desu ka?* "Which one?"

YOU 3　*Aka-i kabaN-desu.* "It's a red bag."

FA 3　*Kore-desu ka?* "This one?"

YOU 4　*Hai, sō-desu!* "Yes, that's it!"
　　　Dōmo arigatō (gozaimasu). "Thank you very much."

(The flight attendant is handing out something.)

YOU 5　*Sore-wa naN-desu ka?* "What is that (in your hand)?"

FA 5　*Nyūkoku kādo-desu.* "(This is) an Embarkation card."
　　　Kai-te kudasai. "Please fill it in." ("fill in" = *kaki-masu*)

YOU 6　*Hai. A, peN-ga ari-maseN.* "Yes. Oh, there isn't a pen."
　　　("there is" = *ari-masu*)

　　　SumimaseN, peN-o kashi-te kudasai maseN ka? "Excuse me, please lend me a pen.

FA 6　*Hai, dōzo.* "Sure. Here you are."

YOU 7　*Dōmo arigatō.* or *SumimaseN.* "Thank you very much."

FA 7　*Dō itashimashite.* "You're welcome."

The Least You Need to Know

- The request form *-te kudasai* (or *-te kudasai maseN ka*) is extremely useful in conversations. Make sure that you learn the *TE*-form by heart (see Chapter 6).
- Master the pointing words *kore* ("this one"), *sore* ("that one [near the listener]"), *are* ("that one [away from the speaker and listener]"), and *dore* ("which one").
- *Onegai shimasu* is a handy expression to use to request something if you can point at the object.
- Politeness is the key to effective requests.
- Be able to identify an object using an adjective such as *kuro-i kabaN* ("black bag").

Is the Flight on Time? Time Expressions

In This Chapter

- Reading the clock
- Point of time
- Duration of time

If you're visiting Japan on business, scheduling might be an important matter. Is the flight on time? Will my friend get to the airport to pick me up as scheduled? Can I catch the connecting flight? You can think of numerous situations in which time is essential. In this chapter, you learn how to tell time in Japanese.

Reading the Clock

First, let's learn how to read the clock in Japanese. The word for "o'clock" is *-ji*, and the word for "minutes" is *-fuN*. (Or *-puN* in some cases, as you'll see soon.) Because you learned the basic numbers in Chapter 7, the following table shouldn't be too difficult. Irregular pronunciations are indicated in bold:

Time Expressions

O'clock	*-ji*	Minutes	*-fuN*
1 o'clock	*ichi-ji*	1 minute	**ip-puN**
2 o'clock	*ni-ji*	2 minutes	*ni-fuN*
3 o'clock	*saN-ji*	**3 minutes**	*saN-puN*
4 o'clock	*yo-ji*	**4 minutes**	*yoN-puN*
5 o'clock	*go-ji*	5 minutes	*go-fuN*

continues

Time Expressions   (continued)

O'clock	-ji	Minutes	-fuN
6 o'clock	*roku-ji*	**6 minutes**	***rop-puN***
7 o'clock	*shichi-ji*	7 minutes	*nana-fuN*
8 o'clock	*hachi-ji*	**8 minutes**	***hap-puN***
9 o'clock	*ku-ji*	9 minutes	*kyū-fuN*
10 o'clock	*jū-ji*	**10 minutes**	***jup-puN***
11 o'clock	*jū ichi-ji*	**11 minutes**	***jū ip-puN***
12 o'clock	*jū ni-ji*	**12 minutes**	***jū ni-fun***
What hour?	*naN-ji*	**What minute?**	***naN-puN***

Let's look at an example. In Japanese, "8:23" is …

> *Hachi-ji ni-jū saN-puN*

Exercise 1

How would you say the following times in Japanese?

1. 10:52 _____

2. 7:34 _____

3. 6:07 _____

If you want to specify A.M. or P.M., add *gozeN*, or *gogo*, respectively, *before you state the time:*

2:55 A.M.   ***GozeN*** *ni-ji gojū go-fuN*

3:03 P.M.   ***Gogo*** *saN-ji saN-puN*

SHORTCUTS TO SUCCESS

Practice makes perfect and proficient. Whenever you have a chance, say the time in Japanese. All you need is a watch!

Useful Time Expressions

 First, let's learn how to ask what time it is now.

Q: *NaN-ji-desu ka?* "What time is it?"

A: *SaN-ji jup-puN-desu.* "It's 3:10."

If you want to specify the exact point at which something happens, you will need to add the time particle *-ni* ("at") to the time, as in the following examples:

Q: *NaN-ji-**ni** iki-masu ka?* "**At** what time are you going?"

A: *Roku-ji-**ni** iki-masu.* "I am going **at** 6 o'clock."

Do you want to know the departure and arrival times for your flight? The verb for "leave" is *de-masu*, and the verb for "arrive" is *tsuki-masu*. Let's suppose that the departure city is Chicago and the arrival city is Tokyo:

*Kono hikōki-wa Shikago-o naN-ji-**ni** de-masu ka?*
"What time will this airplane leave Chicago?"

*Kono hikōki-wa Tōkyō-ni naN-ji-**ni** tsuki-masu ka?*
"What time will this airplane arrive at Tokyo?"

Here are two more important flight schedule words:

shuppatsu "departure"

Shuppatsu-wa naN-ji-desu ka? "What time is the departure?"

tōchaku "arrival"

Tōchaku-wa naN-ji-desu ka? "What time is the arrival?"

 GREEN TEA BREAK

Japanese people make extensive use of military time, especially at work or in publications such as timetables for public transportation. For example, 7:34 P.M. can be said as:

Jū ku-ji saN jū yoN-puN "19:34 (7:34 P.M.)"

As you know, flight departures/arrivals are rarely on schedule, so you really can't ask *exactly* what time the plane leaves or arrives. You might want to attach *goro* ("approximately") to a time expression:

Q: *NaN-ji-**goro** tsuki-masu ka?*   "**About** what time will it arrive?"

A: *Ku-ji-**goro** tsuki-masu.*   "It will arrive **around** 9 o'clock."

Or:

Q: *Tōchaku-wa naN-ji-**goro**-desu ka?*   "What is the **approximate** arrival time?"

A: *Ku-ji-**goro**-desu.*   "It's **around** 9 o'clock."

LIFESAVERS

Here are a couple more useful time expressions:

*Ni-ji **chōdo***	"2 o'clock **sharp**"
*Ni-ji go-fuN **sugi***	"5 minutes **past** 2 o'clock"
*Ni-ji go-fuN **mae***	"5 minutes **before** 2 o'clock"
*Go-ji **haN***	"5:**30**"

Literally, *haN* means "half." Of course, instead of *haN*, you can use *saN jup-puN*, "30 minutes."

Exercise 2

Translate the following dialogues:

1. Q: What time did you wake up today?
    ("wake up" = *oki-masu*)

    _____

    A: I woke up at 7 o'clock.

    _____

2. Q: What time do you go to bed?
    ("go to bed" = *ne-masu*)

    _____

    A: I go to bed around 11 o'clock.

    _____

3. Q: What time will you go to school tomorrow?
    ("school" = *gakkō*)

_____

A: I will go at 8 A.M.

_____

"From" and "Until"

Having learned the basic time expressions, would you now like to ask a flight attendant what time the in-flight movie starts?

> *Ēga-wa naN-ji-**kara**-desu ka?*
> "What time does the movie start?" (*Lit.*) "From what time is the movie?"

HUH?

The particles *-kara* and *-made* can also be used when referring to the flight origin and destination. In this case, *-made* means "to." For example:

> *Tōkyō-kara Nagoya-made iki-masu.*
> "I'm going from Tokyo to Nagoya (but not beyond)."

Notice that *-kara* is a particle indicating "from." An equally important time-related particle is *-made*, meaning "until." How would you ask a flight attendant until what time the in-flight movie is? The answer is …

> *Ēga-wa naN-ji-**made**-desu ka?*
> "What time does the movie end?" (*Lit.*) "Until what time is the movie?"

Combining these two particles, you can say sentences like the following:

> *Ēga-wa naN-ji-**kara** naNji-**made** desu ka?*
> "From what time to what time is the movie?"

> *Ichi-ji-**kara** ni-ji-**made** terebi-o mi-mashita.*
> "I watched TV from 1 o'clock to 2 o'clock."

Exercise 3

Translate the following dialogues:

1. Q: What time does class begin? (*Lit.*) From what time is the class? ("class" = *kurasu*)

   _____

   A: It starts at 4 P.M. (*Lit.*) It's from 4 P.M.

   _____

2. Q: Until what time will you be here? ("be" = *i-masu*; "here" = *koko-ni*)

   _____

   A: I will be here until about 5 o'clock.

   _____

3. Q: From what time till what time did you study? ("study" = *beNkyō shi-masu*)

   _____

   A: I studied from 1 o'clock till 2 o'clock.

   _____

Duration

So far, you've learned the "point" of time. Now let's move on to the "duration" of time. The good news is that duration in terms of minutes follows exactly the same format as the minutes in the preceding table. Again, irregular pronunciations are indicated in bold:

Duration of Time

Hours	-jikaN	Minutes	-fuN
1 hour	*ichi-jikaN*	**1 minute**	***ip-puN***
2 hours	*ni-jikaN*	2 minutes	*ni-fuN*
3 hours	*saN-jikaN*	**3 minutes**	***saN-puN***
4 hours	*yo-jikaN*	**4 minutes**	***yoN-puN***
5 hours	*go-jikaN*	5 minutes	*go-fuN*

Hours	*-jikaN*	Minutes	*-fuN*
6 hours	*roku-jikaN*	**6 minutes**	***rop-puN***
7 hours	*nana-jikaN*	7 minutes	*nana-fuN*
8 hours	*hachi-jikaN*	**8 minutes**	***hap-puN***
9 hours	*ku-jikaN*	9 minutes	*kyū-fuN*
10 hours	*jū-jikaN*	**10 minutes**	***jup-puN***
How many hours?	*naN-jikaN*	**How many minutes?**	***naN-puN***
(For) how long?	*donogurai*		

I have included two important question words in the preceding table—*naN-jikaN* ("how many hours") and *donogurai* "([for] how long"). Let's ask how long the flight is:

> *Furaito-wa naN-jikaN-desu ka?*   "How many hours is the flight?"

Or:

> *Furaito-wa donogurai-desu ka?*   "How long is the flight?"

You might want to ask how long the flight *takes*. The verb for "take" is *kakari-masu*. To ask how long it takes from Seattle to Tokyo, say:

> Q: *Shiatoru-kara Tōkyō-made donogurai kakari-masu ka?*
> "How long does it take from Seattle to Tokyo?"
>
> A: *Ku-jikaN-**gurai** kakari-masu.*   "It takes **about** 9 hours."

Did you notice *-gurai* ("about") in the preceding answer? You've already learned *-goro* ("approximately"), but *-goro* is used only for a specific *point* of time, not the *duration* of time. For the approximate duration of time, use *-gurai*.

The sentence patterns you've learned here are extremely useful not only during flight, but anywhere. You can ask a cab driver how long it takes to get to a destination, so you might be able to avoid paying thousands of *yen* for fare!

Before moving on, let's look at one more useful particle, *-de* ("by means of"). This particle is useful when you have several choices of transportation and want to compare their speeds. Suppose that you're in Tokyo and wonder what transportation is the best for you to get to Yokohama—*by* bus, *by* train, *by* taxi, and so on. Here is one example:

> *Tōkyō-kara Yokohama-made **basu-de** donogurai kakari-masu ka?*
> "How long does it take **by bus** from Tokyo to Yokohama?"

GREEN TEA BREAK

The distance between Tokyo and Yokohama is approximately 25 kilometers (15.5 miles). The Tokyo-Yokohama metropolitan area (a.k.a. the Greater Tokyo area) is probably the most congested in terms of traffic. It sometimes takes three hours to get from Tokyo to Yokohama by car! I would advise you to take the train. It takes only 25 minutes.

The following lists some modes of transportation.

Transportation

airplane	*hikōki*
bicycle	*jiteNsha*
Bullet Train	*shiNkaNseN*
bus	*basu*
car	*kuruma*
motorcycle	*baiku*
subway	*chikatetsu*
taxi	*takushī*
train	*deNsha*
on foot	*aruite*

Please take care when using *aruite*, "on foot." This phrase does not require the particle *-de:*

Aruite iki-masu.   "I'm going on foot."

GREEN TEA BREAK

The Bullet Train, or *shiNkaNseN,* is one of the fastest forms of ground transportation in the world. The Super Express called *Nozomi* can go as fast as 300 kilometers (190 miles) per hour!

Exercise 4

Using the charts for duration of time and modes of transportation, ask the following questions.

1. How long does it take from Tokyo to Osaka by Bullet Train?

2. How many hours does it take from New York to San Francisco by airplane?

_____

3. How many minutes does it take from the university to the bookstore on foot? ("university" = _daigaku_; "bookstore" = _hoNya_)

_____

Answers

Exercise 1

1. 10:52   _jū-ji gojū ni-fuN_

2. 7:34   _shichi-ji saNjū yoN-puN_

3. 6:07   _roku-ji nana-fuN_

Exercise 2

1. Q: What time did you wake up today?
   NaN-ji-ni oki-mashita ka?

   A: I woke up at 7 o'clock.
   Shichi-ni oki-mashita.

2. Q: What time do you go to bed?
   NaN-ji-ni ne-masu ka?

   A: I go to bed around 11 o'clock.
   Jū ichi-ji goro ne-masu.

3. Q: What time will you go to school tomorrow?
   Ashita naN-ji-ni gakkō-ni iki-masu ka?

   A: I will go at 8 A.M.
   GozeN hachi-ji-ni iki-masu.

Exercise 3

1. Q: What time does class begin? (_Lit._) From what time is the class?
   ("class" = _kurasu_)
   Kurasu-wa naN-ji-kara-desu ka?

   A: It starts at 4 P.M. (_Lit._) It's from 4 P.M.
   Gogo yo-ji-kara-desu.

2. Q: Until what time will you be here?
    NaN-ji-made koko-ni i-masu ka?

    A: I will be here until about 5 o'clock.
    Go-ji-goro-made koko-ni i-masu.

3. Q: From what time till what time did you study?
    NaN-ji-kara naN-ji-made beNkyō shi-mashita ka?

    A: I studied from 1 o'clock till 2 o'clock.
    Ichi-ji-kara ni-ji-made beNkyō shi-mashita.

Exercise 4

1. "How long does it take from Tokyo to Osaka by Bullet Train?"
    Tōkyō-kara Ōsaka-made shiNkaNseN-de donogurai kakari-masu ka?

2. "How many hours does it take from New York to San Francisco by airplane?"
    Nyūyōku-kara SaN FuraNshisuko-made hikōki-de naN-jikaN kakari-masu ka?

3. "How many minutes does it take from the university to the bookstore on foot?"
    Daigaku-kara hoNya-made aruite naN-puN kakari-masu ka?

The Least You Need to Know

- Time expressions require that you know the basic number words covered in Chapter 7.
- Note that *-ji* is the counter for "o'clock," *-jikaN* for "hours," and *-fuN* for "minutes."
- Particles such as *-kara* ("from") and *-made* ("until") are useful when you want to specify the starting or ending point.
- Combine time-related phrases with X-*de*, "by means of X"—as in *Basu-de donogurai kakari-masu ka?* ("How long does it take by bus?").

At the Airport

In This Chapter

- Airport protocols
- Counting time length
- Phone numbers

Now the plane has landed in Japan. It has been a long flight, and you might be a little tired. If you are traveling alone, rather than in a tour group, you will have to go through Immigration and Customs on your own before you leave the airport. Of course, many immigration and customs officers do speak English, but it is always nice to be able to communicate in Japanese.

At the Immigration Booth

There are several international airports in Japan, but most international flights arrive at either New Tokyo International Airport, also known as Narita Airport (NRT), or Kansai International Airport (KIX) in Osaka.

The first point you will go through is the immigration booth. There are lines for Japanese nationals and for non-Japanese nationals. By the time you arrive at the booth, you should have your Embarkation card, *nyūkoku kādo*, completely filled out and have your passport in hand. Typical questions that immigration officers ask concern the following:

- Purpose of visit
- Length of stay
- Destination in Japan

"Purpose" is *mokuteki* in Japanese. The officer might first ask you the following:

Pasupōto-o mise-te kudasai. "Please show me your passport."

Ryokō-no mokuteki-wa naN-desu ka? "What's the purpose of the trip?"
(*ryokō* = "travel")

In Chapter 10, you learned some purpose words. Let's review some here:

sightseeing *kaNkō*

business *shigoto*

business trip *shucchō*

study abroad *ryūgaku*

If the purpose of your trip is sightseeing, the answer is simply ...

Kankō-desu. "It is sightseeing."

The officer will then ask how long you will stay in Japan:

NihoN-ni-wa donogurai (or *naN-nichi*) *i-masu ka?*
"For how long (*or* for how many days) will you stay in Japan?"

You have learned hours and minutes, but not days yet. The counter for days is *-nichi*. Unfortunately, from 1 day to 10 days, most of the day words are irregular and don't make use of this counter. If you can't remember those irregular pronunciations, don't worry! You can still use [Number + *-nichi*]. They are somewhat nonstandard but comprehensible by Japanese people. I list both authentic and survival versions of counting days in the following table.

Counting Days

	Authentic Reading	Survival Reading
1 day	*ichi-nichi*	*ichi-nichi*
2 days	*futsuka*	*ni-nichi*
3 days	*mikka*	*saN-nichi*
4 days	*yokka*	*yoN-nichi*
5 days	*itsuka*	*go-nichi*
6 days	*muika*	*roku-nichi*
7 days	*nanoka*	*shichi-nichi*

	Authentic Reading	Survival Reading
8 days	*yōka*	*hachi-nichi*
9 days	*kokonoka*	*ku-nichi*
10 days	*tōka*	*ju-nichi*
11 days	*jū ichi-nichi*	*jū ichi-nichi*
How many days?	*naN-nichi*	

SHORTCUTS TO SUCCESS

The counting system with *ichi, ni, saN*, and so on, was borrowed from Chinese. We also have a traditional Japanese counting system:

1	2	3	4	5	6	7	8	9	10
hi-	fu-	mi-	yo-	itsu-	mu-	nana-	ya-	koko-	tō-

The traditional counting system is used not only for counting days, but also for other items, such as people. In Chapter 10, you learned that "one person" and "two persons" are irregular, but for anything beyond two persons, the counter *-niN* is attached:

hitori	"one person"
futari	"two persons"
saN-niN	"three persons"
yo-niN	"four persons"

You will see some of these counters in the rest of the book, so it's a good idea to become familiar with this system.

If you plan on staying for eight days, your answer looks like this:

Yōka (or hachi-nichi) i-masu.   "I will stay for eight days."

Or simply:

Yōka (or hachi-nichi) desu.   "Eight days."

What if you stay more than just a couple of days, like three weeks, two months, or a year? You will need to know their respective counters. Unlike counting days, these three counters are almost regular. Look at the following table. As usual, irregular instances are indicated in bold.

Counting Weeks, Months, and Years

	Weeks *(-sh-ukaN)*	Months *(-kagetsu)*	Years *(-neN)*
1	***is-sh-ukaN***	***ik-kagetsu***	*ichi-neN*
2	*ni-shūkaN*	*ni-kagetsu*	*ni-neN*
3	*saN-shūkaN*	*saN-kagetsu*	*saN-neN*
4	*yoN-shūkaN*	*yoN-kagetsu*	***yo-neN***
5	*go-shūkaN*	*go-kagetsu*	*go-neN*
6	*roku-shūkaN*	***rok-kagetsu***	*roku-neN*
7	*nana-shūkaN*	*nana-kagetsu*	*nana-neN*
8	***has-sh-ukaN***	*hachi-kagetsu*	*hachi-neN*
9	*kyu-shukaN*	*kyu-kagetsu*	*kyū-neN*
10	***jus-sh-ukaN***	***juk-kagetsu***	*jū-neN*
11	***jū is-sh-ukaN***	***jū ik-kagetsu***	*jū ichi-neN*
How many?	*naN-shūkaN*	*naN-kagetsu*	*naN-neN*

With the duration words "days," "weeks," "months," and "years," you can express a variety of things. Now let me ask you some questions pertaining to duration. First, figure out what you are being asked; then answer the question:

Exercise 1

Q1: *Mainichi, nihoNgo-o naN-jikaN benkyō shi-masu ka?*

(*mainichi* = "everyday"; *benkyō shi-masu* = "study")

A1: _____

Q2: *Is-shūkaN-ni, naN-nichi shigoto-o shi-masu ka?*

(*is-shūkaN-ni* = "in one week"; *shigoto* = "work")

A2: _____

Q3: *Ichi-neN-wa, naN-shūkaN ari-masu ka?*

A3: _____

Okay, let's get back to the immigration booth. The immigration officer might ask what your final destination is or where you will stay:

Q: *NihoN-de-wa doko-ni iki-masu ka?*   "Where will you go in Japan?"

A: *Kyōto-ni iki-masu.*   "I am going to Kyoto."

Q: *Doko-ni tomari-masu ka?*   "Where will you stay?"

A: *Puraza Hoteru-ni tomari-masu.*   "I will stay at the Plaza Hotel."

HUH?

In the first example, because the topic of the sentence is "in Japan," you need to attach the location particle *-de* to nihoN. Note that the particle must be *–de*, not *–ni*, because this sentence has an action verb (*iki-masu*), not an existence verb.

If you're staying at your friend's house, and not in a hotel, your answer will be ...

Tomodachi-no uchi-ni tomari-masu.
"I will stay at my friend's house."
(*tomodachi* = "friend"; *uchi* = "house")

Remember that the particle *-no* in *tomodachi-no uchi* ("friend's house") is a noun connector (see Chapter 6).

If you stay in a private house, you might be asked to give the officer the address of that house. Suppose that the address is ...

800-12 Ogawa-cho
Yokosuka-shi, Kanagawa-ken 238-0004

GREEN TEA BREAK

The suffix *-keN* is equivalent to "province." There are 43 *keN* total in Japan. There are four special districts—Tokyo, Osaka, Kyoto, and Hokkaido—and they have different suffixes:

Tōkyō-to

Ōsaka-fu

Kyōto-fu

Hokkai-dō

The suffix *-cho* (or *-machi*) is for "town," *-shi* for "city," and *-ken* for "prefecture." The Japanese way of reading addresses is the mirror image of the Western style:

〒 *238-0004*
Kanagawa-keN
Yokosuka-shi
Ogawa-chō
800-12 (hap-pyaku-no jū ni)

〒 is a sign placed in front of a postal code. A postal code, or ZIP code, is called *yūbiN baNgō* in Japanese. 〒 238-0004 should be read as …

YūbiN baNgō ni saN hachi-no zero zero zero yoN "〒238-0004"

Well, I guess it would be easier to hand it to the officer in the form of a note that has the address (*jūsho*) on it!

Kore-ga jūsho-desu.   "This is the address."

Oh, No! My Bag Is Missing! At Baggage Claim

After you go through Immigration, you will pick up your luggage and proceed to Customs. What if you can't find your luggage? Don't panic! The good news is that Japanese airports are extremely helpful when your luggage is missing. They will deliver your luggage to your destination by special express as soon as they find it. However, to receive this service, you must file a claim.

GREEN TEA BREAK

These special delivery services are called *takuhaibiN,* "home delivery express." In the past, one of my bags was lost in the New Tokyo International Airport, so I filed a claim. To my surprise, when I arrived at my parents' house three hours later, my bag had already arrived! Of course, it was free of charge! In Japan, you never have to go back to the airport to pick up your lost luggage.

This service can also be used to send your bags to where you'll be staying. Likewise, you can send your bags to the airport before your departure (one to two days in advance). This way, you don't have to carry your luggage to and from the airport.

To claim lost baggage, you must first go to an information booth near any luggage carousel and tell the officer the following:

Watashi-no nimotsu-ga ari-maseN. (*nimotsu* = "luggage")	"My luggage isn't here."

Or:

Watashi-no nimotsu-ga dete ki-maseN. (*dete ki-masu* = "come out")	"My luggage hasn't come out."

You will be asked for your name, your address, your flight number, where you are from, and your contact phone number. You know how to say your name and address already. "Flight *XYZ*" is XYZ-*bin* in Japanese. Suppose that your flight was United 79 and it originated from Chicago:

Q: *BiN-mē-wa naN-desu ka?*	"What is the name of the flight?"
A: *Yunaiteddo-no nana-jū kyū-biN desu.*	"United Flight 79."
Q: *Doko-kara nori-mashita ka?*	"Where did you board the airplane?"
A: *Shikago-kara desu.*	"From Chicago."

Giving a phone number is really very simple, if you are already familiar with the basic number words in Japanese. All you need to do is say each number separately. The hyphen is pronounced as -*no*. Let's say that your contact phone number is 03-5860-3715. The number "03" is the area code.

Q: *DeNwa baNgō-wa naN-desu ka?* (*deNwa* = "phone"; *baNgō* = "number")	"What is the phone number?"
A: *Zero saN-no go hachi roku zero-no saN nana ichi go-desu.*	"03-5860-3715."

GREEN TEA BREAK

Cellular phones are called *kētai deNwa* or simply *kētai*. You can rent or buy a cellular phone at the airport. These phones are usually operated by prepaid calling cards.

Saying phone numbers helps when remembering basic number words. Try to say your phone number:

Uchi-no deNwa baNgō-wa _____-*desu.*

Kaisha-no deNwa baNgō-wa _____-*desu.*

Yes, *uchi* is "home" and *kaisha* is "company."

At the Customs Counter

Okay, you've picked up your luggage at the carousel. You have your bags in hand and proceed to the final checkpoint, Customs. "Customs" is *zēkaN* in Japanese. If you have no taxable items to declare, this is an easy process. However, Customs officers are authorized to check not only for taxable items, but also for illegal objects such as narcotics and firearms. Your bags may be searched here.

LIFESAVERS

The following items are duty-free if they don't exceed the specified quantities:

- Alcoholic beverages—three bottles
- Cigarettes—two cartons
- Perfume—two ounces
- Others—200,000 *yen* (U.S. $2,381, provided that U.S. $1 = 84 *yen*)

Visit the official website of the Japan Customs at www.customs.go.jp/english/passenger/index.htm.

If you have nothing to declare, you can proceed to the Customs counters that are marked by the color green. If you have taxable items or if you don't know whether certain items are taxable, proceed to the Customs counters indicated by the color red. Please note that even in the green line, you will be asked by a Customs officer questions similar to those asked at the immigration booth.

Before learning some Customs-related dialogues, familiarize yourself with some important vocabulary.

Customs	*zēkaN*	something to declare	*shiNkoku-suru mono*
Customs clearance	*tsūkaN*	souvenir	*omiyage*
declaration	*shiNkoku*	tax	*zēkiN*
duty-free	*meNzē*	taxed	*kazē*
duty-free merchandise	*meNzēhiN*		

Here are some typical questions a Customs officer might ask you at the Customs counter:

KabaN-o ake-te kudasai.	"Please open your bag."
Pasupōto-o mise-te kudasai.	"Please show me your passport."
Kore-wa doko-de kai-mashita ka?	"Where did you buy this?"

If the officer asks you whether there is anything to declare and you have nothing to declare, the dialogue should resemble the following:

Q: *ShiNkoku-suru mono-wa ari-masu ka?*   "Do you have anything to declare?"

A: *Īe, ari-maseN.*   "No, I don't."

Suppose that you have a wrapped souvenir for your friends, and the officer asks what it is …

Q: *Kore-wa naN-desu ka?*   "What's this?"

A: *Omiyage-desu. Chokorēto-desu.*   "It's a souvenir. It's chocolate."

Q: *Dare-no desu ka?*   "Whose is it? (For whom?)"

A: *Tomodachi-no desu.*   "It's for my friend."

HUH?

The question seen in the previous example, *Dare-no desu ka?* ("Whose is it?") is the shortened form of …

Dare-no omiyage-desu ka?   "Whose souvenir is it?"

Likewise, the answer *Tomodachi-no desu* ("It's my friend's") is the shortened form of …

Tomodachi-no omiyage-desu.   "It's a souvenir for my friend."

Omission of an understood item is common and acceptable in Japanese.

Immigration and Customs clearance at a Japanese airport used to take a lot of time, but because of the simplification of the procedure, now it is very speedy. Although it might depend on how long it takes to get your luggage from the baggage claim, you can usually get out of the airport within 30–45 minutes after arrival.

If you are expecting someone to pick you up, she or he is most likely to be just beyond the doors of the Customs section. If you are on your own, you need to secure transportation from the airport to the city. You will learn all the necessary transportation-related expressions in Chapter 15. Bon voyage, or *I-i tabi-o!*

Before moving to the next chapter, do the following review exercise. You are at Immigration and Customs. *Q* stands for questions given by an officer, and *A* stands for your answers.

Exercise 2

At Immigration

    Q1: *Pasupōto-o mise-te kudasai.*

    A1: "Yes."

_____

    Q2: *Ryokō-no mokuteki-wa naN-desu ka?*

    A2: "Business."

    Q3: *NihoN-ni-wa donogurai i-masu ka?*

    A3: "One week."

_____

    Q4: *Doko-ni tomari-masu ka?*

    A4: "I will stay at the Plaza Hotel."

_____

At Customs

    Q5: *KabaN-o ake-te kudasai.*

    A5: "Yes."

_____

    Q6: *ShiNkoku-suru mono-wa ari-masu ka?*

    A6: "No, I don't."

_____

    Q7: *Kore-wa naN-desu ka?*

    A7: "It's a souvenir."

_____

    Q8: *Dareno-desu ka?*

    A8: "It's for my friend."

_____

Answers

Exercise 1

Q1: *Mainichi, nihoNgo-o naN-jikaN benkyō shi-masu ka?*   "How many hours do you study Japanese every day?"

A1: *Mainichi, ichi-jikaN benkyō shi-masu.*   "I study Japanese for one hour every day."

Q2: *Is-shūkaN-ni, naN-nichi shigoto-o shi-masu ka?*   "How many days do you work per week?"

A2: *Is-shūkaN-ni, itsuka shigoto-o shi-masu.*   "I work five days per week."

Q3: *Ichi-neN-wa, naN-shūkaN ari-masu ka?*   "How many weeks does one year have?"

A3: *Ichi-neN-wa, gojū ni-shūkaN ari-masu.*   "One year has 52 weeks."

Exercise 2

At Immigration

Q1: *Pasupōto-o mise-te kudasai.*   "Please show me your passport."

A1: *Hai.*   "Yes."

Q2: *Ryokō-no mokuteki-wa naN-desu ka?*   "What is the purpose of the trip?"

A2: *Shigoto-desu.* (or *Shuccho-desu.*)   "Business." (or "Business trip.")

Q3: *NihoN-ni-wa donogurai i-masu ka?*   "How long will you stay in Japan?"

A3: *Is-shūkaN-desu.*   "One week."

Q4: *Doko-ni tomari-masu ka?*   "Where will you be staying?"

A4: *Puraza Hoteru-ni tomari-masu.*   "I will stay at the Plaza Hotel."

At Customs

Q5: *KabaN-o ake-te kudasai.*   "Open your bag, please."

A5: *Hai.*   "Yes."

Q6: *ShiNkoku-suru mono-wa ari-masu ka?*   "Do you have anything to declare?"

A6: *Īe, ari-maseN.*   "No, I don't."

Q7: *Kore-wa naN-desu ka?*   "What is this?"

A7: *Omiyage-desu.*   "It's a souvenir."

Q8: *Dare-no desu ka?*   "For whom?"

A8: *Tomodachi-no-desu.*   "It's for my friend."

The Least You Need to Know

- The questions you will be asked at Immigration and Customs are all predictable, so be prepared.
- Be familiar with time duration words so you can answer the immigration officer's questions about the duration of your stay in Japan.
- The Japanese way of writing addresses is the same as the Western style.
- Saying phone numbers in Japanese is straightforward. Just say each number separately. The hyphen between numbers is pronounced *-no* in Japanese.

Getting to and Around Town

In This Chapter

- Transportation
- Directions and locations
- How to say "I want to ..."

Congratulations! You have successfully gone through Immigration and Customs at the airport all by yourself. If someone is waiting to pick you up and take you to your final destination, you can relax. But what if you are on your own and need to get to your destination by yourself? You can no longer follow the crowd. This is the first time you will find yourself completely relying on your own skills. In this chapter, I show you how to get to your destination without getting lost.

Types of Transportation

 As I told you in Chapter 14, most international flights arrive at either the New Tokyo International Airport in Narita (NRT) or the Kansai International Airport in Osaka (KIX). Because both Tokyo and Osaka are extremely overcrowded and have little space within their city limits, their airports are located outside the city. From NRT to Tokyo, it is 60 kilometers (38 miles), and it is 50 kilometers (31 miles) from KIX to Osaka.

To get to the city from the airport, several options are available:

train	*deNsha*
shuttle bus	*rimujiN basu*
taxi	*takushī*
rental car	*reNtakā*

GREEN TEA BREAK

An old international airport is very close to the center of Tokyo, within a 10-mile radius. It's called the Tokyo International Airport, also known as the Haneda Airport (HND). The new airport was built in the late 1970s because Haneda could not accommodate the ever-growing number of incoming flights to Japan. It now mainly serves domestic flights but has recently been expanding to accommodate more international flights.

Considering the cost and distance from the airport to the city, you probably would want to avoid a taxi or limousine car, so let's focus on a train and limousine bus. Whether you use a train or a limousine bus, you need to do the following:

- Go to the ticket counter and state your destination.

- Check the departure time and location for the train/bus.

- Buy the ticket.

If you are going to stay in a major hotel, I suggest that you take a limousine bus because it stops right in front of major hotels. If not, a train is okay, too.

I personally prefer the train because it is always on schedule and is not affected by stressful traffic jams. In what follows, let's suppose that you have decided to take the train from Narita Airport to Shinjuku, the hub of the city of Tokyo.

LIFESAVERS

The following websites provide extensive information on ground transportation at the New Tokyo International Airport and Kansai International Airport. Remember, these website addresses are subject to change.

New Tokyo International Airport (Narita, Tokyo): www.narita-airport.jp/en/

Kansai International Airport (Osaka): www.kansai-airport.or.jp/en/

Going by Train

You can buy a train ticket from a vending machine. These machines can be a bit complex for a first-time traveler to use. You will probably feel more comfortable and less stressed buying a ticket the old-fashioned way—by purchasing it at a ticket counter.

GREEN TEA BREAK

Japan has a number of private railway companies (*shitetsu*) and a company called JR (pronounced as *jē āru*), which stands for *Japan Railways*. JR serves the majority of major locations in Japan, and although it depends on exactly where you are heading, *JR* is more convenient.

If you plan to travel around Japan by train, I suggest that you purchase a *JR Pass*. Passes are available in the form of 7, 14, or 21 consecutive days. Because a *JR Pass* is not sold in Japan, you must purchase it at a travel agency prior to departure. You will receive a voucher called an "Exchange Order." Exchange this voucher with a pass at a designated station and specify the starting date. For more information, visit the JR East website at www.jreast.co.jp/e/.

Also for planning travel by train, I suggest a handy website called Hypermedia. It instantly gives you the fastest and cheapest route to your destination. Its URL is www.hyperdia.com/en/.

First of all, as shown in the following example, you have to tell the clerk what your destination is. Let's say you are going to the train station called *Shinjuku*:

> *ShiNjuku Eki-ni iki-tai-N-desu ga …*
> "I want to go to the Shinjuku Station, but …" (*eki* = "station")

HUH?

The expression for "I want to" consists of two parts, *tai* ("want") and *N-desu*. The phrase *N-desu* is attached to a predicate when you want to express feelings such as desire, hope, and curiosity, as well as when making an explanation or excuse. You will see more examples of *-N-desu* later.

You have just seen a very important grammatical pattern—"want to." The formation of this pattern looks like the following:

> Verb Stem + *tai-N-desu ga …*

SHORTCUTS TO SUCCESS

Did you notice in the previous example that the word *ga* is attached at the end of the sentence, as in …

> *ShiNjuku Eki-ni iki-tai-N-desu ga …*　　"I want to go to the Shinjuku Station, but …"

This tiny word literally means "but" and is used to soften the tone of a given sentence. You might recall the following expression:

> *SumimaseN ga …*　　"Excuse me, but …"

This is certainly a must-learn expression that makes your Japanese sound natural and polite.

Remember, "verb stem" means a verb without *-masu*. This "want to" pattern is simple and extremely useful. Before we move on, let's practice the pattern here. How would you say the following?

Exercise 1

1. I want to eat *sushi*. ("eat" = *tabe-masu*)

   _____

2. I want to buy a camera. ("buy" = *kai-masu*)

   _____

HUH?

The particle *-to* means "and." This particle connects nouns only.

Now, let's get back to the ticket counter. You have just told the counter clerk that you want to go to the Shinjuku Station. The clerk will give you several departure times, as shown next. Suppose that the train leaves at 3 and 4 o'clock.

SaN-ji to yo-ji-ga ari-masu.   "There is one at 3 and 4."

Dochira-ga i-idesu ka?   "Which would you prefer?"

You want to take the earlier train:

SaN-ji-ga i-idesu.   "I prefer 3:00."

Don't forget to ask how much the ticket costs. The question word for "how much" is *ikura*.

Ikura-desu ka?   "How much is it?"

Suppose the fare from the Narita Airport to the Shinjuku Station is 3,110 *yen*.

SaN-zeN hyaku jū eN-desu.   "It is 3,110 *yen*."

Japanese numbers were introduced in Chapter 7. If you have forgotten them, this is a good time to go back and review them.

In Chapter 13, you learned how to ask how long it takes to get from point X to point Y. The verb for "take" is *kakari-masu*. Let's ask how long it takes to get to the Shinjuku Station.

> *ShiNjuku Eki-made donogurai kakari-masu ka?*
> "How long does it take to get to the Shinjuku Station?"

The answer to your question will be …

> *Ichi-jikaN ni-jup-puN-desu.*   "One hour 20 minutes."

Another important question you should ask is from which track the train is leaving. The verb for "leave" is *de-masu* (see Chapter 13).

> *Doko-kara de-masu ka?*   "Where does it leave from?"

Suppose that it leaves from Track #1. "Track" is *-baNseN*.

> *Ichi-baNseN-kara de-masu.*   "It leaves from Track #1."

Instead of *doko* ("where"), you can also use *naN-baNseN* ("which track"):

> *NaN-baNseN-kara de-masu ka?*   "Which track does it leave from?"

In addition to these expressions and vocabulary, here are some more useful train-related words:

ticket	*kippu*
reserved seat	*shitēseki*
nonreserved seat	*jiyūseki*
nonsmoking seat	*kiNeN seki*
platform	*hōmu*
for (destination)	*-iki* (for example, *Tokyo-iki*)
to transfer	*norikae-masu*
entrance	*iriguchi*
exit	*deguchi*

GREEN TEA BREAK

Every station has a gate where your ticket is checked. This is called *kaisatsu-guchi*. This checkpoint is fully automated. You insert your ticket into the machine, and the gate opens if the ticket is validated. If not, the gate shuts in front of you and makes an annoying beeping sound (a bit embarrassing if this happens …). Oh, there's one more thing. Your validated ticket comes out from the other side of the gate, so don't forget to pick it up because you will need it at your final destination!

If your destination is the last station of the train line, great! But what if you must get off the train at a station before the train's final destination? Suppose that the train is bound for Yokohama, and you need to get off at Shinjuku. The ticket clerk will tell you the following:

> *ShiNjuku-de ori-te kudasai.*   "Please get off at Shinjuku."

The verb *ori-te* is the *TE*-form of *ori-masu,* "to get off." (Just in case, the verb for "get on; ride" is *nori-masu.*)

Now you have finally gotten on the train! You want to make sure that you get off at the right station. Why don't you ask a fellow passenger to signal you when the train approaches the Shinjuku Station? You would want to say "I want to get off at Shinjuku. Please let me know when we get there." You can say this with all the expressions you have learned and one new verb, *oshie-masu* ("tell").

> *ShiNjuku-de ori-tai-N-desu ga, oshie-te kudasai.*
> "I want to get off at Shinjuku, so please let me know."

Did you notice the softening *ga* in the sentence? This would be a perfect setting for you to include the polite marker. Want to sound even more polite? Try the following:

> *ShiNjuku-de ori-tai-N-desu ga, oshie-te kudasaimaseN ka?*
> "I want to get off at Shinjuku, so could you please let me know?"

GREEN TEA BREAK

Big cities also have extensive subway systems. For example, Tokyo has 13 subway lines, and they are closely connected to other subway lines, *JR* lines, and private railways—just like a huge spider web. You can obtain a route map at any subway station. By using the subway system wisely, you can save time and money.

The pattern of requests looks like this:

> *-te kudasaimaseN ka?*   "Could you please do so-and-so?"

If you need to ask a big favor, this pattern is highly recommended.

Riding trains can be stressful. However, after several experiences, the fear will go away and you will start appreciating its convenience. It is fast, inexpensive, and almost always on time. You can travel virtually anywhere in Japan by train!

Going by Taxi

Now you have arrived at the station. The original plan was that your friend was supposed to pick you up at the station, but prior to the departure, you found out she would not be able to be there. You need to get there by yourself, and it looks like the only means of getting there is by taxi. Taking a taxi on your very first day in Japan? Not a problem!

You have the address of your friend's apartment, which looks like the following:

> My Address
> *Maison Shinjuku* #307
> 700-15 Kita-machi
> Shinjuku-ku
> Landmark: Right next to the library

First, hail a taxi. If you are at a station, there is usually a place where taxis are available. This place is called *takushī noriba* ("taxi stand"). It should have a sign with a picture of a taxi.

If you are on the street, look for a taxi that has a red light in its front window because it indicates that the taxi has no passengers. Raise your hand to stop the cab. If the taxi has passengers, the light should be green.

LIFESAVERS

When a cab stops, do not stand right in front of the door. Cab doors in Japan open automatically, and you certainly don't want to be knocked down on the street! This tip is a lifesaver—and kneecap saver!

Now, you have safely gotten into the taxi. The driver will ask you:

> *Dochira-made (desu ka)?*   "Where to?"

Your destination is *Maison Shinjuku*, right?

> *MezoN ShiNjuku-made onegai shimasu.*   "To *Maison Shinjuku*, please."

Or:

> *Mezon ShiNjuku-made iki-tai-N-desu ga …*   "I want to go to *Maison Shinjuku* …"

GREEN TEA BREAK

For some reason, apartments in Japan have very fancy names, like the French word *maison*. Even a mediocre one-bedroom apartment complex can be called *maNshoN* ("mansion") or, a little more modestly, *haimu*, derived from the German *heim* ("apartment").

If the driver does not know where the destination is, you might want to give him the address. Recall that Japanese addresses are the mirror image of Western addresses.

Western Style

Maison Shinjuku #307
700-15 Kita-machi
Shinjuku-ku

Japanese Style

Shinjuku-ku
Kita-machi 700-15
Maison Shinjuku #307

HUH?

An apartment room number ("#") is read as *-gōshitsu*. For example, #307 should be read as *saN-byaku nana-gōshitsu*.

Remember, on the address card, your friend kindly gave you a landmark so that you can easily find her apartment. According to that note, it is located next to the library (*toshokaN*). You can give the directions to the driver, as the next example shows:

> *ToshokaN-no tonari-desu.*   "It's next to the library."
> (*tonari* = "next")

When you give directions, the following pattern is extremely useful:

> [LANDMARK-*no* Direction Word]

The following lists some direction words.

Direction Words

above	*ue*	inside	*naka*
ahead	*saki*	left	*hidari*
back/behind	*ushiro*	next/adjacent	*tonari*
beneath	*shita*	nearby	*chikaku* or *soba*
between	*aida*	outside	*soto*
beyond	*mukō*	right	*migi*
front	*mae*		

If the destination is near the library, you can say:

ToshokaN-no chikaku-desu.   "It's near the library."

The following are some frequently used place names that you might need to use as landmarks when giving directions.

Place Names

art museum	*bijutsukaN*	park	*kōeN*
barber shop	*tokoya*	parking lot	*chūshajō*
beauty salon	*biyōiN*	police station	*kēsatsusho*
bookstore	*hoNya*	post office	*yūbiNkyoku*
Buddhist temple	*otera*	public phone	*kōshū deNwa*
building	*biru*	restaurant	*resutoraN*
bus stop	*basutē*	restroom	*toire*
church	*kyōkai*	school	*gakkō*
city hall	*shiyakusho*	Shinto shrine	*jiNja*
convenience store	*koNbini*	shop	*mise*
department store	*depāto*	supermarket	*sūpā*
drugstore	*kusuriya*	*sushi* bar	*sushiya*
elementary school	*shōgakkō*	theater	*gekijō*
hospital	*byōiN*	train station	*eki*
library	*toshokaN*	university	*daigaku*
movie theater	*ēgakaN*		

Using the words in the previous lists, complete the following exercises. The answers are given at the end of the chapter.

Exercise 2

How would you say the following?

1. "near the bookstore"

   _____

2. "ahead of the city hall"

   _____

3. "in(side) the hospital"

   _____

Exercise 3

Look at the map and answer the following questions. The word *doko* means "where."

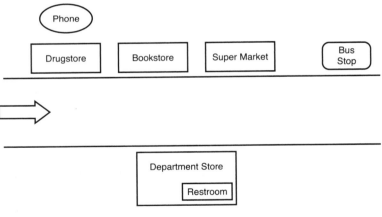

1. Q: *KōshūdeNwa-wa doko-desu ka?*

   A: _____

2. Q: *Basutē-wa doko-desu ka?*

   A: _____

3. Q: *Toire-wa doko-desu ka?*

   A: _____

HUH?

The word for "between" (*aida*) requires the use of two nouns and/or two landmarks. "Between *X* and *Y*" in Japanese is ...

> *X to Y-no aida*

For example, if you want to tell the taxi driver that your destination is between the supermarket and meat shop, you should say:

> *Sūpā-to nikuya-no aida-desu.* "It's between the supermarket and the meat shop."

With the address and simple directions, I am sure that the taxi driver will get you to your friend's apartment. Before ending this section, let me list other expressions that are useful for giving directions:

Koko-desu.	"We're here."
Koko-de tome-te kudasai.	"Please stop here."
Massugu it-te kudasai.	"Please go straight."
Migi-ni magat-te kudasai. (*migi* = "right")	"Please turn to the right."
Hidari-ni magat-te kudasai. (*hidari* = "left")	"Please turn to the left."
Ikura-desu ka?	"How much is it?"

Are You Sure You Want to Drive in Tokyo?

Japan's public transportation system is great! In terms of convenience, areas it serves, and promptness, I believe it is the best system in the world (putting aside the cost). Unless you live in an extremely rural area, you would not even consider driving in Japan. There are traffic jams wherever you go, and gasoline is incredibly expensive.

What? Do you really want to drive in Japan?

> *HoNtōni uNteN shi-tai-N-desu ka?*
> "Do you really want to drive?"
> (*hoNtōni* = "really"; *uNteN* = "driving")

Okay, but there are a few things you should be aware of.

First, the driver's seat is located on the right. Unless you are from the United Kingdom, you'll probably need some time to get used to the feel of it. It's a strange feeling to maneuver a car on the opposite side. When I go back to Japan, I occasionally drive.

Each time, when I intend to use the turn signal, I always turn on the wipers instead! Directional orientation is a hard thing to adjust to.

Second, if you are an American, you'll need to familiarize yourself with the metric system. One mile is equivalent to 1.6 kilometers. So when you see a speed limit sign of 80, do not drive 80 mph; 80 kph (kilometers per hour) is only 50 mph!

LIFESAVERS

Here is a mile-kilometer conversion chart:

10km	6.2 miles
20km	12.5 miles
30km	18.8 miles
40km	25 miles
50km	31.2 miles
60km	37.5 miles
70km	43.8 miles
80km	50 miles
90km	56.3 miles
100km	62 miles

Third, you need to learn the traffic signs. Sure, many Japanese signs are identical or similar to their Western counterparts, but some are unique to Japan and can have Japanese characters on them. Here are some of the signs.

These are frequently seen traffic signs. If you drive in Japan, be familiar with the kanji *characters written on the STOP sign and SLOW DOWN sign.*

The warning I want to give to those who want to drive in Japan is this:

Ki-o tsuke-te!   "Be careful!"

Answers

Exercise 1

1. *Watashi-wa* sushi-o *tabe-tai-N-desu ga …*
2. *Watashi-wa kamera-o kai-tai-N-desu ga …*

Exercise 2

1. *hoNya-no soba* or *hoNya-no chikaku*
2. *shiyakusho-no saki*
3. *byōiN-no naka*

Exercise 3

1. *Kusuriya-no ushiro-desu.* "It's behind the drugstore."
2. *Sūpā-no saki-desu.* "It's ahead of the supermarket."
   Or:
   Sūpā-no chikaku-desu. "It's near the supermarket."
3. *Depāto-no naka-desu.* "It's in the department store."

The Least You Need to Know

- In Japan, the most economical way to get to the city from the airport is either by airport limousine (shuttle) bus or train.
- The Japanese train/subway system is reliable and punctual. You can save time and money by using it, especially if you need to get around a big city.
- You can buy a train/bus ticket using the handy grammatical pattern "want to" (Verb Stem + *tai-N-desu ga …*).
- Use the *-te kudasai maseN ka* request pattern if you need to ask a big favor.
- Learn place names and direction words, and be able to give directions using the [LANDMARK-*no* Direction Word] pattern.

At the Hotel

In This Chapter

* Making a hotel reservation
* Calendar expressions
* *RyokaN*—Japanese-style inn

If you are on business or simply plan to sightsee in the city, staying in a hotel is not a bad idea. You might want to choose a fancy, rather expensive hotel if your budget allows so that you won't have to worry about communicating with a non-English-speaking staff. If you stay in an economy hotel or a hotel in a suburban area, chances are, the hotel staff will not understand English.

Making a Hotel Reservation

The easiest way to make a hotel reservation is through the Internet, as you can imagine. There are numerous bilingual sites where you can make an online reservation.

If you are not using the Internet to make reservations, you probably will need to do so either in person at a travel agency or over the phone. For the latter option, you first need to know some basic telephone expressions, covered in more detail in Chapter 22. Let's suppose that you need to make a reservation at a travel agency counter. You can find such facilities at airports and major train stations.

First, you will want to tell an agent that you want to make a hotel reservation. The word for reservation is *yoyaku*. *Yoyaku-o shi-masu* is the verbal form, meaning "make a reservation." Let's say, "I want to make a reservation." Remember the "want to" pattern introduced in Chapter 14? You got it! It's [Verb Stem + *tai-N-desu ga* …]. Here is the sentence:

Hoteru-no yoyaku-o shi-tai-N-desu ga …
"I want to make a hotel reservation but …"
(*shi-masu* = "do")

You can predict types of questions you will be asked upon making a reservation:

- Where do you want to stay?

- From what date to what date?

- How many people, and what kind of room?

HUH?

Remember the function of the sentence-final *ga?* This *ga* is different from the subject marker *-ga* introduced in Chapter 4. Its English equivalent is "but." By adding *ga,* you make your sentence incomplete, allowing the listener to guess what you want. This is a great strategy to make your Japanese sound polite.

For each of these items, let's learn basic expressions.

Choosing the Hotel

Here are two possible questions you might hear regarding the name of the hotel where you want to stay:

Dochira-no hoteru-desu ka? "What hotel is it (that you want to stay at)?"

Hoteru-no namae-wa (naN-desu ka)?   "(What is) the name of the hotel?"

For either of the previous questions, you can simply mention the name. Let's say that the hotel you have in mind is the Plaza Hotel.

Puraza Hoteru-desu.   "It's Plaza Hotel."

If there is more than one hotel under the name Plaza Hotel, you will be asked:

Dochira-no Puraza Hoteru-desu ka? "Which Plaza Hotel is it?"

Or:

Dochira-no Puraza Hoteru-deshō ka?

HUH?

A question ending with *-deshō ka?* is more polite than one ending with *-desu ka?*

Let's say you want to stay at the Plaza Hotel located in Shinjuku:

> *ShiNjuku-no Puraza Hoteru-desu.*   "It's the Plaza Hotel in Shinjuku."

Simple, isn't it? What if you haven't decided which hotel to stay at? The following expressions would be appropriate:

> *Mada kime-te i-maseN.*   "I haven't decided yet."
>
> *ShiNjuku-ni tomari-tai-N-desu ga …*   "I want to stay in Shinjuku, but …"
>
> *Doko-ga i-idesu ka?*   "Which one would you recommend?"

In reply to this question, you might hear the following:

> *XYZ Hoteru-wa dō-desu ka?*   "How about *XYZ* Hotel?"

Or the agent can reply to your question even more politely:

> *XYZ Hoteru-wa ikaga-deshō ka?*   "How about *XYZ* Hotel?"

The suggestion pattern *-wa dō-desu ka?* (or *-wa ikaga-deshō ka?*—polite version) is extremely useful. You should definitely add this expression to your "must memorize" list!

HUH?

When the question word is predictable in a sentence—as in the example "What is the name of the hotel?"—you can omit that question word and end the sentence with XYZ-*wa?* instead.

Check-In and Check-Out Dates

You need to specify the dates of check-in and check-out. Dates are pronounced almost identically to the way you count days, as you learned in Chapter 14. From the first day to the tenth day, they are all irregular. Beyond the eleventh day, however, most of the days are regularly pronounced except for the fourteenth, twentieth, and twenty-fourth days.

Dates

1st day	*tsuitachi*	10th day	*tōka*
2nd day	*futsuka*	11th day	*jū ichi-nichi*
3rd day	*mikka*	12th day	*jū ni-nichi*
4th day	*yokka*	13th day	*jū saN-nichi*
5th day	*itsuka*	14th day	*jū yokka*
6th day	*muika*	20th day	*hatsuka*
7th day	*nanoka*	24th day	*ni-jū yokka*
8th day	*yōka*	What date?	*naN-nichi*
9th day	*kokonoka*		

How would you say months? The good news is months are pronounced in a completely regular manner:

Months

January	*ichi-gatsu*	August	*hachi-gatsu*
February	*ni-gatsu*	September	*ku-gatsu*
March	*saN-gatsu*	October	*jū-gatsu*
April	*shi-gatsu*	November	*jū ichi-gatsu*
May	*go-gatsu*	December	*jū ni-gatsu*
June	*roku-gatsu*	What month?	*naN-gatsu*
July	*shichi-gatsu*		

Before you forget all the calendar words, answer the following questions. Can you guess what these days are?

1. *Kurisumasu-wa itsu-desu ka?*

2. *Kurisumasu Ibu-wa itsu-desu ka?*

3. *BareNtaiN Dē-wa itsu-desu ka?*

4. *Ēpuriru Fūru-wa itsu-desu ka?*

Did you get it? Yes, you've been asked when (1) Christmas, (2) Christmas Eve, (3) Valentine's Day, and (4) April Fool's Day are, respectively. Now, answer these questions:

Exercise 1

1. *Kurisumasu-wa* _____.

2. *Kurisumasu Ibu-wa* _____.

3. *BareNtaiN Dē* _____.

4. *Ēpuriru Fūru-wa* _____.

SHORTCUTS TO SUCCESS

A useful exercise to practice months and dates is saying people's birthdays, or *taNjōbi*. Ask people this question:

Q: *TaNjōbi-wa itsu-desu ka?*   "When is your birthday?"
A: *SaN-gatsu jū ni-nichi-desu.*   "It's March 12."

 Let's use this opportunity to learn another important calendar expression, days of the week:

Days of the Week

Monday	*getsu-yōbi*	Friday	*kiN-yōbi*
Tuesday	*ka-yōbi*	Saturday	*do-yōbi*
Wednesday	*sui-yōbi*	Sunday	*nichi-yōbi*
Thursday	*moku-yōbi*	What day?	*naN-yōbi*

With all these calendar expressions, let's learn how to specify the dates of your check-in and check-out. The easiest way to specify these dates is to say, "The check-in is so-and-so date and the check-out is so-and-so date." Suppose that you will check in on Tuesday, June 13, and check out on Thursday, June 15:

Chekku iN-wa roku-gatsu jū
saN-nichi ka-yōbi-de,
chekku auto-wa jū go-nichi
moku-yōbi-desu.

"Check-in is Tuesday, June 13,

and check-out is Thursday, the 15th."

Notice that the day of the week follows the date. Also notice that the two sentences are connected by the *TE*-form, *-de*.

Alternatively, using the "want to" pattern, you can specify the check-in date:

Roku-gatsu jū saN-nichi-ni chekku iN shi-tai-N-desu ga …
"I want to check in on June 13 …"

The particle *-ni*, which is attached to the date, means "on." Let me give you another way of specifying check-in and check-out dates:

> *Roku-gatsu jū saN-nichi-<u>kara</u>, jū go-nichi-<u>made</u>-desu.*
> "It's <u>*from*</u> June 13 <u>*to*</u> the 15th."

HUH?

Let's not forget another important calendar-related counter: "year." It is *-neN* and can be used for expressing duration and point of time. Here are some examples:

"five years"	*go-neN*
"1985"	*seN kyū-hyaku hachi-jū go-neN*
"2011"	*ni-seN jū ichi-neN*
"what year; how many years"	*naN-neN*

I think you know by now that particles are extremely important. They make it possible for you to say the same thing in a number of different ways.

Exercise 2

Translate the following by using the expressions you have learned so far.

1. "I want to check in on Wednesday, March 22."

   _____

2. "Check-in is August 2 and check-out is August 3."

   _____

3. "It's from Monday to Friday."

   _____

Number of People and Types of Room

In Chapter 10, you learned how to count people. The counter for _____ people is *-niN*, but "one person" and "two people" are irregular.

Counting People

1	*hitori*	7	*shichi-niN*
2	*futari*	8	*hachi-niN*
3	*saN-niN*	9	*kyū-niN*
4	*yo-niN*	10	*jū-niN*
5	*go-niN*	11	*jū ichi-niN*
6	*roku-niN*	How many?	*naN-niN*

The polite version of the counter *-niN* is *-mēsama*. The clerk at the counter might use *-mēsama* to ask you how many people are staying:

> *NaN-mēsama-desu ka?*   "How many people?"

To reply to this question, just use the regular counter *-niN*:

> *SaN-niN-desu.*   "Three people."

As long as you stay in a Western-style hotel, you can use the same words for room types. But make sure that you *Japanize* them when pronouncing these words!

single	*shiNguru*	double	*daburu*
twin	*tsuiN*	suite	*suīto*

The Japanese word for "room" is *heya* or *oheya* (polite version). Here is a typical dialogue between a clerk and a guest regarding room selection:

> Q: *Donoyōna oheya-ni nasai-masu ka?*   "What kind of room would you like?"

> A: *TsuiN-ni shi-masu.*   "I'll have a twin room."

HUH?

The expression *-ni shi-masu* literally means "decide on …." This expression is often used when placing an order. By the way, the honorific version of *-ni shi-masu* is *-ni nasai-masu.*

Upon making a reservation, you might be asked to leave a deposit. Major credit cards are widely accepted throughout Japan. This can make reserving a room a lot easier.

Check-In and Check-Out

 Now you are in the hotel lobby. You're about to check in. First, you need to tell the front desk who you are and indicate that you have made a reservation:

Yoyaku-o shi-te ari-masu XYZ-*desu ga.* "I am *XYZ*. I have a reservation."

HUH?

The expression *-te ari-masu* is used when talking about something that *has been done in advance.*

Other examples using this pattern are …

Kat-te ari-masu. "Something has been purchased."
(*Kat-te* derives from *kai-masu*.)

TanoN-de ari-masu. "Something has been requested."
(*TanoN-de* derives from *tanomi-masu*.)

Kai-te ari-masu. "Something has been written."
(*Kai-te* derives from *kaki-masu*.)

Upon check-in, it is likely that you will be asked the questions covered in the previous section, such as the check-out date, number of people staying, and type of room. There are a couple of things I want to add here that you might find helpful.

LIFESAVERS

In Japanese hotels, the price for a room might vary depending on how many people stay in the room. For example, the same twin room can cost less if you are staying alone. Make sure that you check the room charge policy prior to making a reservation!

If you are a nonsmoker, you should be sure to ask for a nonsmoking room because smoking rooms still outnumber nonsmoking rooms in Japanese hotels. "Nonsmoking" is *kiNeN*:

KiNeN-no heya-o onegai shimasu. "A nonsmoking room, please."

HUH?

The word *kiNeN* ("No smoking") should be pronounced as *kin en*.

By the way, the phrase for "smoke (a cigarette)" is *tabako-o sui-masu*.

You might want to ask what the check-out time is. You learned the time expressions, so you should have no problem saying the following:

> *Chekku auto-wa naN-ji-desu ka?*   "What time is the check-out?"

There is one more thing—you will need to fill out a registration card. It is called *shukuhaku kādo*. It should look similar to a typical registration card used in Western countries. You will also need to show the hotel clerk your passport so he can make a copy of it. Here are some words you will see on the registration card:

"Name"	*shimē* or *(o)namae*
"Address"	*jūsho*
"Phone number"	*deNwa baNgō*
"Occupation"	*shokugyō*

You can ask if they have an English version of the registration card:

> *Ēgo-no kādo-wa ari-maseN ka?*   "Don't you have an English card?"

Of course, you can use *ari-masu ka*, instead of the negative version *ari-maseN ka*. The negative question such as this, however, sounds softer and more polite. This is another strategy to make your Japanese sound better!

LIFESAVERS

You might want to sightsee in the area using the hotel as the hub. Ask the hotel clerk if there are any places to visit in the area. Suppose that the hotel is in Shinjuku:

ShiNjuku-ni-wa nani-ga ari-masu ka?
"What (kinds of things) are in Shinjuku?"

This pattern (XYZ-*ni-wa nani-ga ari-masu ka?*) is helpful when you are in a new place by yourself and want to explore the area.

When you check out, say the by-now-familiar phrase:

> *Chekku auto, onegai shimasu.*   "Check-out, please."

Or:

> *Kaikē, onegai shimasu.*   "Billing, please."
> (*kaikē* = bill, account)

You might want to tell the front desk how you want to pay for your room. Suppose that you pay by credit card:

> *Kādo-<u>de</u> onegai shimasu.*   "By credit card, please."

The particle *-de* means "by means of." If paying in cash, say *kyasshu* or *geNkiN*, as in:

> *Kyasshu-<u>de</u> onegai shimasu.*   "In cash, please."
>
> *GeNkiN-<u>de</u> onegai shimasu.*   "In cash, please."

If you need a receipt, you should say:

> *Ryōshūsho-o onegai shimasu.*   "Receipt, please."

Instead of *ryōshūsho*, its loanword version *reshīto* can also work.

Staying in a *RyokaN*—a Japanese-Style Inn

It is certainly more convenient to stay in a Western-style hotel because you will be familiar with the room arrangement, amenities, check-in/check-out procedures, and so forth. However, if you want to experience traditional Japanese accommodations, try a Japanese-style inn, or *ryokaN*. In what follows, I briefly explain the major differences between Western-style hotels and Japanese-style inns.

LIFESAVERS

For more information about *ryokaNs,* check out the official website of the Japan Ryokan Association at www.ryokan.or.jp.

A *ryokaN* guest room generally has no bed, couch, or carpet. Instead, it has a *futon*, low table, and *tatami* mat. You might know this already, but a *futon* is a foldable mattress with a comforter. A Japanese-style low table is called *chabudai*. *Tatami* is a straw mat that is about two inches thick.

GREEN TEA BREAK

Some larger *ryokaN* have Western-style rooms available. A Japanese-style room is called *washitsu* or *nihoNma*, and a Western-style room is *yōma*.

Perhaps the best part of staying in a *ryokaN* is that breakfast and dinner are included in the accommodations. Typically, a room service person in charge of your room (called *nakaisaN*) takes you to your room after check-in. She then makes tea for you and asks what time you want the meal served in your room. The questions look like the following:

Oshokuji-wa, naN-ji-goro-ga yoroshi-idesu ka?
"Around what time would you like to have the meal?"

Oshokuji is the politer version of *shokuji* ("meal"), and *yoroshi-idesu* is a polite equivalent of *i-idesu* ("all right").

GREEN TEA BREAK

Tipping is not required in Japan, but it will definitely be appreciated in a *ryokaN*. Give it to the room service person when she takes you to the room. A 1,000-*yen* bill would be great! "Tip" in Japanese is *chippu*.

If you want the meal served around 6 o'clock, say:

Roku-ji-goro onegai shimasu.   "Around 6, please."

In general, *nakaisaN*, a person in charge of your room, ensures that you have all you need during your stay.

Before dinner, you might want to relax, take a bath, and put on a *yukata* (a casual-style *kimono*).

Here comes dinner! It is usually served on a high tray and placed in front of you as you sit on the *tatami*. Because the food is not at eye-level, you have to bend over slightly to eat. (If you are not comfortable, you can request that the meal be placed on a *chabudai*, the low table. But you still have to sit on the *tatami*, or floor.)

After the meal, the room service person will put away the tray and then start laying out a *futon*. After you wake up in the morning, she will put away the *futon* for you. This is how Japanese people make the best use of their living space.

LIFESAVERS

If you request it in advance, the *ryokaN* will even make lunch for you (for an extra charge). If you plan to venture out and do some activities the following day, you can use this service so you won't have to eat fast food on the street. By the way, the Japanese words for "breakfast," "lunch," and "dinner" are …

"breakfast"	*asa-gohaN* or *chō-shoku*
"lunch"	*hiru-gohaN* or *chū-shoku*
"dinner"	*baN-gohaN* or *yū-shoku*

Your room might have a bathtub, but I highly recommend that you use the huge guest bath located away from the guest rooms. This is called *dai-yokujō* ("big bath for guests") or simply *ofuro*. If your travel destination is famous for hot springs (*oNseN*), it would be criminal not to try the *dai-yokujō!* Some *ryokaN* inns have several baths, which look like swimming pools. (I first learned how to swim in a *dai-yokujō!*) Some baths are even located outdoors (called *roteNburo*). Taking a bath is a serious form of recreation for Japanese people!

> **GREEN TEA BREAK**
>
> Each *oNseN* is unique in terms of minerals contained in the water. They are therapeutic and can be good for backaches, gastritis, arthritis, and other maladies. The website hosted by *Outdoor Japan* has extensive coverage of Japanese *oNseN*. Check out www.outdoorjapan.com.

There are several manners you should obey when using *ofuro*:

- Wash your body thoroughly before entering the bath.
- Do not put your hand towel in the bath water. Put it outside the tub or on your head.
- Never use soap in the bath!
- Don't drain the bath water after using it.

Taking a dip in a nice and relaxing *oNseN* hot spring and enjoying delicious Japanese cuisine personally served in your room will make staying at a *ryokaN* a memorable experience for you!

Answers

Exercise 1

1. *Kurisumasu-wa jū ni-gatsu ni-jū go-nichi-desu.*

2. *Kurisumasu Ibu-wa jū ni-gatsu ni-jū yokka-desu.*

3. *BareNtaiN Dē-wa ni-gatsu jū yokka-desu.*

4. *Ēpuriru Fūru-wa shi-gatsu tsuitachi-desu.*

Exercise 2

1. *SaN-gatsu ni-jū ni-nichi suiyō-bi-ni chekku iN shi-tai-N-desu ga.*
2. *Chekku iN-wa hachi-gatsu futsuka-de, chekku auto-wa hachi-gatsu mikka-desu.*
3. *Getsu-yōbi-kara kiN-yōbi-made desu.*

The Least You Need to Know

- Learn calendar expressions and counting people for making a reservation (*yoyaku*).
- Practice basic dialogues for check-in and check-out.
- Try a *ryokaN*, a Japanese-style inn. There, you can enjoy delicious meals served in your room and relax in an *oNseN*, or hot spring bath.
- Here are three points to remember when you take a Japanese-style bath: (1) wash your body before entering; (2) don't use soap in the bath; and (3) don't drain the bath water after using it.
- At a *ryokaN*, a *nakaisaN* is in charge of your room and makes sure your stay is comfortable by serving you meals, making a bed, and so on. Tipping a *nakaisaN* (commonly a 1,000-*yen* bill) is a good idea.

At the Bank

In This Chapter

- Japanese bills and coins
- Counting money
- Currency exchange
- Opening a bank account

At least two things have changed the world of traveling in recent years—the Internet and credit cards. Thanks to the Internet, you can find the cheapest possible plane tickets, make a reservation for a hotel, rent a car, and come up with a precise itinerary. And thanks to credit cards, you can travel almost anywhere in the world without carrying a large sum of cash. You can withdraw cash from an ATM at a nearby convenience store or even make an international phone call using a plastic card.

Even though you can rely on your credit card pretty much anywhere in Japan, you should know that Japan is still a cash-oriented society. In some establishments, especially in rural areas, credit cards are not accepted or a processing charge is added to your purchase. So you'd better know how to deal with *yen*. In this chapter, I first give you basic facts about Japanese money and then give you expressions you might use at a bank.

HUH?

All the denominations of paper *yen* end with the sound *N*, as in *seN,* "1,000." Make sure you pronounce this sound correctly so that you don't pronounce ¥1,000 as *seneN*. It should be *seN eN*. For more details on this sound, refer to Chapter 3.

Bills and Coins

In several previous chapters, we dealt with Japanese number words, but most were small numbers. With money in hand, now we have to deal with bigger numbers. I certainly don't want you to lose your money due to a miscalculation or simply because you don't know how to count Japanese money! To make this chapter easier, I suggest you go back to Chapter 7 and review the counting basics in Japanese.

The monetary unit used in Japan is *yen*, but it is actually pronounced as *eN*. Its international symbol is ¥, which comes before the amount. First, let's take a look at paper *yen*. There are four kinds of bills: ¥1,000; ¥2,000; ¥5,000; and ¥10,000. Here is how to pronounce each denomination:

 Japanese Bills

Denomination	Pronunciation
¥1,000	*seN-eN*
¥2,000	*ni-seN-eN*
¥5,000	*go-seN-eN*
¥10,000	*ichi-maN-eN*

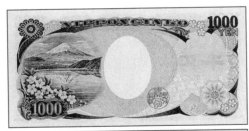

Japanese ¥1,000; ¥2,000; ¥5,000; and ¥10,000 bills (back and front). The ¥2,000 bills are not widely circulated.

 GREEN TEA BREAK

Because the bills are slightly different in size (the higher the denomination, the bigger its size!), it is easy to organize your wallet. Also, specially imprinted Braille appears on the left corner, so visually impaired persons can recognize each bill:

- ¥1,000: One round dot
- ¥2,000: Three dots (vertical)
- ¥5,000: Two dots (vertical)
- ¥10,000: Two dots (horizontal)

How would you say "coins"? There are six kinds of coins.

Japanese Coins

Denomination	Pronunciation
¥1	*ichi-eN*
¥5	*go-eN*
¥10	*jū-eN*
¥50	*go-jū-eN*
¥100	*hyaku-eN*
¥500	*go-hyaku-eN*

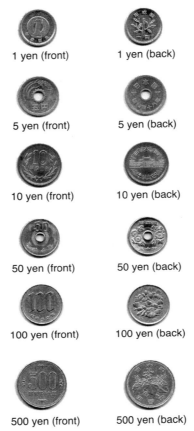

1 yen (front)   1 yen (back)

5 yen (front)   5 yen (back)

10 yen (front)   10 yen (back)

50 yen (front)   50 yen (back)

100 yen (front) 100 yen (back)

500 yen (front) 500 yen (back)

There are six kinds of coins circulated in Japan. The 1 yen coins are made of aluminum; 5 yen coins are made of copper; 10 yen coins are made of bronze; and 50, 100, and 500 yen coins are all made of nickel.

Counting in Japanese can be a challenging task, but it is absolutely essential when counting your money! If you are not confident about counting, refer to Chapter 7.

Now, how about a short exercise? How do you say the following in Japanese?

Exercise 1

1. ¥24 _____

2. ¥805 _____

3. ¥7,000 _____

4. ¥46,100 _____

5. ¥100,000 _____

Now with all the basics covered, the following sections cover various tasks that are useful at a bank, or *giNkō:*

- Currency exchange
- Sending money
- Opening a bank account

Currency Exchange

The top reason a foreign traveler uses a bank is to exchange money. The expression for "to exchange" is *ryōgae shi-masu*. Suppose that you have U.S. dollars and want to exchange them to Japanese *yen*. Using the "want to" pattern, say the following:

> *Amerika doru-o, nihoN eN-ni ryōgae shi-tai-N-desu ga …*
> "I want to exchange U.S. *dollars* to Japanese *yen*."

The formula for currency exchange is …

> (Original Currencies)-*o*, (Desired Currencies)-*ni ryōgae shi-tai-N-desu ga …*

Note that in the preceding example, "dollar ($)" is pronounced *doru.*

What do you call other countries' currencies in Japanese?

Canadian dollar	*Kanada doru*
Euro	*yūro*
U.K. pound	*poNdo*
Mexican peso	*peso*

Now you are at a currency exchange. Exchange your money as instructed:

Exercise 2

1. From Japanese *yen* to Canadian dollars

   _____

2. From euros to Japanese *yen*

   _____

A bank clerk will ask you how much in U.S. dollars you want to exchange by asking the following:

> *Amerika doru-o, ikura-desu ka?*   "How much of U.S. dollars?"

Let's say that you have $1,000 to exchange:

> *SeN-doru onegai shimasu.*   "$1,000, please."

Using the XYZ-*wa ikura-desu ka* pattern, the following expressions can also be useful when exchanging money:

> *Tesūryō-wa ikura-desu ka?*   "How much is the processing fee?"
>
> *Rēto-wa, ikura-desu ka?*   "What is the (exchange) rate?"

LIFESAVERS

Usually the processing (or handling) fee for currency exchange is included in the exchange rate.

Suppose the rate is U.S. $1 = ¥130. Then the answer to the previous rate question is:

> *Ichi-doru-wa hyaku saN-jū-eN-desu.*   "U.S. $1 = ¥130."

Note that the by-now-familiar X-*wa* Y-*desu* pattern is just like a mathematical equation, as explained in Chapter 9.

The word *ryōgae* is used not only for international exchanges, but also for just breaking a big bill into smaller denominations. Requesting an exchange is easy!

> *Ryōgae shi-te kudasai.*   "Exchange, please."

Or:

> *Ryōgae onegai shimasu.*   "Exchange, please."

SHORTCUTS TO SUCCESS

As of this writing, U.S. $1 is equal to ¥84. However, because the commodity price of Japan is higher than that of the United States, what you can buy with $1 in the United States costs about ¥150 despite the exchange rate. For example, a canned beverage in a vending machine (about 75¢ in the United States) is ¥120. A McDonald's value meal with a Big Mac (about $3.50 in the United States) is about ¥550.

What if you have a ¥10,000 bill and want to exchange it for ¥1,000 bills?

> *Ichi-maN-eN-o seN-eN-ni ryōgae shi-te kudasai.*
> "Please exchange a ¥10,000 bill to ¥1,000s."

Exercise 3

Ask to break the following bills to smaller bills.

1. A ¥1,000 bill to ¥100s

_____

2. A ¥10,000 bill to a ¥5,000 bill *and* ¥1,000s (use *to* for "and")

_____

Opening a Bank Account

If you plan to stay in Japan for a longer period of time, you will probably need to open a bank account, or *kōza*. You will be dealing with your money in a foreign country, so you want to be very cautious about bank-related business. If you have a Japanese friend, ask her or him to help you do all the paperwork when opening a new account. If not, I suggest that you go to a branch office of a major Western bank, such as Citibank, where many of the clerks are bilingual. However, if you live in a rural area where there is no Western bank branch and you need to do it on your own, here is how you go about it.

 GREEN TEA BREAK

You can also open your account at a local post office (*yūbiNkyoku*). One of the advantages of using the post office as a bank is that you can withdraw your money at any post office in Japan. This way, you won't have to pay a service charge for using other banks' ATMs. On a related note, ATMs might not be open 24 hours, especially in small towns.

First of all, you should know that in Japanese business, signatures or autographs are not used for identification purposes. Instead, you must use an impression seal (or signature stamp) called *haNko* or *iNkaN*. It is about 2.5 inches long (7cm), its diameter is a .5 inch (12mm) to 1 inch (25mm), and it is usually made of wood or plastic. You can purchase a *haNko* at a local department store in Japan. Unless you are of Japanese descent, you probably don't have a Japanese name. In such a case, it will have to be custom-made and it will take a couple of days to get your own *haNko*.

A sample impression of haNko (signature stamp). It says "Fujita" in kanji.

  GREEN TEA BREAK

If you do not have your *haNko,* you might be asked to use your thumbprint to identify yourself. This method is called *boiN.*

With your *haNko* in hand now, you are ready to open your new account.

> *Atarashi-i kōza-o tsukuri-tai-N-desu ga ...*
> "I want to make (open) a new account ..."

Note that *atarashi-i* means "new" and *tsukuri-masu* means "to make." Also remember the "want to" pattern:

> Verb Stem + *tai-N-desu ga ...*   "I want to VERB"

You will be given an application form. (Most major banks have a form written in English.) Next to your name, you will be asked to put a *haNko* impression. This impression is registered in the bank as a means of your identification. Therefore, when you need to withdraw money from your account, you will need your *haNko* (except when you withdraw your money from an ATM, of course).

Here are other important bank-related words:

certificate of deposit (CD)	*tēki yokiN* (or "term saving")
regular savings	*futsū yokiN*
interest	*risoku*
cancellation of account	*kaiyaku*
ATM card	*kyasshu kādo*
account number	*kōza baNgō*
account record book	*chokiN tsūchō*

You might be wondering why the list did not include the words for "checking account" or "personal check." In Japan, there is no checking account simply because personal checks are not commonly available. Checks are limited to corporate use in general.

The phrase *chokiN tsūchō* ("account record book") might not be a familiar concept to you. This is a tiny booklet that shows your account record. When you go to your bank to deposit or withdraw money from your account, you need to show this booklet along with your *haNko* ("signature stamp"). After a transaction, the bank clerk will insert the booklet into a machine and print the transaction activities and balance on it.

Keeping this record of your own bank account makes a few things easier. For example, you can easily cash your traveler's checks or send money to your home country (and receive money by wire to your account from abroad).

First, here is how you request cashing traveler's checks. The expression for "to cash" is *kaNkiN shi-masu*:

> *Toraberāzu chekku-o kaNkiN shi-tai-N-desu ga …*
> "I want to cash my traveler's checks …"

When you cash traveler's checks, you will be asked to show your ID:

> *MibuN shōmēsho-o mise-te kudasai.*
> "Please show me your ID." (*mise-masu* = "to show")

Possible IDs you might have are …

pasupōto	passport
kokusai meNkyoshō	international driver's license

 LIFESAVERS

If you stay in Japan for more than 90 days, you need to obtain a *gaikokujiN tōrokushō* (Alien Registration Card). You can get one at your local city hall (*shiyakusho*) and use this card as your ID as well.

Let's learn some essential phrases for sending (or wiring) money to your home country. The phrase for "send (wire) money" is *sōkiN shi-masu*. Suppose that you want to send money to the United States:

> *Amerika-ni sōkiN shi-tai-N-desu ga …*
> "I want to wire money to the United States …"

You will have to give the bank clerk the following information:

> *Amerika-no* XYZ *GiNkō-desu.*   "It's the Bank of XYZ in the United States."
>
> ABC *ShiteN-desu.*   "It's the ABC Branch."

UketoriniN-wa John Smith-desu. "The recipient is John Smith."

Kōza baNgō-wa XXX-desu. "The account number is XXX."

LIFESAVERS

When you read a series of numbers, such as a phone or account number, say each digit separately and use *no* for a dash (-). If your account number is 346-2687-1, say:

SaN yoN roku no ni roku hachi nana no ichi

Learning Japanese number words can be a lot of work, but learning them will make your life much less stressful when it comes to money and banking.

Answers

Exercise 1

1. ¥24 *ni-jū yo-eN*

2. ¥805 *hap-pyaku go-eN*

3. ¥7,000 *nana-seN-eN*

4. ¥46,100 *yoN-maN roku-seN hyaku-eN*

5. ¥100,000 *jū-maN-eN*

Exercise 2

1. From Japanese *yen* to Canadian dollars
   NihoN eN-o, Kanada doru-ni ryōgae shi-tai-N-desu ga ...

2. From euros to Japanese *yen*
   Yūro-o, nihoN eN-ni ryōgae shi-tai-N-desu ga ...

Exercise 3

1. A ¥1,000 bill to ¥100s
   SeN-eN-o hyaku-eN-ni ryōgae shi-te kudasai.

2. A ¥10,000 bill to a ¥5,000 bill *and* ¥1,000s
   Ichi-maN-eN-o go-seN-eN to seN-eN-ni ryōgae shi-te kudasai.

The Least You Need to Know

- Familiarize yourself with Japanese bills and coins. There are four kinds of bills: ¥1,000; ¥2,000; ¥5,000; and ¥10,000. There are also six kinds of coins: ¥1, ¥5, ¥10, ¥50, ¥100, and ¥500.

- The ability to count numbers in Japanese is a true lifesaver!

- Be able to ask for currency exchange and know how to cash your traveler's checks.

- In Japan, a *haNko,* or seal impression, is used for bank transactions in place of a signature.

Japanese for Fun

This part covers four fun activities: shopping, dining, home-stay, and leisure time. You learn all the must-know shopping phrases and expressions. Dining is also a fun part of traveling—especially in Japan. With the expressions covered in these chapters, you can decide what to eat and order your favorite dishes, not to mention learn about Japanese dining etiquette.

If possible, try arranging a home-stay. Nothing is a more exciting and authentic experience than living in a real Japanese house with Japanese people. I take you on a virtual house tour and explain in detail what you are or are not expected to do in a Japanese home.

If you're an independent person and want to explore Japan on your own, Chapter 21 is for you. After reading the chapter, you will be able to make plans for a short trip. You also discover the kinds of popular events that are held during each season.

Let's Go Shopping!

In This Chapter

- Buying what you want
- Four basic counters
- Use of adjectives

We dealt with Japanese money in Chapter 17. While your memory is still fresh, let's move on to shopping! There is no doubt that shopping is one of the best parts of traveling. If you like shopping, you will find this chapter very helpful.

Types of Shops

One thing I noticed when I first came to the United States was that supermarkets in the United States are so big that you can buy almost anything there. Consequently, I noticed that specialty shops such as vegetable shops, meat shops, and small general stores are extremely scarce in the States, compared to Japan.

In Japan, the number of supermarkets (*sūpā*) has grown rapidly in recent years, but there are still many traditional small retail stores. Here is a list of the Japanese names for common retail stores:

Shops

bakery	*paNya* (or *paNya-saN*)
bookstore	*hoNya* (or *hoNya-saN*)
cleaner	*kurīniNguya* (or *kurīniNguya-saN*)
convenience store	*koNbini*
department store	*depāto*
drug store	*kusuriya* (or *kusuriya-saN* or *yakkyoku*)

electronics store	*deNkiya*
fish market	*sakanaya* (or *sakanaya-saN*)
florist	*hanaya* (or *hanaya-saN*)
fruit store	*kudamonoya*
liquor store	*sakaya* (or *sakaya-saN)*
meat shop	*nikuya* (or *nikuya-saN*)
office supply store	*buNbōguya* (or *buNbōguya-saN*)
shoe store	*kutsuya* (or *kutsuya-saN*)
shop (in general)	*mise*
supermarket	*sūpā*
vegetable shop	*yaoya* (or *yaoya-saN*)

HUH?

You might have noticed that many of the shop names end in *ya,* "shop." So by looking at *hoNya* ("bookstore"), you know that the Japanese word for "book" is *hoN.* There are two exceptions: *yaoya* ("vegetable shop") and *sakaya* ("liquor shop"). The words for "vegetable" and "liquor" are *yasai* and *sake,* respectively, not *yao* and *saka.* Also, as shown in the list, businesses ending with *ya* often end with -*saN*, as in *hoNya-saN.* This way, these names sound more personable.

As you know, shopping at a supermarket is easy. You just put merchandise in your shopping cart, take it to the cashier, and then pay. But what if the item you are looking for can only be found in a small retail shop? If so, you will need to converse with a shop clerk to get what you want.

LIFESAVERS

A convenience store, or *koNbini,* does more than just sell a variety of goods. You can use dry-cleaning services, send packages via an express home delivery service called *takuhaibiN,* use a photocopier, buy a concert ticket, pay for utility bills, and so on. In some *koNbini,* you can withdraw money (Japanese *yen*) from your own bank account. Even in rural areas, you can find at least one *koNbini* near you.

Let's learn some basic dialogues that contain essential shopping expressions.

Shop Talk

 When you enter a shop, you will be greeted with …

>   *Irasshai mase.*   "Welcome!"

This is a ritualized expression, so you don't have to reply to this greeting. The shop clerk will then ask you if she or he can be of assistance:

>   *Nanika osagashi-desu ka?*   "Looking for something?"

LIFESAVERS

If you are just looking, the following phrase can be handy:
>   *Mi-te iru dake-desu.*   "Just looking."

The basic expression that you should use when you buy something is very simple, as shown here:

>   XYZ-*o kudasai.*   "Please give me *XYZ*."

Alternatively, you can say "I want *XYZ*":

>   XYZ-*ga hoshi-i-N-desu ga …*   "I want *XYZ* …"

HUH?

The word *hoshi-i* ("want") is an adjective in Japanese. So "I don't want (it)" should be …

>   *Hoshi-kuna-idesu.*   "I don't want (it)."

If you use "want" with a verb (as in "want to do so-and-so"), use the following pattern:

>   Verb Stem + <u>*tai*</u>-*N-desu ga …*

Refer to Chapter 5 for adjective conjugation.

These expressions will suffice if you purchase just one item, but what if you want to buy more than one? You should know how to attach the desired number to a noun.

Basic Counters

 One of the notable characteristics of Japanese is that when you count objects, you must attach an appropriate counter to the number. In English, when you count "uncountable" substances such as paper, salt, and water, you use phrases such as "three sheets of paper," "a pinch of salt," or "two glasses of water." Japanese counters are in a sense similar to "sheet," "pinch," and "glass," but they are not limited to uncountable objects.

You have already seen two counters in Chapter 10: *-niN* for counting people and *-sai* for ages. In this chapter, you learn four types of counters that are useful when counting objects for shopping: *-mai*, *-satsu*, *-boN*, and *-tsu/-ko*.

Counter	Used For	Examples
-mai	flat objects	paper, CDs, pizza, stamps, plates
-satsu	bound objects	books, magazines
-boN	long objects	pens, bananas, bottles
-tsu/-ko	miscellaneous objects	vegetables, eggs, erasers, paper clips, fruit, chairs

I referred to *-tsu* as the counter for miscellaneous objects. This is the general counter, so if you are not sure exactly which counter to use, you can always use it as a default. This counter behaves in a slightly complicated way. But don't worry about that now. We will look at how it works shortly. Just remember that these four counters should cover most merchandise you might need to buy at Japanese shops.

Now, let's look at each of the first three counters from 1 to 11. The pronunciation pattern of words from 11 on is just the same as that for words between 1 and 10. As always, irregular pronunciations are indicated in bold-face.

Three Basic Counters

	Flat	Bound	Long
One	*ichi-mai*	**is-satsu**	**ip-poN**
Two	*ni-mai*	*ni-satsu*	*ni-boN*
Three	*saN-mai*	*saN-satsu*	**saN-boN**
Four	*yoN-mai*	*yoN-satsu*	*yoN-boN*
Five	*go-mai*	*go-satsu*	*go-boN*
Six	*roku-mai*	*roku-satsu*	**rop-poN**
Seven	*nana-mai*	*nana-satsu*	*nana-boN*
Eight	*hachi-mai*	**has-satsu**	**hap-poN**
Nine	*kyū-mai*	*kyū-satsu*	*kyū-boN*
Ten	*jū-mai*	**jus-satsu**	**jup-poN**
Eleven	*jū ichi-mai*	**jū is-satsu**	**jū ip-poN**
How many?	*naN-mai*	*naN-satsu*	**naN-boN**

When you want to specify the quantity of an object, you should use the following sentence pattern:

[ITEM-*particle* QUANTITY-*counter* ... Predicate]

With this pattern in mind, let's say both "Please give me five pens" and "I want five pens."

PeN-o go-boN kudasai.   "Please give me five pens."

PeN-ga go-boN hoshi-i-N-desu ga... "I want five pens..."

Now, answer the following questions for practice. An item and its quantity are provided. The answers are given at the end of this chapter.

Exercise 1

1. "I want five Japanese language books." (Hint: books = bound)

   _____

2. "I bought eleven blue pencils." ("blue" = *aoi*; "pencil" = *eNpitsu*)

   _____

3. "There are thirteen books." ("there are *X*" = X-*ga ari-masu*)

   _____

4. "Please buy six bottles of beer." (Hint: beer bottle = long)

   _____

5. "Eight '10-*yen*' stamps, please." ("10-*yen* stamps" = *jū-eN kitte*)

   _____

Let's move on to the counters used for miscellaneous objects: *-tsu* and *-ko*. Miscellaneous objects are things such as (lumpy) vegetables, eggs, erasers, paper clips, (lumpy) fruit, chairs, and so on.

 LIFESAVERS

In Chapter 10, we learned the counter *-sai* for age. The *-tsu* counter can also be used for age.

The Counters for Miscellaneous Objects

	-tsu	*-ko*
One	*hito-tsu*	**ik-ko**
Two	*futa-tsu*	*ni-ko*
Three	*mit-tsu*	*saN-ko*
Four	*yot-tsu*	*yoN-ko*
Five	*itsu-tsu*	*go-ko*
Six	*mut-tsu*	**rok-ko**
Seven	*nana-tsu*	*nana-ko*
Eight	*yat-tsu*	**hak-ko**
Nine	*kokono-tsu*	*kyū-ko*
Ten	*tō*	**juk-ko**
Eleven	*jū ichi*	**jū ik-ko**
Twelve	*jū ni*	*jū ni-ko*
How many?	*iku-tsu*	*naN-ko*

Note 1: For "ten," the counter -tsu *does not accompany the number.*

Note 2: For "eleven" and beyond, the counter -tsu *is not used. Instead, regular numbers such as* jū ichi *("eleven"),* jū ni *("twelve"),* jū saN *("thirteen"), and so on, are used.*

As you see in the chart, the *-tsu* counter is complicated. I was tempted to teach you just the *-ko* counter because it's much simpler. However, you will hear the *-tsu* counter often, so you should at least know how it works. It's perfectly okay to stick to *-ko* when you count objects.

Let's do an exercise, focusing on the *-tsu* counter. Again, an item and its quantity are provided. How would you say the following?

Exercise 2

1. Please give me three apples. ("apple" = *riNgo*)

   _____

2. I want four balls. ("ball" = *bōru*)

   _____

3. I ate nine *sushi*!

   _____

HUH?

The general counters *hito-tsu, futa-tsu,* and so on, are the native Japanese version of the now-familiar counting system starting with *ichi, ni, saN,* and so on, which is actually of Chinese origin. If you recall, this native counting system was already introduced in counters for people (see Chapter 10) and counters for days and reading a calendar (see Chapters 14 and 16).

I Want *This* One, Not *That* One!

You should be able to let the shop clerk know exactly what you want. The easiest way is just to point at the item and say "this one." I introduced pointing words in Chapter 9. Let's review them:

Pointing Words: Nouns

kore	this one
sore	that one (near the listener)
are	that one (away from the speaker and listener)
dore	which one

If the item of interest is near you, point to it and say:

Kore-o kudasai.   "Please give me this one."

If the item is on the clerk's side, use *sore* instead:

Sore-o kudasai.   "Please give me that one (near you)."

On the other hand, if it is away from you and the clerk, use *are*:

Are-o kudasai.   "Please give me that one over there (away from both of us)."

If the clerk still cannot figure out which one you mean, she or he will ask you:

Dore-desu ka?   "Which one?"

GREEN TEA BREAK

If you love shopping or even window shopping, try a department store, or *depāto*. Japanese department stores have virtually everything—clothes, bags, shoes, jewelry, books, toys, furniture, a food court, and restaurants. Interestingly, all department stores look alike in terms of their floor plans, so you can expect to find the same setup at any store.

Basement: Food court, coffee shops

First floor: Cosmetics, ladies' purses and hats, shoes, and so on

Second and third floors: Ladies' clothes, handbags, and so on

Fourth floor: Children's and babies' clothes, ladies' clothes, and so on

Fifth floor: Men's clothes, shoes and accessories, eyeglasses, sporting goods, and so on

Sixth floor: Furniture, household goods, jewelry, *kimono,* and so on

Seventh floor: Restaurants, special sales, toys, office supplies, books, CDs, and so on

Rooftop: Pet-shop, gardening, game-center, and so on

In the summer, several department stores have a beer garden on their rooftops. Last but not least, try checking out the food court in the basement. You will have a good time not only looking at a variety of foods, but also trying free samples. (You can have a light meal there!) This is where you can practice the pointing words like *kore, sore,* and *are.* It can be a free Japanese lesson with free food! A department store is one of the best places for a student of Japanese.

Sometimes, instead of using just "this one" or "that one," you might want to be more specific. Suppose that you want a pen, but there are many kinds of items other than pens in the showcase—pencils, erasers, notebooks, ink, and so on. In such a case, you need to use an appropriate pointing word as an adjective:

Pointing Words: Adjectives

kono X	this X
sono X	that X (near the listener)
ano X	that X (away from the speaker and listener)
dono X	which X

Here is an example:

Sono peN-o kudasai.   "Please give me that pen (near you)."

Here is another useful expression when you're looking for something at a shop. If you just want to take a look at the item, try this request pattern:

XYZ-*o mise-te kudasai.* "Please show me *XYZ*."

If you have found what you really want to buy, ask the clerk how much it is:

Ikura-desu ka? "How much is it?"

Or:

XYZ-*wa ikura-desu ka?* "How much is *XYZ*?"

You might think that just pointing is not enough. Do you want to be more specific in describing the item of interest? Okay, then you need to learn more adjectives. Here is a list of adjectives frequently used in shopping.

Shopping-Related Adjectives

big	*ōki-i*	black	*kuro-i*
small	*chīsa-i*	white	*shiro-i*
long	*naga-i*	red	*aka-i*
short	*mijika-i*	yellow	*kīro-i*
new	*atarashi-i*	brown	*chairo-i*
light	*karu-i*	thin	*usu-i*
heavy	*omo-i*	thick	*atsu-i*

Now, combining everything you have learned so far, translate the following.

Exercise 3

1. Please give me that black pencil (near you). ("pencil" = *eNpitsu*)

   _____

2. I want two of those white bags over there. ("bag" = *kabaN*)

   _____

3. Please show me those big suitcases over there. ("show me" = *mise-masu*; "suitcase" = *sūtsu kēsu*)

   _____

4. How much are those brown shoes (near you)? ("shoes" = *kutsu*)

   _____

5. Please give me three sheets of that red paper over there. ("paper" = *kami*)

Here's one more important word. The word for "change" is *otsuri*.

LIFESAVERS

Don't forget to add 5 percent government sales tax. "Sales tax" is *shōhi zē*.

Don't You Have a Cheaper One?

Compromise isn't a good thing when it comes to shopping because you don't want to end up buying something you are not really happy with. In this section, you learn how to ask a shop clerk whether there is anything else of a similar kind.

Suppose that you are looking for a pair of shoes, *kutsu*. The pair you tried on is a little too tight, so you want to ask the clerk for a bigger size.

> *Mō sukoshi ōki-i no-wa ari-maseN ka?*
> "Isn't there (*or* Don't you have) a little bigger one?"

Remember two important phrases here:

mō sukoshi	"a little more/slightly"
no	"one"

Note that the tiny word *no* attaches to an adjective. What if you don't like the color and want a red one instead?

> *Aka-i no-wa ari-maseN ka?*   "Isn't there (*or* Don't you have) a red one?"

LIFESAVERS

When you are asked a negative question such as "*Aka-i no-wa ari-maseN ka?*" ("Don't you have a red one?"), you must be careful how you answer with *hai* or *īe*. *Hai* means "what you said is *right*," whereas *īe* means "what you said is *not right*." So when you are asked, "Don't you have a red one?" and you *do* have it, you should use *īe*, as in:

Īe, ari-masu. "(What you said is not right.) I do have it."

On the other hand, if you *don't* have it, you should use *hai*, as in:

Hai, ari-maseN. "(What you said is right.) Right, I don't have it."

Now how would you say the following?

Exercise 4

1. Don't you have a slightly cheaper one? ("cheap" = *yasu-i*)

   _____

2. Please give me a black one. ("black" = *kuro-i*)

   _____

Here is another important word: *hoka* ("other"). If you want to see other kinds of merchandise, this word is useful:

Hoka no-wa ari-masu ka?	"Do you have other ones?"
Hoka no-o mise-te kudasai.	"Please show me other ones."

While showing you other items, the clerk will say either one of the following:

Kore-wa dō-desu ka?	"How about this one?"
Kore-wa ikaga-desu ka?	"How about this one?"

SHORTCUTS TO SUCCESS

The [X-*wa dō-desu ka?*] pattern is useful for any situation in which you need to make a suggestion.

The word *ikaga* is the polite version of *dō*. If you still do not like what the clerk has suggested, it's perfectly okay to say so, but the following reply would sound very polite:

Ē … chotto …	"Well …"

When you decide on something, say either one of the following:

Kore-o kudasai.	"This one, please."
Kore-ni shi-masu.	"I'll take this one."
(X-*ni shi-masu* = "decide on X")	

Before wrapping up this chapter, I want you to take part in the following rather lengthy dialogue. Don't panic! You can do it! This dialogue contains some materials from the previous chapters, so it is a good review exercise, too. Good luck!

Exercise 5

SHOP 1 _____

"Welcome!"

YOU 1 _____

"I want (some) paper."   ("paper" = *kami*)

SHOP 2 _____

"What kind of paper?"   ("what kind" = *doNna*)

YOU 2 _____

"Blue one."

SHOP 3 _____

"How about this one?"

YOU 3 _____

"How much is it?"

SHOP 4 _____

"It's 20 *yen* per sheet." (*Lit.* "One sheet, 20 *yen*.")

YOU 4 _____

"Isn't there a slightly cheaper one?"

SHOP 5 _____

"Yes. This is 10 *yen* per sheet."

YOU 5 _____

"I'll take this one. Please give me 10 sheets."

SHOP 6 _____

"100 *yen*."

YOU 6 _____

"Here, 1,000 *yen*."

SHOP 7 _____

"The change, 900 *yen*. Thank you very much."

YOU 7 _____

"Thanks!"

Answers

Exercise 1

1. "I want five Japanese language books."
   NihoNgo-no hoN-ga go-satsu hoshi-i-N-desu ga.

2. "I bought eleven blue pencils."
   (Watashi-wa) ao-i eNpitsu-o jū ip-poN kai-mashita.

3. "There are thirteen books."
   HoN-ga jū saN-satsu ari-masu.

4. "Please buy six bottles of beer."
   Bīru-o rop-poN kat-te kudasai.

5. "Eight '10-*yen*' stamps, please."
   Jū-eN kitte-o hachi-mai onegai shimasu.

Exercise 2

1. "Please give me three apples."
   RiNgo-o mit-tsu kudasai.

2. "I want four balls."
   Bōru-ga yot-tsu hoshi-i-N-desu ga.

3. "I ate nine *sushi*!"
   (Watashi-wa) sushi-o *kokono-tsu tabe-mashita.*

Exercise 3

1. "Please give me that black pencil (near you)."
   Sono kuro-i eNpitsu-o kudasai.

2. "I want two of those white bags over there."
   Ano shiro-i kabaN-ga futa-tsu hoshi-i-N-desu ga.

3. "Please show me those big suitcases over there."
   Ano ōki-i sūtsu kēsu-o mise-te kudasai.

4. "How much are those brown shoes (near you)?"
   Sono chairo-i kutsu-wa ikura-desu ka?

5. "Please give me three sheets of that red paper over there."
   Ano aka-i kami-o saN-mai kudasai.

Exercise 4

1. "Don't you have a little cheaper one?"
   Mō sukoshi yasu-i no-wa ari-maseN ka?

2. "Please give me a black one."
   Kuro-i no-o kudasai.

Exercise 5

SHOP 1   *Irasshai mase.* "Welcome!"

YOU 1   *Kami-ga hoshi-i-N-desu ga.* "I want (some) paper."

SHOP 2   *DoNna kami-desu ka?* "What kind of paper?"

YOU 2   *Ao-i no-desu.* "Blue one."

SHOP 3   *Kore-wa ikaga-desu ka?* "How about this one?"

YOU 3   *Ikura-desu ka?* "How much is it?"

SHOP 4   *Ichi-mai, ni-jū-eN-desu.* "It's 20 *yen* per sheet."

YOU 4   *Mō sukoshi yasu-i no-wa ari-maseN ka?* "Isn't there a slightly cheaper one?"

SHOP 5   *Hai, kore-wa ichi-mai, jū-eN-desu.* "Yes. This is 10 *yen* per sheet."

YOU 5   *Kore-ni shi-masu. Jū-mai kudasai.* "I'll take this one. Please give me 10 sheets."

SHOP 6   *Hyaku-eN-desu.* "100 *yen*."

YOU 6   *Hai, seN-eN.* "Here, 1,000 *yen*."

SHOP 7   *Otsuri, kyū-hyaku-eN-desu. Arigatō gozai mashita.* "The change, 900 *yen*. Thank you very much."

YOU 7   *Dōmo (arigatō).* "Thanks!"

The Least You Need to Know

- Four types of counters (*-mai*, *-satsu*, *-hoN*, and *–tsu/-ko*) will take care of your basic shopping needs.
- Pointing words (such as *kore*, *sore*, and *are*) and adjectives are useful for specifying the item of interest.

- Don't compromise! Use the phrases you learned in this chapter to keep asking until you find what you want.

- A department store is an ideal place for a student of Japanese to practice the language, shop, and taste free Japanese food samples.

More Than Just *Sushi*: Dining Out in Japan

In This Chapter

* Likes and dislikes
* Making a comparison
* How to order food
* Tips for eating at a Japanese restaurant

Japanese people take eating seriously. They don't mind paying a fortune at a restaurant if the food is great. Customers expect excellence in cooking, and their high standards have brought about the high quality of dining establishments. Please note that dining can be expensive in Japan, but of course, you can find good, moderately priced restaurants, too.

If you want to enjoy dining in Japan, take a close look at the useful dining vocabulary and phrases in this chapter. Okay, *tabe-ni iki-mashō!* Let's go out to eat!

Likes and Dislikes

Japanese cuisine is called *nihoN ryōri* or *washoku*. You might be curious about what other cuisines are called in Japanese:

Western food	*Sēyō ryōri* or *Yōshoku*	Indian food	*INdo ryōri*
Chinese food	*Chūka ryōri*	Mexican food	*Mekishiko ryōri*
Korean food	*KaNkoku ryōri*	German food	*Doitsu ryōri*
French food	*FuraNsu ryōri*	American food	*Amerika ryōri*
Italian food	*Itaria ryōri*	British food	*Igirisu ryōri*
Spanish food	*SupeiN ryōri*		

As you can see, you can be specific about cuisine by adding the country name to the word *ryōri*, such as *Burajiru ryōri* ("Brazilian food"). The word for "restaurant" is *resutoraN*, but for Asian food restaurants, either *ryōri-ya* or *ryōri-teN* is preferred.

LIFESAVERS

Here is how to say "I'm hungry!" and "I'm thirsty!":

Onaka-ga suki-mashita.	"I'm hungry!"
Nodo-ga kawaki-mashita.	"I'm thirsty!"

If you are talking with your friends in a casual setting, I recommend the following alternatives:

Onaka-ga suita!	"I'm hungry!"
Nodo-ga kawaita!	"I'm thirsty!"

If you are going out to eat with other people, you might have to decide what kind of food you will eat.

DoNna ryōri-ga suki-desu ka?   "What kind of cuisine do you like?"

Instead of *ryōri*, you can use *tabemono*, "food."

DoNna tabemono-ga suki-desu ka?   "What kind of food do you like?"

What if you are determined to eat Japanese food, particularly *sushi*, and you want to see if your Japanese friend also feels like eating *sushi*?

Sushi-wa *suki-desu ka?*   "Do you like *sushi*?"

If your friend does not like *sushi*, she will say either one of the following:

Māmā-desu.	"So-so."
Amari suki-jana-idesu.	"I don't like it very much."
Kirai-desu!	"I hate it!"

Note that *kirai* is a very strong word for dislike, so I suggest that you not use it as a reply.

If you want your Japanese to sound natural, keep in mind that the key to success is indirectness. Don't hesitate to use vague expressions such as *māmā* ("so-so") and *amari* ("(not) very"). I recommend putting *Sō-desu nē …* ("Well, let's see …") at the beginning of your reply, as shown here:

Q: Sushi-wa *suki-desu ka?* "Do you like *sushi*?"

A: *Sō-desu nē … Amari suki-jana-idesu.* "Well, let's see … not very much …"

This way doesn't sound self-centered but is emphatic.

If, on the other hand, your friend likes *sushi* very much, the reply will be:

Daisuki-desu!   "I love it!"

Totemo suki-desu.   "I like it very much."

 LIFESAVERS

Chapter 11 has extensive coverage of helpful expressions you can use when you ask people to go out to eat.

Even though Japanese food is delicious, there might be something you cannot eat. In such a case, you will find the like/dislike expressions in this section helpful.

Exercise 1

Complete the following dialogues.

1. Q: "What kind of Japanese food do you like?"

   _____

   A: "I like *sukiyaki*."

   _____

2. Q: "Do you like Spanish cuisine?"

   _____

   A: "I love it!"

   _____

3. Q: "Do you like *natto* (fermented soybeans)?"

   _____

   A: "Well, let's see … not very much …"

   _____

Making Comparisons

Let's learn another useful pattern called comparative questions. If you and your friend have not decided between two choices—say, Japanese or Chinese food—ask her the following:

> *NihoN ryōri-to, chūka ryōri-to, dochira-no hō-ga i-idesu ka?*
> "Between Japanese and Chinese food, which is better?"

The schematic pattern is …

> X-*to*, Y-*to*, *dochira-no hō-ga* PREDICATE *ka?*

LIFESAVERS

Because a number of vegetables and fruits are of foreign origin, they are pronounced as loanwords, such as *asuparagasu* ("asparagus") and *painappuru* ("pineapple"). Make sure that you Japanize the words!

The predicate part does not have to be an adjective like *i-idesu*, "is good," as shown here:

> Sushi-*to*, *teNpura-to*, *dochira-no hō-ga <u>suki</u>-desu ka?*
> "Between *sushi* and tempura, which do you <u>like</u> better?"

Answering this question is easy! Remember, when you answer a question in Japanese, all you need to do is replace the question word with your answer. If you like *sushi* better, you would say:

> Sushi-*no hō-ga suki-desu.*   "I like *sushi* better."

HUH?

If you have three or more items to compare, the pattern looks slightly different:

> X-*to*, Y-*to*, Z-<u>*de*</u>, *dore-ga <u>ichibaN</u>* PREDICATE *ka?*
> "Among X, Y, and Z, which is the most …?"

Here is an example:

> Q: Sushi-*to*, *teNpura-to*, sukiyaki-*de*, *dore-ga ichibaN oishi-idesu ka?*
>   "Among *sushi*, tempura, and *sukiyaki*, which is the most delicious?"
> A: Sushi-*ga ichibaN oishi-idesu!*
>   "*Sushi* is the most delicious!"

The question word *dore* is used when comparing three or more items, whereas *dochira-no hō* is used when comparing two items.

Before we move on to the next section, here are some common foods in Japanese:

Foods

meat	*niku*	fruit	*furūtsu*
beef	*gyū-niku/bīfu*	apple	*riNgo*
chicken	*tori-niku/chikiN*	cantaloupe	*meroN*
pork	*buta-niku/pōku*	grape	*budō*
fish	*sakana*	peach	*momo*
crab	*kani*	tangerine	*mikaN*
shellfish	*kai*	watermelon	*suika*
shrimp/prawn	*ebi*	beverage	*nomimono*
tofu	*tōfu*	liquor (and *sake*)	*sake*
vegetable	*yasai*	milk	*gyūnyū/miruku*
cabbage	*kyabetsu*	water	*mizu*
carrot	*niNjiN*	condiment	*chōmiryō*
garlic	*niNniku*	horseradish	*wasabi*
green pepper	*pīmaN*	mustard	*karashi/masutādo*
(round) onion	*tamanegi*	oil	*abura/oiru*
potato	*jagaimo/poteto*	pepper	*koshō*
scallion	*negi*	salt	*shio*
squash	*kabocha*	sugar	*satō*
sweet potato	*satsumaimo*	soy sauce	*shōyu*
bread	*paN*	vinegar	*osu*
egg	*tamago*	rice	*kome* (grain) or *gohan* (cooked)

Exercise 2

Using the given words, make a comparative question and answer. Use the English-Japanese dictionary in Appendix B for vocabulary.

1. Q: _____

   [apples, peaches, like better?]

   A: _____

   [I like peaches better.]

2. Q: _____

   [skiing, skating, more fun?]

   A: _____

   [skiing is more fun]

Ordering

You and your friend have decided on Japanese food, and here you are in a Japanese restaurant! Many Japanese restaurants have Japanese-style rooms with *tatami* (straw) mats. This individually separated room is called *ozashiki*. You take your shoes off before you sit on the *tatami* mat. If you prefer an *ozashiki* room, say the following to the waiter:

> *Ozashiki-wa aite i-masu ka?*　　　"Is the *ozashiki* available?"
> (*aite i-masu* = "vacant")

GREEN TEA BREAK

Most restaurants have a nicely decorated display case next to the entrance. In the display are realistic food models made out of wax. You can point to the dish you would like when ordering if you don't want to order from the menu. These food models look so real that you may be tempted to eat them! Many tourists actually buy these wax models as souvenirs.

Upon being seated, you will be given a hot steamed towel to wipe your hands (and face, if you wish). It is so refreshing, especially on a hot, muggy summer day!

If reading a Japanese menu is challenging for you, ask for an English version:

> *Ēgo-no menyū-wa ari-masu ka?*　　　"Do you have an English menu?"
> (*Ēgo* = "English")

Here is a list of popular dishes you will find on the menu.

Japanese Dishes

sushi	*sushi*
makizushi	*sushi* roll
sashimi	sashimi (sliced raw fish)
udoN	thick flour noodles
soba	thin buckwheat noodles
yakisoba	fried noodles
yakiniku	grilled meat
katsu	cutlet
katsudoN	rice bowl with cutlet
gohaN	steamed rice
onigiri	rice ball
teNpura	battered, deep-fried fish/vegetables

teNdoN	rice bowl with tempura
tōfu	tofu
yakizakana	broiled fish
nabe	a dish served in a pot
sukiyaki	*sukiyaki* (Japanese stew)
rāmeN	ramen (Japanized Chinese noodles)
tsukemono	pickled vegetables
misoshiru	miso soup (with soybean-paste base)
tsukidashi or *otōshi*	assorted appetizers
ocha	green tea

GREEN TEA BREAK

As defined in the previous list, *tsukidashi* or *otōshi* is a mixed appetizer, like Italian *antipasto*. Each restaurant has its own *tsukidashi,* ranging from pickled vegetables to broiled fish. It is usually complimentary, especially when you order an alcoholic beverage.

Mmmm! Aren't you getting hungry? Let's order some dishes! The Japanese word for "ordering" is *chūmoN.* After a short while, the waiter will ask you whether you have decided:

Go-chūmoN-wa okimari-desu ka?
"Have you decided what you would like to order?"

HUH?

The prefix *go-,* as seen in *go-chūmoN* ("order"), is another marker to indicate politeness.

In Chapters 12 and 18, you learned an important expression that can be used when making a decision:

XYZ-*ni shi-masu.*   "I've decided on *XYZ.*"

If you want to order *sushi,* say:

Sushi-ni *shi-masu.*   "I'll have *sushi.*"

Of course, you can use the handy *onegai shimasu:*

Sushi-o *onegai shimasu.*   "*Sushi,* please."

The waiter will ask if you want anything to drink (*nomimono* = "beverage"):

> *O-nomimono-wa?* "Anything to drink?"

If you are thirsty and want something, use either the preceding XYZ-*ni shi-masu* pattern or the XYZ-*o onegai shimasu* pattern. If you don't want anything, here is what you should say:

> *Kekkō-desu* or *I-idesu.* "No, thanks."

When you order *sushi*, a plate comes with assorted *sushi*. If there is any particular *sushi* you cannot eat, you should tell the waiter so that he will get you something different. Suppose that you are allergic to shrimp (*ebi*). Here is an easy way to say "I cannot eat shrimp":

> *Ebi-wa dame-naN-desu.* "I cannot eat shrimp."

The word *dame* literally means "no good." In general, the XYZ-*wa dame-naN-desu* pattern can be used when you cannot do *XYZ*. For example, if you cannot speak Spanish, you can say *SupeiN-go-wa dame-naN-desu.* You should definitely memorize this handy expression.

Alternatively, you can say "I'm allergic to shrimp," as in:

> *Ebi arerugī-naN-desu.* "I'm allergic to shrimp."
> (*arerugī* = "allergy")

XYZ *arerugī-naN-desu* is also a handy expression when you want to let people know that you are allergic to *XYZ*.

HUH?

In *dame-naN-desu* and *arerugī-naN-desu*, *naN* does not have grammatical meaning because it is an emphatic idiomatic expression.

Even if you are not comfortable using chopsticks (*hashi*), don't feel embarrassed! Tell the waiter you cannot use them and ask for a fork. Here again, you should use the XYZ-*wa dame-naN-desu* pattern:

> *Hashi-wa dame-naN-desu ga … Fōku-wa ari-maseN ka?*
> "I cannot use chopsticks. Isn't there a fork?"

Actually, it is perfectly acceptable to eat *sushi* using your hands, so you might not need a fork after all!

GREEN TEA BREAK

Sushi is raw fish served on a rice ball, usually with *wasabi*, a spicy Japanese horseradish paste, whereas *sashimi* is sliced raw fish without rice. *Sushi* or *sashimi* tastes better with only a small amount of soy sauce. This way, you can appreciate the texture of the fish. Don't soak it in the sauce! Dip only the fish side into the sauce, not the rice. This is another reason it's better to use your hand rather than chopsticks—with chopsticks, you could easily drop the *sushi* on the sauce plate!

Learning Eating Etiquette

The food is now served. It would be nice if you said the following ritual expression before eating:

> *Itadakimasu.*

Itadakimasu literally means "I humbly accept the food."

By the way, when you finish eating, don't forget to say the following:

> *Gochisōsama (deshita).*

Gochisōsama (deshita) literally means "That was a feast!"

If you would like seconds of something such as rice or *miso* soup or a refill of tea or coffee, you can use the following handy phrase:

> *Okawari (onegai shimasu).*   "May I have another serving?"

Here is another useful phrase. If you'd like your friend to pass you something like soy sauce or salt, use the following pattern:

> XYZ-*o tot-te kudasai.*   "Please pass me *XYZ*."

Here is an example:

> *Shōyu-o tot-te kudasai.*   "Please pass me the soy sauce."

If you are with Japanese people, or there is a waiter/waitress nearby, go ahead and ask them manner-related questions. The first step in asking such questions is to find out whether a certain behavior is acceptable. Here is a perfect sentence pattern that can be used to ask these questions:

> -*TE-mo i-idesu ka?* "Is it okay to …?"

I explained the *TE*-form in Chapter 6 and introduced several usages of this form in previous chapters. Again, this form is used for the "Is it okay?" pattern. For example, if you want to ask whether it's okay to use a fork to eat *sushi*, say the following:

> *Fōku-o tsukat-te-mo i-idesu ka?*   "Is it okay to use a fork?"
> (*tsukai-masu* = "to use")

Or:

> *Te-de tabe-te-mo i-idesu ka?*   "Is it okay to eat with my hands?"
> (*te* = "hand"; *-de* = "with")

If it is acceptable, your Japanese friend or the waiter will say:

> *Ē, i-idesu yo!*   "Sure, it's okay!"

Or:

> *Ē, mochiroN!*   "Yes, of course!"

If it is not acceptable, she or he will say:

> *Chotto …*   "Well …"

SHORTCUTS TO SUCCESS

The *TE-mo i-desu ka* pattern can also be used when you ask for permission, as in the following example:

Q: *Tabako-o sut-te-mo i-desu ka?*   "May I smoke?"
   (*sui-masu* = "to smoke")

A: *Ē, dōzo.*   "Sure."

When you hear *chotto* in a hesitant tone, that's an indirect way of saying "no."

Asking manner-related questions with the food in front of you should be a lot of fun, and your Japanese friend or waiter will be happy to answer your questions. This is a much better way to learn the etiquette than reading a book on manners.

GREEN TEA BREAK

Slurping is perfectly okay when you eat noodles, especially when they are hot. It's difficult not to eat without slurping anyway, so why not? A friend of mine who owns a noodle shop even told me that he checks the quality of the noodle by carefully listening to customers' slurping. It's true!

Here are some things you should or should not do at a Japanese restaurant:

- Don't drink the soup first. Drink it as you eat the main dish.
- Don't use a spoon when drinking soup. Bring the bowl to your mouth and sip it.
- It's okay to make subtle noises when eating.
- Don't leave your chopsticks sticking up in your rice! This is taboo! The only time you can do so is when making offerings for the spirits of the dead in front of the family altar (*butsudaN*).
- When you eat rice from a bowl, never pour soy sauce on it. It's culturally unacceptable and considered low-class.
- "Doggie-bagging" is not a common practice.
- Tipping is not necessary.

Just by observing people around you, you will learn the culture of eating in Japan. But don't spend too much time on observation. Take time to appreciate the food, too!

Exercise 3

Translate the following permission sentences.

1. "Is it okay to drink?" ("drink" = *nomi-masu*)

   _____

2. "Is it okay to go home?" ("go home" = *kaeri-masu*)

   _____

3. "Excuse me. Is it okay to go to the bathroom?" ("go to the bathroom" = *toire-ni iki-masu*)

   _____

Taste Words

If you have never eaten a certain food, you might want to ask how it tastes. The word for "taste" is *aji*. The following question will be helpful:

DoNna aji-desu ka?   "How does it taste?"

Here is a list of commonly used taste words:

Taste Words

sweet	*ama-i*	sour	*suppa-i*
spicy; hot	*kara-i*	bitter	*niga-i*
salty	*shiokara-i* or *shoppa-i*		

If it is a little bit sour, say:

Chotto suppa-i-desu.   "It is a little bit sour."

If you want to be more specific in explaining what the food tastes like, use *mitai-desu:*

ChikiN mitai-desu.   "It tastes like chicken."

The *mitai-desu* expression can be used in any situation when you make an analogy. For example, if your friend looks like a movie star, give him a compliment using this form:

Ēga sutā mitai-desu ne!   "You look like a movie star!"

Check, Please!

Now you have just finished eating. If you are ready for your check, you must ask for it. Here is how to ask for a check:

OkaNjō-o, onegai shimasu.   "Check, please."

If you forget the word *okaNjō*, you can use the loanword *chekku* as the last resort.

Generally, in a Japanese restaurant, your waiter/waitress is not your cashier. Instead, you take the check to the cashier at the door and pay there. By the way, as I mentioned previously, you do not have to leave a tip for the waiter.

HUH?

Note that *oishi-kattadesu* is the past tense of the adjective *oishi-idesu*. Refer to Chapter 5 if you want to review adjective conjugation.

Unless they are students, Japanese people hardly go Dutch, or pay 50/50. For example, suppose that you and I go to eat and I decide to pay. You don't have to feel that you owe me. You can pay the next time we go out to eat. This is how we break even!

Sometimes you will see people fighting over a check at a restaurant, saying "No, I will pay!" or "You paid last time, so let me pay this time!" If you would like to pay, when the waiter brings a check to the table, quickly grab it and tell your friends the following:

> *Watashi-ga harai-masu.*   "I will pay."
> *(harai-masu* = "to pay")

After you pay the cashier, the host/hostess will say to you upon leaving the restaurant:

> *Dōmo arigatō gozai-mashita.*   "Thank you very much (for coming)!"

You can reply by saying *gochisōsama (deshita).* Additionally, if the food was delicious, give them a compliment:

> *Oishi-kattadesu!*   "It was delicious!"

With the expressions introduced in this chapter, you should be able to have a stress-free dining experience. After all, dining should be fun. So enjoy Japanese food!

Exercise 4

Complete the dialogue between you and the waiter (abbreviated as *WTR*).

- WTR 1   *Go-chūmoN-wa okimari-desu ka?*

  "Have you decided what you would like to order?"

- YOU 1   "I'll have tempura."

  _____

- WTR 2   *O-nomimono-wa?*

  "Anything to drink?"

- YOU 2   "Do you have *sake?*"

  _____

- WTR 3   *SumimaseN,* o-sake-wa *arimaseN ga ... Bīru-wa ikaga-desu ka?*

  "Sorry, we don't have *sake.* How about beer?"

- YOU 3   "No, thank you. I cannot drink beer."

  _____

Answers

Exercise 1

1. Q: "What kind of Japanese food do you like?"
   DoNna NihoN-no tabemono-ga suki-desu ka?

   A: "I like *sukiyaki*."
   Sukiyaki-ga suki-desu.

2. Q: "Do you like Spanish cuisine?"
   SupeiN ryōri-ga suki-desu ka?

   A: "I love it!" *Daisuki-desu!*

3. Q: "Do you like *natto* (fermented soybeans)?"
   Nattō-ga suki-desu ka?

   A: "Well, not very much …"
   Sō-desu nē … Amari suki-jana-idesu.

Exercise 2

1. Q: "Which do you like better, apples or peaches?"
   RiNgo-to, momo-to dochira-no hō-ga suki-desu ka?

   A: "I like peaches better."
   Momo-no hō-ga suki-desu.

2. Q: "Which is more fun, skiing or skating?"
   Sukī-to, sukēto-to dochira-no hō-ga tanoshi-idesu ka?

   A: "Skiing is more fun."
   Skī-no hō-ga tanoshi-idesu.

Exercise 3

1. "Is it okay to drink?"
   NoN-de mo i-idesu ka?

2. "Is it okay to go home?"
   Kaet-te mo i-idesu ka?

3. "Excuse me. Is it okay to go to the bathroom?"
   SumimaseN. Toire-ni it-te mo i-idesu ka?

Exercise 4

WTR 1   *Go-chūmoN-wa okimari-desu ka?*
        "Have you decided what you would like to order?"

YOU 1   *TeNpura-ni shi-masu.*
        "I'll have tempura."

WTR 2   *O-nomimono-wa?*
        "Anything to drink?"

YOU 2   O-sake-wa *ari-masu ka?*
        "Do you have *sake*?"

WTR 3   *SumimaseN*, o-sake-wa *arimaseN ga ... Bīru-wa ikaga-desu ka?*
        "Sorry, we don't have *sake*. How about beer?"

YOU 3   *Kekkō-desu. Bīru-wa dame-naN-desu.*
        "No, thank you. I cannot drink beer."

The Least You Need to Know

- Be familiar with Japanese names for food.

- *Kirai* is a very strong word for expressing dislikes. It's better to use an expression such as *Māmā-desu* ("So-so").

- Learn the pattern for asking a comparative question—X-*to*, Y-*to*, *dochira-no hō-ga* PREDICATE *ka*—which gives the listener a wider range of choices when answering.

- Order food using X-*ni shi-masu*, "I will decide on X."

- Learn etiquette for dining in Japan by using the pattern -*TE-mo i-idesu ka ...?* "Is it okay to ...?"

Touring a Japanese House

In This Chapter

- Getting to know the structure and layout of a Japanese house
- Making yourself at home
- Learning important Japanese household items

Staying in a fancy hotel is worry-free and can be great if you plan to sightsee only. However, those who want to experience the lifestyle of ordinary Japanese people should try a home-stay program. This is the best way to improve your Japanese, too, because you will be totally immersed in a Japanese-speaking environment, 24 hours a day, while becoming accustomed to the way Japanese people live.

Even if the primary purpose of your trip is conventional sightseeing, a number of "short home-stay" programs are available in Japan. Such information can be obtained via the Internet or at a travel agency specializing in Japan. Alternatively, you can stay in a home-style inn called *miNshuku*. This is similar to a bed and breakfast (B&B), but unlike a B&B, a *miNshuku* offers supper as well.

Let's imagine that you are now home-staying at your host family's house and are learning what a typical Japanese house looks like and how Japanese people live.

A Typical Japanese Household

Many things in Japan are now westernized, and houses are no exception. It's hard to see a purely traditional Japanese house nowadays unless you go to a rural region. A typical contemporary Japanese house is wooden and two story. You'll find both Western-style rooms and traditional Japanese-style rooms in one house. Here is a list of house-related words in Japanese:

House-Related Words

bathroom	*furo* or *basu rūmu*	kitchen	*kicchiN* or *daidokoro*
bedroom	*beddo rūmu*	room	*heya*
family room	*ima* or *chanoma*	room (Japanese-style)	*nihoNma* or *washitsu*
living room	*ribiNgu rūmu*	room (Western-style)	*yōma*
entryway	*geNkaN*	toilet	*toire* or *otearai*
futon storage	*oshīre*	stairs	*kaidaN*
hallway	*rōka*	slide door	*fusuma*

Okay, here you are! You have just arrived at your host family's house. You are welcomed by the family at the door. Let's have a virtual home-stay experience. Along with information about each room, I will give you helpful tips as well as do's and don'ts.

Entering the House—*GeNkaN*

When you enter the house, you will see a tiny area called the *geNkaN*, where you take off your shoes and leave them before entering the house. Even a completely Western-style house has a *geNkaN*. Remember that in Japan, you cannot enter the house with your shoes on! The *geNkaN* floor is one step lower than the rest of the house, so you can sit in the hallway and easily take off or put on your shoes there. Here are the words for "take off" and "put on" shoes (*kutsu*):

kutsu-o nugi-masu	"to take off shoes"
kutsu-o haki-masu	"to put on shoes"

When you leave your shoes in the *geNkaN*, make sure that you put the heels of your shoes against the wall. Indoor slippers (*surippa*) might be available for you.

Take off your shoes at the geNkaN *before entering the house. As seen in this figure, place your shoes with the heels against the wall.*
(Photo courtesy Agency for Cultural Affairs of Japan)

If you recall, in Chapter 8, I introduced several ritualized expressions to be uttered when entering the house. Upon entering the house, say either one of the following:

Shitsurē shimasu.	*"(Lit.)* Excuse me."
Ojama shimasu.	*"(Lit.)* Sorry to intrude upon your privacy."

After you become introduced to the host family, you are part of the family. From that time on, upon returning home, you should say something different:

Tadaima.	"I'm home."

Your family will welcome you home by saying:

Okaeri nasai.	"Welcome back."

By the way, when you leave home for work, for school, or to do errands, say the following fixed expression:

Itte kimasu.	*"(Lit.)* I am going and coming back."

Your (host) family will send you off by saying:

Itte rasshai.	*"(Lit.)* Please go and come back."

Japanese-Style Room—*NihoNma*

By the time you are taken to your room, you and your host family should have exchanged greetings and self-introductions. You might want to go back to Chapter 9 to review useful expressions for meeting people.

Your room might be either a Western-style room (*yōma*) or a Japanese-style room (*nihoNma*). In the latter case, keep these points in mind. A *nihoNma* is a multipurpose room. In general, it simply has *tatami* mats on the floor, a Japanese dresser called *taNsu*, an easily removable low table called *chabudai*, and floor cushions called *zabutoN*. Each *nihoNma* has built-in *futon* storage called *oshīre*.

The main concept of a *nihoNma* is that, by making everything removable, you can convert the room into any type of room, like a guest room, a bedroom, or even a temporary storage room. You can even make more space by removing the *fusuma*, sliding doors, between the rooms.

HUH?

A Japanese-style room is also called *washitsu*. *Wa* is a prefix whose meaning is "Japanese." For example, *washoku* means "Japanese food" and *wafuku* means "kimono."

Family Room—*Ima* or *Chanoma*

It's dinner time! The dinner might be served in the *ima* (or *chanoma*), "family room." In the *ima*, you must sit on the *tatami* floor. You might find this practice a little challenging. Here is a tip. Try not to sit straight because your legs will probably go numb within five minutes. Dinner time should be fun, not a pain, so you are allowed to be relaxed. If you are male, you can sit with your legs crossed. If you are female, you can extend your legs to the side (not forward), "side saddle."

In winter, instead of an ordinary low table (*chabudai*), a heated table called *kotatsu* is used. It has an infrared heater inside it. You remove the tabletop, put a thin *futon* over the table frame, and place the tabletop back on top of the *futon*. The thin *futon* is designed to trap the heat in the table frame, so you can warm your legs. This is quite comfortable, especially on a cold winter night, because most Japanese homes do not have central heating.

At meals, always remember that you must say something before and after you eat:

> [Before the meal] *Itadakimasu.*

> [After the meal] *Gochisōsama deshita.*

Your host might offer you something to eat or drink by saying:

> *Kore, dō-desu ka?*　　　　"How about this?"

Or:

> *Dōzo.*　　　　"Here you are."

If you want it, say either *Itadakimasu* or

> *Onegai shimasu.*　　　　"Yes, please."

If you don't want it, politely decline the offer:

> *Arigatō gozaimasu. Demo, kekkō-desu.*　　"Thank you for the offer, but
> (*demo* = "but")　　　　　　　　　　no thank you."

The expression "I'm full!" also works in Japanese:

> *Onaka-ga ippai-desu! Arigatō gozaimasu.*　　"I'm full! Thank you."
> (*onaka* = "stomach"; *ippai* = "full")

If the meal was fantastic, don't forget to give your host mother a compliment on her cooking:

Totemo oishi-kattadesu!   "It was very delicious!"

"Bathroom"—*Ofuro*

The concept of a Japanese bathtub, or *ofuro*, is quite different from that of a Western bathtub. It is a place to warm yourself, not to wash your body. The tub is deep enough to cover up to your shoulders. So the word for "take a bath" in Japanese is actually "enter a bath":

ofuro-ni hairi-masu   "take a bath"
(*hairi-masu* = [*Lit.*] "to enter")

Because warming your body and relaxing are the most important concepts of taking a Japanese-style bath, most people take one before going to bed.

GREEN TEA BREAK

Nowadays, more and more houses have a 24-hour-ready bath. The water heater has a thermostat, so the bath water can remain comfortably warm.

Unlike a Western-style bath, you do not pour hot water into the bathtub. A tiny water heater (or boiler) is attached to the bath. To conserve energy, your host family might not set up the bath in the morning, even if you have a habit of taking a bath in the morning. You might be able to take only a shower in the morning. However, you might want to ask the family if it is okay to do so. Remember the "permission" pattern introduced in Chapter 19? Using *-TE-mo i-idesu ka*, ask the following question:

Asa, shawā-o abi-te-mo i-idesu ka?   "May I take a shower in the morning?"
(*asa* = "morning")

Just like at an *oNseN* (hot spring), as explained in Chapter 16, before you enter the bath, you wash yourself outside the tub using either the bath water or a shower. This "washing area" is called *araiba*. This is to keep the bath water clean so that the water can be shared. Important things to note are that you neither use soap in the water nor empty the bathtub after using it!

Ofuro *consists of a bathtub and washing area.*
(Photo courtesy Agency for Cultural Affairs of Japan)

Many Western people feel uncomfortable sharing bath water with other people because it is considered to be unsanitary. I think, however, that this is based on the misconception that Japanese people wash themselves in the bath water, which is not true, as mentioned previously. Consider a Japanese bath to be like a swimming pool. You don't mind sharing pool water, and you certainly don't empty the pool after use, right? The Japanese bath is the same thing.

GREEN TEA BREAK

In case you choose to experience home-stay, it's comforting to know that most host families are aware that Western people are not comfortable sharing bath water, so they will let you take a bath first. Plus, you're their guest, and Japanese families will offer the bath to their guests first anyway!

The room next to the bathroom is the *datsuijo,* (un)dressing room. The expression for "to undress" is *nugi-masu.* As for the expression for "to dress; to put on (clothes)," there are two verbs. For wearing clothes above the waist line, use *ki-masu,* and for wearing clothes below the waist line, use *haki-masu.* Although most clothes-related items are loanwords, let's see how they are pronounced in Japanese.

Clothes

blouse	*burausu*	panty	*paNti*
bra	*burajā*	pantyhose	*paNti sutokkiNgu*
coat	*kōto*	shirt	*shatsu*
hat	*bōshi*	skirt	*sukāto*
jacket	*jaketto*	socks	*kutsushita*
jeans	*jīNzu*	stockings	*sutokkiNgu*
men's underwear	*paNtsu*	sweater	*sētā*
pants	*zuboN* or *paNtsu*	underwear	*shitagi*

For example, you use *ki-masu* for sweaters and *haki-masu* for jeans:

Sētā-o ki-masu.	"I wear a sweater."
JīNzu-o haki-masu.	"I wear a pair of jeans."

While staying with a home-stay family, there will be many occasions when you go out with the host family and need to change your clothes or get dressed. You will find the following expressions handy:

Kigaete ki-masu.	"I'm going to change my clothes."
Fuku-o ki-te ki-masu.	"I'm going to get dressed."

For the second pattern, you can substitute *fuku* ("clothes") with a specific item. For example, on a very cold day, you might want to say:

Kōto-o ki-te ki-masu.	"I'm going to put my coat on."

Bedtime

Before you go to bed, make sure that you say "good night" to your host family:

Oyasumi nasai.	"Good night."

Your host family might have laid out a *futon* for you before you go to your room. If not, just remember that a *futon* is stored in the *oshīre*, a kind of closet attached to your room. Make sure that you fold the *futon* and put it back in the *oshīre* storage the next morning.

The futon *is stored in the* oshīre. *After waking up, fold the* futon *and put it back into the* oshīre.

Perhaps you want to use the bathroom before going to bed. You might have heard from somebody a horrifying story about Japanese toilets. That is, you don't sit on the toilet seat but step over the toilet and squat. Or you might have heard that Japanese toilets do not use the flushing method but the dropping method instead. Sure, if you go to the countryside of Japan and stay in a 50-year-old house, you might be able to see a nonflushing, squat-type toilet. But Japan is more civilized than you might think!

LIFESAVERS

In public restrooms such as those in train stations or department stores, the majority of toilets are still squat-type (flushing, of course). But Western-style toilets are usually available in at least one or two stalls.

Although it might not be intuitive to Westerners, when you enter the stall, face the rear of the stall.

Warning: Some restrooms in public places such as a park do not carry toilet paper, but there is usually a toilet paper vending machine nearby.

It is more than 95 percent probable that your host family's house has a Western-style toilet. Even more amazingly, Japanese toilets have undergone a revolution in the past decade. More and more houses now have a paperless toilet called a "washlet," or *uosshuretto*.

A washlet looks like an ordinary Western-style toilet, but an adjustable nozzle does the cleaning. In a sense, it's like an automatic *bidet*. By using the control panel, you can change the direction of water, water pressure, and water temperature. You can even heat the toilet seat in winter! Make sure that you flush the toilet before using the washlet. For those who are not comfortable using it or are simply unfamiliar with the instructions, you can use the old-fashioned paper method!

 GREEN TEA BREAK

There are a couple more toilet-related cautions. First, it is best that women not flush feminine products because they might plug up the toilets (usually because of narrower plumbing pipes).

Second, in the toilet area, you'll find a pair of slippers you must change into as you enter. Don't continue to wear them outside of the toilet room! Likewise, don't forget to remove your house slippers upon entering the toilet room.

Now, the morning comes. Did you have a good sleep? Oh, don't forget to say "Good morning" when you see your host family in the morning!

> *Ohayō gozaimasu.* "Good morning."

Okay, this is it for the virtual house tour! The most important thing is not to hesitate to ask questions whenever you are not sure about something. There is an old proverb in Japanese that says:

> *Kiku-wa ittoki-no haji.* "Better to ask the way than go astray."

Asking is the fastest way to learn the culture and language. Don't spend too much time looking at a dictionary or at a guidebook—just ask Japanese people around you!

Household Items

Let's finish the chapter with some lists of Japanese words for important household items (room by room).

Kitchen Items

chopsticks *hashi*

cleaning cloth *fukiN*

cooking range *reNji*

cupboard *shokkidana*

cutting board *manaita*

deep pan *nabe*

detergent *seNzai*

frying pan *furaipaN*

glass *koppu*

Japanese teapot *kyūsu*

knife *hōchō* or *naifu*

microwave oven *deNshireNji*

plate *osara*

refrigerator *rēzōko*

rice bowl/tea cup *chawaN*

rice cooker *suihaNki*

sink *nagashi*

Bathroom Items

blow-dryer *doraiyā*

conditioner *riNsu*

laundry basket *datsuikago*

mirror *kagami*

shampoo *shaNpū*

soap *sekkeN*

toothbrush *haburashi*

toothpaste *hamigaki*

towel *taoru*

wash bowl/wash basin *seNmeNki*

washing machine *seNtakuki*

water (cold) *mizu*

water (hot) *oyu*

water faucet *jaguchi*

water heater (for bathtub) *yuwakashiki*

Room Items

alarm clock *mezamashi dokē*

blanket *mōfu*

bookcase *hoNdana*

chair *isu*

chest *taNsu*

clock *tokē*

desk *tsukue*

futon *futoN*

iron *airoN*

pillow *makura*

trashcan *gomibako*

vacuum cleaner *sōjiki*

Items Outside the House

bonsai plants *boNsai*

doghouse *inugoya*

garage *garēji*

gate *moN*

mailbox *yūbiN uke* or *yūbiN bako*

plants *ueki*

pond *ike*

porch *pōchi*

yard; garden *niwa*

As I said at the beginning of this chapter, doing a home-stay is definitely an invaluable experience. By living in a traditional house, with "real" people, you can get the feel of how Japanese people live. And most importantly, you can learn Japanese at a much faster speed. So if there is an opportunity, try living in a house with a host family.

The Least You Need to Know

- You will gain a lot from home-stay experiences, especially insight into the way Japanese people communicate. Home-stay is a great way to improve your Japanese.
- Always leave your shoes in the *geNkaN* when entering a Japanese house.
- Get to know culturally specific things about Japanese houses such as how to use a Japanese bath, lay out a *futon*, and so on.
- Be familiar with basic household items, especially regularly used items such as utensils, bathroom items, and so on.
- Remember the old Japanese proverb, *Kiku-wa ittoki-no haji* ("Better to ask the way than go astray").

Spending Leisure Time

In This Chapter

- Planning activities in chronological order
- Weather and climate
- Annual traditional events in Japan

Even if you are traveling in Japan with a large tour group, you might have a day off, which you can spend with a few good friends. You should go out and explore the country. It's a lot of fun to make a travel plan by yourself, without relying on a group tour. This chapter gives you tips that will make your day trip enjoyable.

Where Do You Wanna Go?

 If you have a day off, where can you possibly go? You know by now that the Japanese public transportation system is so great that you can go anywhere. Here is a list of places you might want to consider going:

Places to Go

amusement park *yūeNchi* or *amyūzumeNto pāku*	mountain *yama*
art museum *bijutsukaN*	movie theater *ēgakaN*
bar *bā*	museum *hakubutsukaN*
bowling alley *bōriNgujō*	restaurant *resutoraN*
Buddhist temple *otera*	sea *umi*
bus tour *basu tsuā*	Shinto shrine *jiNja*
castle *oshiro*	shopping *kaimono*
coffee shop *kissateN*	shopping center *shoppiNgu seNtā*
department store *depāto*	shopping mall *mōru*
festival *(o)matsuri*	sumo (stadium) *sumō*
kabuki (theater) *kabuki*	swimming pool *pūru*

If you're going with someone else (especially a Japanese person), the following questions might be helpful. All these questions have been introduced in previous chapters. Do you remember them? I've also provided a sample answer to each question:

Q: *Doko-ni iki-mashō ka?* "Where shall we go?"

A: *Mōru-wa dō-desu ka?* "How about the shopping mall?"

Q: *NaN-yōbi-ni shi-mashō ka?* "What day shall we decide on?"

A: *Do-yōbi-ni shi-maseN ka?* "Won't we go on Saturday?"

Q: *NaN-de iki-masu ka?* "How will we get there?" (*Lit.*) "By what means will we go there?"

A: *DeNsha-de iki-mashō!* "Let's go by train!"

SHORTCUTS TO SUCCESS

In addition to *naN-de* ("by what means"), *nani-de* is also acceptable.

If you've forgotten the words for days of the week, refer to Chapter 16.

It is important to decide by what means you will go to your destination. I introduced some forms of transportation in Chapter 13; let's review them here.

Means of Transportation

airplane	*hikōki*	on foot	*aruite*
Bullet Train	*shiNkaNseN*	sightseeing bus	*kaNkō basu*
bus	*basu*	subway	*chikatetsu*
car	*kuruma*	taxi	*takushī*
monorail	*monorēru*	train	*deNsha*

Caution: aruite *("on foot") does not require the particle* -de.

LIFESAVERS

If you want to have a worry-free short trip, try a guided tour, or *gaido tsuā,* a bus tour with a tour guide. You can find such tours in most major cities, and you can obtain information about a special tour for foreign visitors with a bilingual tour guide. If you are staying in a major hotel, chances are they will pick you up at the hotel.

In Tokyo, there is a sightseeing tour company called *Hato Basu.* It provides a variety of day, half-day, and evening tours to various destinations. Many such tours include a famous Japanese restaurant in the itinerary so that you can enjoy traditional cuisine! You can make a reservation at major hotels, train terminals, and travel agencies. For more information, visit the *Hato Bus* website at www.hatobus.com/en/.

Let's suppose that you and your friends have decided to take a day trip to Mt. Fuji (*Fuji-saN*) on Saturday by means of a highway bus:

> *Do-yōbi-ni kōsoku basu-de Fuji-san-ni iki-masu.*
> "We will go to Mt. Fuji by highway bus on Saturday."

Make a Plan

One of the fun aspects of traveling is planning. Let's make a travel schedule in Japanese for our day trip to Mr. Fuji.

06:00	Wake up	*Oki-masu*
06:30	Breakfast	*AsagohaN-o tabe-masu*
07:00	Leave the hotel	*Hoteru-o de-masu*
07:15	Go to Shinjuku by train	*DeNsha-de ShiNjuku-ni iki-masu*
08:00	Buy tickets	*Kippu-o kai-masu*
08:30	Ride the highway bus	*Kōsoku basu-ni nori-masu*
11:30	Arrive at Mt. Fuji	*Fuji-saN-ni tsuki-masu*
12:00	Lunch	*HirugohaN-o tabe-masu*
01:00 to 04:00	Free time	*Jiyū jikaN*
04:00	Buy souvenirs	*Omiyage-o kai-masu*
04:30	Ride the bus	*Basu-ni nori-masu*
07:30	Arrive at Shinjuku	*ShiNjuku-ni tsuki-masu*
08:00	Dinner	*BaNgohaN-o tabe-masu*
09:00	Go back to the hotel by taxi	*Takushī-de hoteru-ni kaeri-masu*
10:00	Take a shower	*Shawā-o abi-masu*
11:00	Go to bed	*Ne-masu*

This schedule might look a little detailed, but there are two reasons for that. The first reason is that I want you to remember all the important vocabulary. The second reason is that I want to introduce a new grammatical pattern for listing activities in a chronological order.

You can connect "activity" verbs using the *TE*-form, and when you do so, the connected sentences show a chronological sequence. (If you have forgotten the formation of the *TE*-form, refer to Chapter 6.)

HUH?

In Chapter 10, you learned how to connect "nonactivity" verbs using the *TE*-form. Here is an example:

Watashi-wa kekkoN shite i-te, kanai-no namae-wa Risa-desu.
"I am married, and my wife's name is Lisa."

"Being married" is not an "activity" verb. When the *TE*-form connects "non-activity" verbs or predicates, chronological order is not specified.

Looking at the schedule, let's connect the first three activities—"waking up at 6," "eating breakfast at 6:30," and "leaving the hotel at 7." The sentence should look like this:

Roku-ji-ni oki-te, roku-ji haN-ni asagohaN-o tabe-te, shichi-ji-ni hoteru-o de-masu.
"I will wake up at 6, eat breakfast at 6:30, and leave the hotel at 7."

Remember, for "half an hour," you can simply say *haN* (refer to Chapter 13). Now, for your exercise, connect the following activities with the times. The answers are provided at the end of the chapter.

Exercise 1

1. Go to Shinjuku by train (at 7:15)—Buy tickets (at 8)—Ride the highway bus (at 8:30)

_____

2. Buy souvenirs (at 4)—Ride bus (at 4:30)—Arrive at Shinjuku (at 7:30)

_____

3. Go back to the hotel by taxi (at 9)—Take a shower (at 10)—Go to bed (at 11)

_____

HUH?

According to the explanation given in Chapter 6 for the formation of the *TE*-form, you might suppose that the *TE*-form of *oki-masu* ("wake"), *iki-masu* ("go"), and *abi-masu* ("take [a shower]") would be *oi-te, ii-te,* and *aN-de,* respectively. However, these are exceptions, and *oki-te, it-te,* and *abi-te* are the correct forms. These are irregular *TE*-forms that you'll need to memorize.

The *TE*-form is probably the most challenging grammatical pattern introduced in this book. However, it is also one of the most important and useful grammatical concepts. It appears in various patterns, such as making requests, connecting sentences, and asking permission. Because of the limitation of space in this book, I cannot include all the patterns that make use of the *TE*-form. If you want to continue to study Japanese and go beyond this book (I hope you will do so), the mastery of the *TE*-form will definitely help you grasp the grammar more easily.

Weather and Climate

 For any type of outdoor activities, it is important to know what weather and climate your destination has. Let's learn some basic vocabulary for weather and climate.

Before getting into these topics, however, let's learn the words for "seasons":

season	*kisetsu*
spring	*haru*
summer	*natsu*
autumn	*aki*
winter	*fuyu*

Now answer the following question:

Dono kisetsu-ga suki-desu ka?

Did you get it? The words *dono* and *suki-desu* mean "which" and "to like," respectively. So the question is "What is your favorite season?" My answer would be …

(Watashi-wa) haru-ga suki-desu.   "I like spring."

If you want to ask a superlative question—such as "Which season do you like *the most?*"—just add *ichibaN* to the predicate:

Q: *Dono kisetsu-ga ichibaN suki-desu ka?*   "Which season do you like the most?"

A: *Haru-ga ichibaN suki-desu.*   "I like spring the most."

In the next two subsections, you learn some essential vocabulary and expressions for weather and climates.

Weather

The Japanese word for "weather" is *teNki*. Here is a list of basic weather nouns:

sunny (weather)	*hare*
cloudy (weather)	*kumori*
rainy (weather)	*ame*
snowy (weather)	*yuki*
windy	*kaze ga tsuyo-i*
stormy	*ōame*

If you want to ask how today's weather is, say the following:

Kyō-no teNki-wa dō-desu ka?   "How's today's weather?"

LIFESAVERS

Usually from mid-June to mid-July, there is a rainy season called *tsuyu* all over Japan, except Hokkaido. Because the weather is not very predictable during this season, avoid traveling if possible, especially if you plan to do outdoor activities.

Because the preceding weather words are all nouns, your answer should end with *-desu:*

Ame-desu.   "It's rainy."

Nobody can predict the weather with 100 percent accuracy. If you want to sound presumptive, use *-deshō* instead of *-desu:*

Q: *Kyō-no teNki-wa dō-deshō ka?*   "How will today's weather be?"

A: *Ame-deshō.*   "I suppose it'll be rainy."

The verbal forms of the preceding weather words are shown next. Note that when they end with *-masu*, they usually refer to a future event:

Hare-masu.	"It will become sunny."
Kumori-masu.	"It will become cloudy."
Ame-ga furi-masu.	"It will rain."
Yuki-ga furi-masu.	"It will snow."

How do you say "It will snow tomorrow"?

Ashita-wa yuki-ga furi-masu.   "It will snow tomorrow."

LIFESAVERS

In Japan, temperature is indicated by Celsius (= °C), *sesshi,* not Fahrenheit (= °F), *kashi.* (Refer to Chapter 2 for Celsius-Fahrenheit conversion.) Whether Celsius or Fahrenheit, the word for "degree" is *-do,* as in *sesshi ni-jū-do* ("20°C").

You have just seen the time reference words for "today" (*kyō*) and "tomorrow" (*ashita*). Let's learn time reference words for days, weeks, months, and years.

In the following pattern, "0" means present, "+" means future, and "-" means past. The accompanying number is an indication of how far into the past or future we're talking about. For example "-2" day (*ototoi*) is "the day before yesterday," "-1" day (*kinō*) is "yesterday," "0" day (*kyō*) is "today," "+1" day (*ashita*) is "tomorrow," and "+2" day (*asatte*) is "the day after tomorrow":

	-2	-1	0	+1	+2
Day	*ototoi*	*kinō*	*kyō*	*ashita*	*asatte*
Week	*seNseNshū*	*seNshū*	*koNshū*	*raishū*	*saraishū*
Month	*seNseNgetsu*	*seNgetsu*	*koNgetsu*	*raigetsu*	*saraigetsu*
Year	*ototoshi*	*kyoneN*	*kotoshi*	*raineN*	*saraineN*

But let's get back to the weather. When you describe the current weather, you must change the verb form to the *TE*-form and attach *i-masu* to the verb:

Hare-te i-masu.	"It is sunny (now)."
Kumot-te i-masu.	"It is cloudy (now)."
Ame-ga fut-te i-masu.	"It is raining (now)."
Yuki-ga fut-te i-masu.	"It is snowing (now)."

Climates

Most of the climate words are adjectives and end with *-idesu:*

"It's hot."	*Atsu-idesu.*
"It's warm."	*Atataka-idesu.*
"It's humid."	*Mushiatsu-idesu.*
"It's cold."	*Samu-idesu.*
"It's cool."	*Suzushi-idesu.*

HUH?

The word for "cold" is *samu-i*, but this refers to cold *air*. When you want to refer to cold *substances*, such as liquids, use *tsumeta-i*. On a related note, *tsumeta-i* also refers to personality, as in …

> *tsumeta-i hito*   "a cold person"
>
> *Watashi-wa tsumeta-idesu.*   "I am a cold person." (personality)

Compare the second sentence with the following:

> *Watashi-wa samu-idesu.*   "I am cold." (temperature)

By the way, *atsu-i* ("hot") refers to temperature only. When it refers to "spicy hot," use *kara-i*, as introduced in Chapter 19.

Now, using "season" and "climate" words, answer the following questions. As usual, the answers are at the end of this chapter.

Exercise 2

1. *Arasuka-no fuyu-wa dō-desu ka?* (*Arasuka* = "Alaska") (Cold)

   _____

2. *Furorida-no natsu-wa dō-desu ka?* (*Furorida* = "Florida") (Humid)

   _____

Answers

Exercise 1

1. Go to Shinjuku by train (at 7:15)—Buy tickets (at 8:00)—Ride the highway bus (at 8:30)

   Shichi-ji jū go-fuN-ni deNsha-de ShiNjuku-ni it-te—hachi-ji-ni kippu-o kat-te—hachi-ji haN-ni kōsoku basu-ni nori-masu.

2. Buy souvenirs (at 4:00)—Ride bus (at 4:30)—Arrive at Shinjuku (at 7:30)

   Yo-ji-ni omiyage-o kat-te—yo-ji haN-ni basu-ni not-te—shichi-ji haN-ni ShiNjuku-ni tsuki-masu.

3. Go back to the hotel by taxi (at 9:00)—Take a shower (at 10:00)—Go to bed (at 11:00)

   Ku-ji-ni takushī-de hoteru-ni kaet-te—jū-ji-ni shawā-o abi-te—jū ichi-ji-ni ne-masu.

Exercise 2

1. Q: *Arasuka-no fuyu-wa dō-desu ka?* "How is the winter in Alaska?"
   A: *Arasuka-no fuyu-wa samu-idesu.*

2. Q: *Furorida-no natsu-wa dō-desu ka?* "How is the summer in Florida?"
   A: *Furorida-no natsu-wa mushiatsu-idesu.*

The Least You Need to Know

* Using the *TE*-form, you can connect sentences in chronological order.
* Knowing weather/climate expressions will help you plan wisely.
* Important weather-related words are *hare* ("sunny"), *ame* ("rainy"), *kumori* ("cloudy"), and *yuki* ("snowy"). Some climate-related words are *atsu-idesu* ("hot"), *atataka-idesu* ("warm"), *samu-idesu* ("cold"), and *suzushi-idesu* ("cool").
* Experience Japanese culture and tradition by checking out various annual events.

Troubleshooting

Life is full of unexpected events, sometimes good and sometimes challenging. The chapters in this part provide useful information for those challenging events.

This part covers all the facts and expressions you need to make a phone call, domestic or international. You also learn information in case you need to seek medical assistance or encounter other kinds of emergencies. Helpful phrases and tips in case you experience inconveniences at a hotel, restaurant, or shop are also provided. In addition, Chapter 26 provides essential signs and symbols so that you won't miss important information or lose your way.

Better preparation makes you feel secure and confident. Even if you are not in trouble, the expressions you learn in these chapters will be lifesavers for you.

Talking on the Phone

In This Chapter

- The telephone system in Japan
- Calling home from Japan
- A sample phone conversation

In this chapter, you will first learn some basic facts about Japanese phones and then learn two useful tasks—making an international call to your home country and having a simple telephone conversation.

Japanese Phone Facts

First of all, here is a list of essential telephone vocabulary:

telephone; telephone call	*deNwa*
cellular telephone	*kētai deNwa* or *kētai*
public pay phone	*kōshū deNwa*
telephone number	*deNwa baNgō*
make a phone call	*deNwa-o shi-masu*
collect call	*korekuto kōru*
operator	*operētā*
phone book	*deNwachō*

GREEN TEA BREAK

In Japan, almost everyone has a cellular phone, or *kētai*. Use of a *kētai* is a serious public concern nowadays. It's wise to turn off your *kētai* in a public place such as on a train, at a train station, or in a movie theater. At a hospital, it is mandatory to turn off your *kētai* so as to not disturb patients with pacemakers.

If you go to Japan on a business trip, you will find a cellular phone, or *kētai*, essential. You might already have a special calling plan or calling card that allows you to use your existing phone for international calls from abroad. If your cellular phone does not work in Japan and you want to have one, you have two options: You can rent a *kētai* phone with a prepaid calling plan, or you can purchase a package containing a *kētai* phone and a prepaid calling card. For either option, you can find vendors at the airport. You can even reserve them online, before you leave for Japan. Likely, they will be waiting at your hotel for you.

Let's move on to Japanese public pay phones, or *kōshū deNwa*. How do they work? Most public phones accept coins (10 *yen* coin or 100 *yen* coin) and a prepaid calling card called *terefoN kādo*. If you use coins, please note that it is not an unlimited call even if you are making a local call. With 10 *yen*, you can make a local call for 1 minute.

When you use a prepaid calling card in the United States or Canada, you enter your PIN. Japanese prepaid cards work differently. In Japan, you insert a prepaid *terefoN kādo* into the upper slot of a telephone. There is no PIN because the telephone reads your card and verifies its remaining time. After use, your card is ejected from the lower slot, leaving a punch hole indicating how many minutes remain on the card.

 LIFESAVERS

When "0" appears in a phone number (other than at the beginning), it can be pronounced as *maru,* instead of *zero,* as in:

41-8096   *YoN ichi no hachi maru kyū roku*

Pronouncing telephone numbers is quite easy. You just say each number separately and use *no* for a hyphen between numbers. For example, 0423-41-8796 is pronounced as …

Zero yoN ni saN no yoN ichi no hachi nana kyū roku

Area codes such as 0423 in the preceding example are called *shigai kyokubaN*. Note that all Japanese area codes start with 0. If you are making a local call, you don't have to dial the area code.

Exercise 1

Write the following phone numbers in Japanese.

1. 0426-63-2154 _____

2. 03-3950-4672 _____

Now you are ready to make a phone call. The most important phrase in a telephone conversation is …

Moshi moshi.   "Hello."

SHORTCUTS TO SUCCESS

English speakers tend to pronounce this phrase like *mòshi MÓshi,* putting a strong accent on the second *mo* and a weak accent on the first *mo.* As explained in Chapter 3, the Japanese accent does not work like the English accent. Make sure that you do not give a strong intonation to the word, but put a slight stress on the first *mo.* Calmness in pronunciation will make your Japanese more natural.

Let's Call Home!

If you are staying in a hotel, there should be detailed instructions in your room as to how to make an international call from the room phone.

If you are calling from an ordinary hotel room telephone, you must first dial the selected phone company's access number. For example, the telephone company access code of *KDDI* (a Japanese phone company) is 001. Then you would dial the country code, the area code, and the rest of the phone number:

001 + COUNTRY CODE + AREA CODE + NUMBER

Here are the country codes of some English-speaking countries:

United States	1
Canada	1
United Kingdom	44
Australia	61
New Zealand	64

LIFESAVERS

The country code of Japan is 81. If you are making an international call to Japan from the United States and the phone number you are calling is 0425-76-2795, dial the following:

011-81-425-76-2795

The access number from the United States to other countries is 011. Note that you do not dial the first digit of the area code, 0.

What if you want to call collect to your home country? Again, let's use *KDDI* because it is probably the most foreigner-friendly phone company and many of its operators are bilingual. The number to remember for a collect call is:

Collect Call (KDDI): 0051

When you call, the operator will answer like this:

Hai, KDDI-desu. "This is KDDI."

You could ask him or her to speak in English because the operator will probably be bilingual:

Ēgo-de onegai shimasu. "In English, please."

You might want to try your Japanese first, though. You can always switch to English later. First, tell the operator that you want to make a collect call:

Korekuto kōru-o shi-tai-N-desu ga … "I want to make a collect call."

Or simply:

Korekuto kōru-o onegai shimasu. "Collect call, please."

You can make your request more specific by adding which country you want to call:

<u>*Amerika-ni*</u> *korekuto kōru-o onegai shimasu.*
"Collect call to the USA, please."

The operator will ask you several questions:

Dochira-no kuni-ni okake-desu ka?
"Which country are you calling?" (*kuni* = country)

Aite-no deNwa baNgō-wa naN-baN-desu ka?
"What is the phone number of the other party?"

Aite-no o-namae-wa naN-desu ka?
"What is the name of the other party?"

An important word is *aite*, literally meaning "the other party"—in this case, "the person you are calling."

A telephone conversation can be a challenging task because, unlike in an ordinary conversation, you cannot see the listener. So if you do not understand what the operator says, you should not be ashamed about asking the operator to repeat him- or herself! The following expressions might be useful:

SumimaseN, wakari-maseN.	"Sorry, I don't understand."
SumimaseN, kikoe-maseN.	"Sorry, I cannot hear you."
Mō ichido it-te kudasai. (*mō ichido* = "one more time")	"Please say it again."
Mō sukoshi yukkuri hanashi-te kudasai. (*mō sukoshi* = "little more"; *yukkuri* = "slow")	"Please speak a little more slowly."
Mō sukoshi ōki-i koe-de hanashi-te kudasai. (koe = "voice")	"Please speak a little louder."

If you really cannot communicate in Japanese any further, say the following as the last resort:

Ēgo-de i-idesu ka?	"Would English be okay?"

Or:

Ēgo-de onegai shimasu.	"In English, please."

HUH?

Remember the permission pattern (*TE-mo i-desu ka*) that was introduced in Chapter 18? This can be used not only with a verb, but also a noun, as in *Ēgo-de-mo i-desu ka* ("Would English be acceptable?"). Note that the *TE*-form of a noun is XYZ-*de*.

When You Must Call Someone's House

Suppose that there is an urgent matter that you must let your Japanese friend, *Yumiko*, know about, so you are calling her house. Yumiko is fluent in English. However, what if she is not at home and someone in the family, who does not understand English, picks up the phone? Leaving an accurate message in Japanese might be a little too challenging at this point, so let's focus on the following simpler tasks:

- Ask if your friend is home.

- Provided that she is not home, ask the family member to tell your friend to call you.

- Identify yourself and leave your phone number.

Let's look at a simulated telephone conversation. Here is the situation:

- Yumiko's family name is Tanaka.

- Yumiko's mother picks up the phone.

- Your name is John Brown (*JoN BrauN*).

- Your phone number is 03-4213-8267.

Study the whole conversation first. Then we'll divide it into parts and examine it more closely.

Telephone Dialogue

TANAKA 1	*Moshi moshi, Tanaka-desu ga.* "Hello, this is the Tanakas."
YOU 1	*Moshi moshi, JoN BrauN to mōshi-masu ga, Yumiko-saN onegai shimasu.* "Hello, my name is John Brown. May I talk to Yumiko?"
TANAKA 2	*SumimaseN, Yumiko-wa rusu-desu ga.* "Sorry, Yumiko is out."
YOU 2	*Sō-desu ka. Jā, atode deNwa shi-te hoshi-i-N-desu ga.* "I see. Then, I would like her to call me later."
TANAKA 3	*Hai. DeNwa baNgō-wa naN-baN-desu ka?* "Certainly. What is your phone number?"
YOU 3	*Zero saN no yoN ni ichi saN no hachi ni roku nana-desu.* "03-4213-8267."
TANAKA 4	*Hai, wakari-mashita.* "Yes, I got it."
YOU 4	*Onegai shimasu. Shitsurē shimasu.* "Thank you. Good-bye."
TANAKA 5	*Shitsurē shimasu.* "Good-bye."

 LIFESAVERS

In a telephone conversation, it is wise to avoid the verb *i-masu*, as in *Yumiko-saN-wa i-masu ka*, "Is Yumiko there?" This might sound a little rude.

In what follows, I will explain the dialogue in detail, segment by segment.

Segment 1

TANAKA 1   *Moshi moshi, Tanaka-desu ga.*
"Hello, this is the Tanakas."

YOU 1   *Moshi moshi, JoN BurauN to mōshi-masu ga, Yumiko-saN onegai shimasu.*
"Hello, my name is John Brown. May I talk to Yumiko?"

What is important in this segment is your self-introduction. Because you are not sure who you are talking with at this point, you need to be polite. As discussed in Chapter 9, the pattern NAME *to mōshi-masu* is a very polite expression for self-introduction.

Instead of *Yumiko-saN onegai shimasu*, you could ask a much more formal question such as the following:

Yumiko-saN-wa irasshai-masu ka?   "Is Yumiko at home?"

The verb *irasshai-masu* is the super-polite version of *i-masu*, "to be."

Segment 2

TANAKA 2   *SumimaseN, Yumiko-wa rusu-desu ga.*
"Sorry, Yumiko is out."

YOU 2   *Sō-desu ka. Jā, atode Yumiko-san-ni deNwa shi-te hoshi-i-N-desu ga.*
"I see. Then, I would like her to call me later." (*atode* = "later")

The word *rusu* means "not at home." Note that this sentence ends with the familiar *ga*, the conversation softening marker. Instead of *rusu-desu*, you could say

SumimaseN, Yumiko-wa ori-maseN ga   "Sorry, Yumiko is not here."

This segment contains a very important expression pattern:

PERSON-*ni* VERB-*te hoshi-i-N-desu ga* ...   "I want PERSON to do so-and-so."

In Segment 2, you want Yumiko to call you later. This expression is handy when you indirectly ask someone to do something. Let's practice using this pattern. The answers are at the end of this chapter.

SHORTCUTS TO SUCCESS

As you know, in Japanese, you can omit items that are known to both the speaker and listener. So if I want *you* to call me later, I can omit both *watashi* ("I") and *anata* ("you"):

Atode deNwa shi-te hoshi-i-N-desu ga.   "I want you to call me later."

HUH?

Remember in Segment 1, you learned *irasshai-masu,* "to be." Now you learned *ori-masu,* which also means "to be." Both are polite verbs, but *irasshai-masu* is used when you refer to someone besides you or your family members, whereas *ori-masu* is used when you refer to yourself or your family members. In the previous case, because Yumiko is a family member of Mrs. Tanaka, she uses *ori-masu.* On the other hand, in Segment 1, you used *irasshai-masu* because Yumiko is not your family member.

Exercise 2

1. I want Mr. Tanaka to come to my party.
   ("come" = *ki-masu*)

   _____

2. I want you to speak in English.
   ("speak" = *hanashi-masu;* "in English" = *ēgo-de*)

   _____

SHORTCUTS TO SUCCESS

The adjective *hoshi-i* literally means "desirable." Besides the usage that I have just introduced here, it can be used when you want something (noun), as explained in Chapter 18.

Watashi-wa riNgo-ga hoshi-i-N-desu ga.   "I want an apple."

Segments 3, 4, and 5

TANAKA 3   *Hai. DeNwa baNgō-wa naN-baN-desu ka?*
             "Certainly. What is your phone number?"

YOU 3   *Zero saN no yoN ni ichi saN no hachi ni roku nana-desu.*
             "03-4213-8267."

TANAKA 4   *Hai, wakari-mashita.*
             "Yes, I got it."

YOU 4   *Onegai shimasu. Shitsurē shimasu.*
               "Thank you. Good-bye."

TANAKA 5   *Shitsurē shimasu.*
               "Good-bye."

These segments are relatively straightforward. Make sure that you say your phone number clearly, digit by digit. Here again, there is a handy expression, *onegai shimasu.* Use this phrase when you ask someone to take care of a certain task.

Important Numbers

You should know some important phone numbers in Japan:

Ambulance (*kyūkyūsha*)	119
Fire (*shōbōsho*)	119
Police (*kēsatsu*)	110

Chapter 23 covers useful Japanese expressions for medical emergencies, and Chapter 24 covers other kinds of emergencies.

Here are some more nonemergency, but useful, phone numbers:

Time (*jihō*)	117
Weather forecast (*teNki yohō*)	177
Phone directory (*baNgō aNnai*)	104

Here is information for English-speaking countries' embassies in Tokyo. The area code (03) is not necessary if you're calling within the metropolitan Tokyo area.

American (U.S.) Embassy
Phone: (03) 3224-5000 (Tokyo)
Website: tokyo.usembassy.gov/
Address: 1-10-5 Akasaka, Minato-ku, Tokyo 107-8420

Canadian Embassy
Phone: (03) 5412-6200 (Tokyo)
Website: www.canadainternational.gc.ca/japan-japon/index.aspx?lang=eng
Address: 7-3-38 Akasaka, Minato-ku, Tokyo 107-8503

British Embassy
Phone: (03) 5211-1100 (Tokyo)
Website: ukinjapan.fco.gov.uk/en/e.html
Address: 1 Ichibancho, Chiyoda-ku, Tokyo 102-8381

Australian Embassy
Phone: (03) 5232-4111 (Tokyo)
Website: www.australia.or.jp/en/
Address: 2-1-14 Mita, Minato-ku, Tokyo 108-8361

New Zealand Embassy
Phone: (03) 3467 2271 (Tokyo)
Website: www.nzembassy.com/japan
Address: 20-40 Kamiyama-cho, Shibuya-ku, Tokyo 150-0047

You might have noticed that talking on the phone does not require a lot of new vocabulary. However, you really have to listen carefully to the person on the other end because you cannot see her or him. Remember, nothing is wrong or inappropriate about asking the other party to repeat something or to speak slowly or louder.

Answers

Exercise 1

1. 0426-63-2154   *zero yoN ni roku no roku saN no ni ichi go yoN*

2. 03-3950-4672   *zero saN no saN kyū go zero no yoN roku nana ni*

Exercise 2

1. "I want Mr. Tanaka to come to my party."
   Tanaka-saN-ni watashi-no pāti-ni ki-te hoshi-i-N-desu ga.

2. "I want you to speak in English."   *Ēgo-de hanashi-te hoshi-i-N-desu ga.*

The Least You Need to Know

* Most public phones in Japan accept 10 *yen* coins or 100 *yen* coins and a prepaid calling card called *terefoN kādo*.

* To pronounce telephone numbers, just say each number separately and use *no* for a hyphen between numbers.

* Say *Moshi moshi* ("hello") when answering the telephone in Japan. Remember not to accent any of the syllables.

* As always, politeness is important. The pattern NAME *to mōshi-masu* is a polite expression for self-introduction over the telephone.

* Remember, nothing is wrong or inappropriate about asking the other party to repeat something or to speak slowly or louder.

I'm Sick! Call 911? No, Call 119!

In This Chapter

- Health-related and body-part vocabulary
- Telling a doctor how you feel
- Buying medicine

Sickness is the last thing you want to encounter when traveling abroad. But this can happen to anyone, and I want you to be prepared. In this chapter, I introduce health-related expressions you will find helpful if you get sick.

Health-Related Expressions

First of all, let's take a look at some important health-related expressions:

Health-Related Vocabulary

ambulance *kyūkyūsha*

be hospitalized *nyūiN shi-masu*

doctor/doctor's office *isha*

emergency hospital *kyūkyū byōiN*

first aid *ōkyū shochi*

first aid room *imushitsu*

handicapped person *shiNshōsha*

health insurance *keNkō hokeN*

hospital *byōiN*

hospitalization *nyūiN*

I feel sick. *KibuN-ga waru-i-N-desu.*

I'm injured. *Kega-o shi-mashita.*

injury *kega*

insurance card *hokeNshō*

medicine *kusuri*

pharmacy *kusuriya* or *yakkyoku*

pharmacist *yakuzaishi*

prescription *shohōseN*

see a doctor *isha-ni iki-masu*

sickness *byōki*

take a lab test *keNsa-o shi-masu*

take medicine *kusuri-o nomi-masu*

If you don't feel well, you should let people know by saying …

> *Guai-ga waru-i-N-desu ga.* "I am not feeling well."

If you are on your own and want to find out where the hospital is, say

> *ByōiN-wa doko-desu ka?* "Where is the hospital?"

HUH?

The word *byōiN* refers to a hospital as well as a doctor's office. On a street map, a *byōiN* is indicated by a "cross" symbol.

If you are staying in a fairly large hotel, it might have a medical room where first aid is available. This is called an *imushitsu*, "first aid room."

In case of a medical emergency, say the following to someone near you:

> *Kyūkyūsha-o yoN-de kudasai.* "Please call an ambulance."

If you must call an ambulance yourself, call 119. Don't confuse it with 911!

LIFESAVERS

The emergency number 119 is for both medical emergencies and fire. In case of fire, say *Kaji-desu*, "Fire." In case of a medical emergency, say *Kyūkyūsha onegai shimasu*, "Ambulance, please." The number for the police is 110.

You can obtain hospital information in English at the following phone numbers:

03-5285-8181

03-5285-8088

Both of these are Tokyo numbers. If you are calling within the city of Tokyo, you do not have to dial the area code 03.

At a Doctor's Office

Before seeing a doctor at a hospital, you will need to check in. The check-in booth is called *uketsuke*. They will ask you several questions, such as:

name	*(o)namae* or *shimē*	age	*neNrē*
address	*(go)jūsho*	occupation	*shokugyō*
phone number	*deNwa baNgō*	birth date	*sēneN gappi*

You might be asked to fill out a registration form with the preceding information. Many hospitals have an English registration form. Here is how you ask for an English version:

Ēgo-no fōmu-wa ari-masu ka?   "Do you have an English form?"

Upon check-in, you will be asked to show your insurance card to the receptionist:

HokeNshō-o mise-te kudasai.   "Please show me your insurance card."

LIFESAVERS

If your trip to, or stay in, Japan is less than one year, I strongly suggest that you obtain short-term travel health insurance before leaving for Japan. Your existing health insurance might cover medical expenses incurred in a foreign country; however, it requires a tremendous amount of paperwork and documentation written by your doctor. If it is written in Japanese, it must be translated into English. Travel health insurance might be slightly expensive, but it is definitely less of a hassle.

If your situation is not an emergency, you might have to wait in a waiting room near the examination room until you are called. The waiting room is called *machiai shitsu;* the examination room is *shiNsatsu shitsu.*

Parts of the Body

When you see a doctor, you will need to describe your medical condition. You should be familiar with the Japanese words for parts of the body.

SHORTCUTS TO SUCCESS

It's effective to categorize body-part vocabulary according to areas and memorize them. For example, memorize all the face-related words at once.

Parts of the Body

cheek	*hō*	face	*kao*	mouth	*kuchi*
chin	*ago*	gum	*haguki*	nose	*hana*
ear	*mimi*	hair	*kami*	teeth	*ha*
eye	*me*	head	*atama*	throat	*nodo*
eyelid	*mabuta*	lip	*kuchibiru*	tongue	*shita*

continues

continued

Parts of the Body

arm *ude*	crotch; groin *mata*	heart *shiNzō*
back *senaka*	knee *hiza*	intestines *chō*
belly *onaka*	leg/foot *ashi*	kidney *jiNzō*
chest *mune*	thigh *momo*	liver *kaNzō*
elbow *hiji*	toe *tsumasaki*	lung *hai*
finger *yubi*	waist *koshi*	lymph node *riNpaseN*
hand *te*	appendix *mōchō*	perspiration *ase*
shoulder *kata*	blood *chi*	saliva *tsuba*
ankle *ashikubi*	genitals *iNbu*	stomach *i*
buttocks *oshiri*		

GREEN TEA BREAK

The name of each finger is as follows:

thumb	*oya-yubi*
index finger	*hitosashi-yubi*
middle finger	*naka-yubi*
ring finger	*kusuri-yubi*
little finger	*ko-yubi*

By the way, *oya* means "parent," *hitosashi* means "pointing at people," *naka* means "middle," *kusuri* means "medicine," and *ko* means "child." The ring finger is the "medicine finger" in Japanese because this finger was used to mix a certain kind of medicine in old days.

Symptoms

Before examining you, your doctor will ask you the following question:

Dō shi-mashita ka? "What is the problem?"

Let's familiarize ourselves with some common symptoms.

Symptoms

I broke a bone.	*Hone-o ori-mashita.*
I caught a cold.	*Kaze-o hiki-mashita.*
I don't have an appetite.	*Shokuyoku-ga ari-maseN.*

I feel a chill.	*Samuke-ga shi-masu.*
I feel dizzy.	*Memai-ga shi-masu.*
I feel itchy in the *X*.	*X-ga kayu-i-N-desu.*
I feel tired.	*Tsukare-te i-masu.*
I got a cut on *X*.	*X-o kiri-mashita.*
I got burnt.	*Yakedo shi-mashita.*
I have a cough.	*Seki-ga de-masu.*
I have a fever.	*Netsu-ga ari-masu.*
I have a headache.	*Atama-ga ita-idesu.*
I have a heavy discharge.	*Orimono-ga hido-idesu.*
I have a runny nose.	*Hana-ga de-te i-masu.*
I have a sore throat.	*Nodo-ga ita-idesu.*
I have a sprain.	*NeNza shi-mashita.*
I have a stomachache.	*Onaka-ga ita-idesu.*
I have a stuffy nose.	*Hana-ga tsumat-te i-masu.*
I have a toothache.	*Ha-ga ita-idesu.*
I have back pain.	*Koshi-ga ita-idesu.*
I have cramps.	*Sēritsū-ga ari-masu.*
I have diarrhea.	*Geri-o shi-te i-masu.*
I have nausea.	*Hakike-ga shi-masu.*
I'm bleeding.	*Shukketsu shi-te i-masu.*
I'm constipated.	*BeNpi-o shi-te i-masu.*
I'm having my period.	*Sēri-desu.*
I'm sweating.	*Ase-o kai-te i-masu.*
I'm pregnant.	*NiNshiN shi-te i-masu.*
I vomited.	*Haki-mashita.*
My period is late.	*Sēri-ga okure-te i-masu.*
X hurts.	*X-ga ita-i-N-desu.*

GREEN TEA BREAK

The general term for "doctor" is *isha,* but when you address a doctor, you should call her or him *seNsē.* This is an honorable term for a medical professional. Yes, *seNsē* can also refer to teachers.

The first expression in the preceding table is particularly useful when you describe your symptoms. All you need to do is replace *X* with the appropriate part of the body.

X-ga ita-i-N-desu.	"X hurts."
Atama-ga ita-i-N-desu ga.	"I have a headache."
X-o kiri-mashita.	"I got a cut on X."
Yubi-o kiri-mashita.	"I got a cut on my finger."

HUH?

Notice that the word *ita-i* ends with *N-desu*. This <u>N</u> is a "feeling" marker. When you want to emphasize the expression of a feeling, this marker is effective. Other than *ita-i,* this emotion marker <u>N</u> is also seen in "desire" constructions:

NihoN-ni <u>iki-ta-i</u>-N-desu.	"I want to go to Japan."
RiNgo-ga <u>hoshi-i</u>-N-desu.	"I want an apple."

"Wanting" is an internal feeling of the speaker.

You might want to describe to the doctor what kind of pain you are experiencing:

I have a dull pain.	*Nibuku ita-i-N-desu.*
I have a slight pain.	*Sukoshi ita-i-N-desu.*
I have an intense pain.	*Totemo ita-i-N-desu.*
I have a pricking pain.	*Chiku-chiku ita-i-N-desu.*
I have a throbbing pain.	*Zuki-zuki ita-i-N-desu.*
I have a burning sensation.	*Hiri-hiri ita-i-N-desu.*
I have an itchy pain.	*Itagayu-i-N-desu.*
I have a massive headache.	*Atama-ga gaNgaN shi-masu.*

Common Requests a Doctor Makes

Your doctor might make the following requests during the examination:

Yoko-ni nat-te kudasai.	"Please lie down."
(*yoko-ni nari-masu* = "lie down")	
Aomuke-ni nat-te kudasai.	"Please lie on your back."
(*aomuke-ni nari-masu* = "lie on your back")	

Utsubuse-ni nat-te kudasai.	"Please lie on your stomach."
(*utsubuse-ni nari-masu* = "lie on your stomach")	
Fuku-o nui-de kudasai.	"Please take off your clothes."
(*fuku* = "clothes"; *nugi-masu* = "take off")	
Fuku-o ki-te kudasai.	"Please put on your clothes."
(*ki-masu* = "wear")	
Iki-o sut-te kudasai.	"Please breathe."
(*iki* = "breath"; *sui-masu* = "inhale")	
Iki-o hai-te kudasai.	"Please exhale."
(*haki-masu* = "exhale")	
Kuchi-o ake-te kudasai.	"Please open your mouth."
(*ake-masu* = "open")	
Tat-te kudasai.	"Please stand up."
(*tachi-masu* = "stand up")	
Suwat-te kudasai.	"Please sit down."
(*suwari-masu* = "sit down")	
Ā-to it-te kudasai.	"Please say 'ah.'"
(*ii-masu* = "say")	

Whether at a hospital or doctor's office, if a prescription is given, you must purchase the medicine prescribed at the same office. Pharmacies you find in town sell only over-the-counter drugs.

Last, but not least, if you are in a general hospital, you need to know which medical department you are supposed to go to, such as "internal medicine," "dermatology," or someplace else.

Medical Departments

dentist	*shika*	pediatrics	*shōnika*
dermatology	*hifuka*	psychiatric	*sēshiNka*
gynecology	*fujiNka*	radiology	*hōshaseNka*
internal medicine	*naika*	surgery	*geka*
neurology	*shiNkēka*	urology	*hinyōkika*
otolaryngology	*jibika*		
(ears, nose, and throat)			

Before moving on to the next section, here is a list of names of diseases.

Names of Medical Problems

appendicitis	*mōchōeN*	headache	*zutsū*
burn	*yakedo*	heart attack	*shiNzō hossa*
cancer	*gaN*	hemorrhoid	*ji*
cavity (tooth decay)	*mushiba*	migraine	*heNzutsū*
common cold	*kaze*	miscarriage	*ryūzaN*
ear infection	*chūjieN*	muscle sprain	*neNza*
flu	*iNfurueNza*	pneumonia	*haieN*
food poisoning	*shokuchūdoku*	sexually transmitted disease	*sēbyō*
food poisoning (mild)	*shokuatari*	sinus (infection)	*bieN*
fracture	*kossetsu*	stroke	*nōsocchū*
gastritis	*ieN*		

At the Pharmacy

If your medical problem is a rather minor one and you think that over-the-counter medicine will take care of it, the best place to go is a *kusuriya* or *yakkyoku*, which both mean "pharmacy."

 GREEN TEA BREAK

In Japan, many prescribed medicines come in powder form in packets rather than in capsules. You pour the powder into your mouth and use water to help you swallow.

Because thousands of drugs are available at a pharmacy and their directions and indications are written in Japanese, I think that the best way to find the most suitable medicine is to ask a pharmacist, or *yakuzaishi*. You have just learned in the previous section how to describe your medical condition, right?

When you find the right medicine, ask the pharmacist questions such as how many times a day to take it, how many tablets to take each time, and so on. Here is how to ask these questions:

Ichi-nichi naN-kai-desu ka?   "How many times a day?"
(*naN-kai* = "how many times")

Ik-kai naN-jō-desu ka?   "How many tablets each time?"
(*naN-jō* = "how many tablets")

You have just seen two new counters, *-kai* ("times; rounds") and *-jo* ("tablets"). What if you should take the medicine three times a day?

Ichi-nichi saN-kai-desu.   "Three times a day."

Likewise, what if you should take two tablets each time?

Ik-kai ni-jō-desu.   "Two tablets each time."

Some medicine should be taken before or after a meal.

ShokuzeN-ni noN-de kudasai.   "Take (it) before a meal."
(*shokuzeN* = "before meal")

Shokugo-ni noN-de kudasai.   "Take (it) after a meal."
(*shokugo* = "after meal")

You might have noticed that the verb for "take (medicine)" is *nomi-masu*, which literally means "drink; swallow." This verb applies to liquid, tablets, and powder.

Okay, before closing this chapter, let's list some common drugs.

Common Drugs and Medical Supplies

antibiotics *kōsē busshitsu*	for cold/flu *kazegusuri*
Band-Aid *baNsōkō*	for coughing *seki-no kusuri*
bandage *hōtai*	for headache *zutsūyaku*
cane *tsue*	for itchiness *kayumidome*
cast *gipusu*	for motion sickness *yoidome*
compress (for muscle pain) *shippu*	for reducing fever *genetsuzai*
contraceptive *hiniNgu*	for stomachache *onaka-no kusuri*
cough drop *nodoame*	painkiller *itamidome*
cream *kurīmu*	sanitary napkin *napukiN*
crutch *matsubazue*	tampon *taNpoN*
disinfectant solution *shōdokuyaku*	vitamin *bitamiN*
eye drop *megusuri*	wheelchair *kurumaisu*
eye patch *gaNtai*	women's sanitary products *sēri yōhiN*

I hope your trip is safe, fun, and—most importantly—that you won't have to count on this chapter. But it is better to be prepared, just in case. Have a safe trip!

GREEN TEA BREAK

If you visit Japan in the winter, you will be surprised to see many people on the street wearing surgical masks, or *masuku*. No, they aren't surgeons! They wear these cotton masks to prevent the spread of germs. They might appear bizarre to you at first, but remember their motive and be grateful for their thoughtfulness!

The Least You Need to Know

- The Japanese number for medical emergencies is 119, not 911!
- Body-part words are essential in daily conversations, too.
- Master the pattern *[Body part]-ga ita-i-N-desu*, "X hurts."
- Be familiar with the words for basic medicines.
- Pharmacies in town sell only over-the-counter drugs. So if a doctor gives you a prescription, you must purchase the medicine right there at the doctor's office.

I Lost My Wallet! Nonmedical Emergencies

Chapter 24

In This Chapter

- Important facts for your safety
- Reporting a lost or stolen item
- Use of "if"
- Describing an activity in the past
- What to do when you get lost on the street

I know you are a wise traveler, but no matter how careful you are, unexpected things can happen, such as getting sick (discussed in Chapter 23). In this chapter, I talk about other kinds of emergencies like lost articles or theft. I'm sure that your trip will be safe and fun, but this chapter is just for your peace of mind.

Safety Facts and Japanese Police

Japan is a pretty safe country. The crime rate is very low compared with that in many Western countries. You can walk alone at night in downtown Tokyo without worrying about being robbed or attacked. Public transportation is also safe and clean, so getting around town is a piece of cake.

 GREEN TEA BREAK

Gun-related crimes are extremely scarce in Japan due to strict laws that restrict the possession of firearms. Similarly, the crime rate for possession of illegal drugs is low for two reasons: severe punishment (imprisonment and a steep fine) and the law enforcement authorities' hard work against drug trafficking at the borders.

One unique thing contributing to community safety in Japan is the presence of KOBAN (pronounced *kōbaN*), or "community police stands." A *kōbaN* is a small, houselike building where two or three police officers are stationed and patrol the neighboring community.

You can report any matters such as theft, lost articles, or criminal offences you might have witnessed at a nearby *kōbaN*. For travelers, a *kōbaN* is especially helpful when you get lost and want to find your destination. Huge local maps are available there, and the officers know the area very well. If your destination is near, she or he will even take you there!

When you have a nonmedical emergency and need immediate attention, you should call the police. The phone number is 110—it is not 911. Also remember, as noted in Chapter 23, you should dial 119 for a medical emergency or fire.

LIFESAVERS

There is a phone number at which you can talk with the police in English:

Police Foreign Language Hotline: 03-3503-8484

The 03 is the area code for the City of Tokyo. If you're calling within Tokyo, dial without using 03.

Because I introduced a few police-related words, let me list some more:

police	*kēsatsu*
police station	*kēsatsusho*
police officer	*kēkaN* or *omawarisaN*
police car	*patokā*

HUH?

The word *omawarisaN* is an informal and frequently used term for a police officer. This literally means "a person who patrols."

Just in case you experience any trouble, I want to make sure that you can speak or understand well enough to have the problem taken care of. In the following sections, I talk about three possible emergencies:

- You lost something.
- Your belonging was stolen.
- You got lost in town.

Lost and Found

The word for a "lost article" is *otoshimono*. What kinds of belongings are you likely to lose while walking? Here are some possible items:

bag	*baggu* or *kabaN*	passport	*pasupōto*
camera	*kamera*	pen	*peN*
cellular phone	*kētai deNwa* or *kētai*	ring	*yubiwa*
credit card	*kurejitto kādo*	sunglasses	*saNgurasu*
day planner	*techō*	ticket (for theater)	*chiketto*
eyeglasses	*megane*	ticket (for transportation)	*kippu*
handbag	*haNdobaggu*	umbrella	*kasa*
hat	*bōshi*	wallet; purse	*saifu*
jacket	*jaketto* or *uwagi*	wrist watch	*tokē*
laptop computer	*nōto pasokoN*		

If you lost something on the street, I suggest that you go to a nearby police stand (*kōbaN*) or police station (*kēsatsusho*). On the other hand, if you lost something in a public place such as a train station (*eki*), department store (*depāto*), or theater (*gekijō*), the place to go is an information booth. (There is hardly any place called "Lost and Found" in Japan.) The word for "information booth" is either *aNnaijo* or *iNfomēshoN*.

You should tell the police officer or information officer that you lost, say, your wallet:

> *Saifu-o otoshi-mashita.*   "I lost my wallet."

Then, ask her or him whether it has been reported to the station or booth:

> *Koko-ni ki-te i-maseN ka?*   "Hasn't it been reported here?"
> (*ki-te i-masu* = [Lit.] "has come")

She or he might ask you what your wallet looks like:

> *DoNna saifu-desu ka?*   "What kind of wallet is it?"

Suppose that your wallet is a black leather one.

> *Kuro-i kawa-no saifu-desu.*   "It's a black leather wallet."
> (*kawa* = "leather")

Does this answer sound familiar? Yes, in Chapter 12, you learned how to describe a noun in terms of color and size. Now, given the following description, describe the lost article, using the preceding answer as a template. You can find all the description items in Appendix B. As usual, the answers are given at the end of this chapter.

Exercise 1

1. "It's a blue American passport."

   _____

2. "It's a small Nikon camera." ("*Nikon*" = *nikoN*)

   _____

3. "It's a ticket for the Bullet Train."

   _____

If they have your wallet, their answer will be …

   Hai, ari-masu yo.   "Yes, we have it."

If not, unfortunately, it will be …

   SumimaseN, ari-maseN (nē).   "No, we don't."

Even if the wallet is yours, they won't give it to you unless you prove that it's yours. They might ask you a question that only the real owner of the wallet would be able to answer:

   Saifu-ni-wa nani-ga hait-te i-masu ka?
   "What is in the wallet?"
   (*hait-te i-masu* = "be put [in]")

Your answer should be as specific as possible. Suppose that your wallet contains your driver's license and a Citibank credit card:

   MeNkyoshō-to Shitī BaNku-no kurejitto kādo-ga hait-te i-masu.

Here are the words for items commonly found in one's wallet:

business card	*mēshi*	international driver's license	*kokusai meNkyoshō*
credit card	*kurejitto kādo*	money	*okane*
driver's license	*meNkyoshō*	photograph	*shashiN*
ID card	*mibuNshōmēshō*		

Other than the identification question shown previously, the police or information officer might also ask you basic questions such as your name, address, age, and occupation. Refer to Chapter 23, where these words are listed, for a review.

If ... Then

If, unfortunately, you cannot find your wallet, leave your phone number so that they will be able to contact you when they receive it. Let's learn how to say "Please call me <u>when</u> (*or* <u>if</u>) you find it."

Mitsukari-mashita <u>ra</u> deNwa shi-te kudasai. (*mitsukari-masu* = "find")	"<u>When</u> (*or* <u>If</u>) you find it, then please call me."

Notice that the word *ra* follows the past tense of the verb, as in *mitsukari-mashita <u>ra</u>,* "when you find it, then." *Ra* literally means "when/if ... then."

Let's practice the *ra* pattern. Translate the following sentences.

Exercise 2

1. "When I arrive at the hotel, then I will call you." ("arrive at X" = X-*ni tsuki-masu*)

_____

2. "If it rains, then I will not go." ("it rains" = *ame-ga furi-masu*)

_____

HUH?

Here are the words for other theft crimes:

stealing (general term)	*dorobō* or *nusumi*
purse-snatching	*hittakuri*
robbery	*gōtō*
shoplifting	*maNbiki*

Theft!

As I mentioned at the beginning of this chapter, Japan is a relatively safe country, but this doesn't mean it is completely crime-free. There is still a chance you might encounter a pickpocket (*suri*) when you walk in a crowded place such as a shopping center or ride a packed train. Also, don't leave your luggage unattended to avoid baggage theft (*okibiki*).

Imagine this scenario. After you leave a department store, you notice that your purse or wallet, which was in your backpack, is gone! So you go to a nearby police stand, or *kōbaN*, to talk with a police officer (*kēkaN*). Now, let's take a look at a likely conversation between you and the police officer step-by-step.

Like a medical doctor, the officer will ask you what brought you there. Do you remember the expression?

> *Dō shi-mashita ka?*   "What is the problem?"

You want to tell the officer that your wallet was stolen. An important expression you should know is …

> XYZ-*o nusumare-mashita.*   "My *XYZ* was stolen."

In this case, you should say:

> *Saifu-o nusumare-mashita.*   "My purse was stolen."

Other than basic questions about your identification, which have just been mentioned, the officer will ask you *where* it was stolen. Now, can you answer the following question? Suppose the name of the department store you were at is Mitsukoshi Department Store in Ginza:

> Officer: *Doko-de nusumare-mashita ka?*   "Where was it stolen?"
>
> You: _____

How did you do? The answer is …

> You: *GiNza-no Mitsukoshi Depāto-de nusumare-mashita.*
> "It was stolen at the Mitsukoshi Department Store in Ginza."

The officer will then ask you the following question. Can you figure out what he is asking?

> Officer: *Itsu-desu ka?*

Yes, good job! The word *itsu* means "when." You think it happened at about 2 o'clock.

> You: *Ni-ji-goro-desu.*   "Around 2 o'clock." (*goro* = "around")

Because this incident happened in the department store, the next likely question will be on what floor it happened. The counter for "floor" is -*kai*. Look at the following counter chart for "floors." Irregular pronunciation is indicated in bold.

Counters for "Floor" (-kai)

1st floor	**ik-kai**	7th floor	*nana-kai*
2nd floor	*ni-kai*	8th floor	*hachi-kai*
3rd floor	*saN-kai*	9th floor	*kyū-kai*
4th floor	*yoN-kai*	10th floor	**juk-kai**
5th floor	*go-kai*	11th floor	**jū ik-kai**
6th floor	**rok-kai**	What floor?	*naN-kai*

LIFESAVERS

Refer to Chapter 18 for more information on the floor setting of a department store.

If you think it happened on the seventh floor, a dialogue between the officer and you should look like this:

Officer: *NaN-kai-desu ka?*   "Which floor?"

You: *Nana-kai-desu.*   "Seventh floor."

What Were You *Doing* That Time?

The officer might be curious about what you were doing at that time. Suppose that you were browsing the bookstore. Here is another important pattern, an expression that allows you to say, "I *was doing* so-and-so." (It's a past-progressive pattern, technically speaking.) Note that this pattern makes use of the *TE*-form:

-te i-mashita.   "was doing"

HUH?

Of course, the progressive pattern can be used for the present tense as well.

-te i-masu   "is doing"

An example is:

Q: *Ima, nani-o shi-te i-masu ka?*   "What are you doing now?"

A: *Terebi-o mi-te i-masu.*   "I'm watching TV."

A typical dialogue regarding this question might resemble the following:

Officer: *Nani-o shi-te i-mashita ka?*   "What were you doing (then)?"

You: *HoN-o mi-te i-mashita.*   "I was looking at books."

Let's practice this past-progressive pattern.

Exercise 3

Translate both questions and answers into Japanese. Use Appendix B for help with vocabulary.

    1. Q: What were you doing yesterday?

        _____

        A: I was sleeping all day. ("all day" = *ichinichijū*)

        _____

    2. Q: What were you doing from 1:00 to 2:00 today?

        _____

        A: I was studying Japanese!

        _____

After a series of questions, a police officer or an information officer will ask for your contact address or phone number:

contact person	*reNrakusaki*
contact address	*reNrakusaki-no jūsho*
contact phone number	*reNrakusaki-no deNwa baNgō*

Well, I suppose rather than memorizing all these expressions, it might be more efficient to just be cautious when traveling!

Help! I Think I'm Lost!

 Do you have a good sense of direction? If you don't, you will need to pay extra attention when traveling in Japan, not only because of language barriers, but also because many signs are written only in Japanese.

In Chapter 15, you learned how to ask for directions. In this section, we look at the same issue from a different angle. Suppose you get lost somewhere in a busy town. You want to go to your destination, but you don't have time to ask people for detailed directions.

GREEN TEA BREAK

In Western countries, addresses are given in reference to a street, such as 345 Baker Street. So once you find Baker Street, it's easy to find the house because it is *on* the street. The Japanese address system is not based on reference to a street. Instead, it is area-based, for example:

Tokyo	"Tokyo"
Shinjuku-ku	"Shinjuku District"
Kita-machi 700	"Kita Town 700"

This "700" could be in the middle or at the end of the *Kita* area. Before you visit someone's house, make sure that you ask her or him to draw a map for you!

You know how to ask where a certain thing is …

> *XYZ-wa doko-desu ka?*   "Where is *XYZ*?"

Using this pattern, you can ask where you are now:

> *Koko-wa doko-desu ka?*   "Where am I?" (*koko* = "here")

Or you can say that you are lost:

> *Michi-ni mayoi-mashita!*   "I'm lost!"

If you are truly desperate, the following sentence might also be appropriate:

> *SumimaseN, chotto komatte i-masu.*   "Excuse me, I'm in trouble."
> (*komatte i-masu* = "be in trouble")

Okay, maybe you are not that desperate. Perhaps you still want to find the way out on your own. Good for you! However, even if that's the case, I think it's wise to ask whether your destination is near or far away from where you are now.

> *Chika-idesu ka?*   "Is it near?"
> *Tō-idesu ka?*   "Is it far away?"

If it is near but seems hard to get to by yourself, try the following question:

> *SumimaseN, tsure-te it-te kudasai maseN ka?*   "Excuse me, but could you
> *tsure-te iki-masu* = (take [someone])   please take me there?"

If your destination is far away, why don't you ask her or him to draw you a map?

> *SumimaseN, chizu-o kai-te kudasai maseN ka?*
> (*chizu* = "map")

> "Excuse me, could you draw a map for me?"

LIFESAVERS

If you desperately need help and need to communicate in English, you can count on the free telephone consultation service called Japan Helpline. The following telephone number is toll-free (only within Japan):

Japan Helpline: 0120-46-1997

The number 0120 is equivalent to 800 in the United States. Numbers beginning with 0120 are toll-free (*furī daiaru*, "free dial").

An online help service operated by a nonprofit organization is called jhelp.com:

www.jhelp.com

This site also provides a number of useful telephone numbers.

As this is a Japanese textbook, I encourage you to use Japanese, but if you are seriously in need of help, use the wild card:

> *Ēgo-ga hanase-masu ka?*
> (*hanase-masu* = "can speak")

> "Do you speak English?"

Having read this chapter and Chapter 23, I bet you are well-prepared and worry-free. Enjoy your stay in Japan. And remember, when something unexpected happens, don't panic. Panicking makes you forget all the Japanese expressions you have learned. Only a calm state of mind will help you in an emergency!

Answers

Exercise 1

1. "It's a blue American passport."
   Ao-i Amerika-no pasupōto-desu.

2. "It's a small Nikon camera."
   Chīsa-i nikoN-no kamera-desu.

3. "It's a ticket for the Bullet Train."
   ShiNkaNseN-no kippu-desu.

Exercise 2

1. "When I arrive at the hotel, then I will call you."
   Hoteru-ni tsuki-mashita ra deNwa shi-masu.

2. "If it rains, then I will not go."
   Ame-ga furi-mashita ra iki-maseN.

Exercise 3

1. Q: *Kinō, nani-o shi-te i-mashita ka?*

   A: *Ichinichijū ne-te i-mashita.*

2. Q: *Kyō, ichi-ji-kara ni-ji-made nani-o shi-te i-mashita ka?*

   A: *NihoNgo-o beNkyō shi-te i-mashita!*

The Least You Need to Know

- A *kōbaN* is a community police box. You can report any lost articles or crime to them. You can also use a *kōbaN* when you need directions.

- When you are in trouble, remain calm so that you can tell people exactly what has happened.

- Be able to describe a past event using *–te imashita,* "I was doing X."

- The word *-ra* ("if") broadens your language capability.

- When you are seriously in need of help, don't hesitate to count on English. *Ēgo-ga hanase-masu ka?* ("Do you speak English?") is a handy expression. When you speak English to Japanese people, speak slowly and clearly.

Making Complaints

In This Chapter

- Dealing with poor service at a hotel, restaurant, and shop
- How to make a complaint
- Making a request without being blunt

I have mentioned throughout this book that Japanese people tend not to show their emotions in public, especially frustration or anger. This does not mean, however, that the Japanese are always content and never make complaints. They do complain when necessary. While you are in Japan, you might encounter some inconveniences or frustrating circumstances. In this chapter, I teach you how to make complaints without being blunt or offensive.

As a traveler or businessperson, the following are likely settings in which you might have to make a complaint:

- Hotels
- Restaurants
- Shops

Let's look at each one and learn some useful complaint expressions.

Staying at a Not-So-Great Hotel

Not everyone stays in a luxurious, five-star hotel when traveling. If your travel budget is tight, the first thing to cut is probably the accommodation budget. Inconveniences are likely to occur at an economy hotel. Let's suppose that you are staying at a so-so hotel and are facing various inconveniences.

Room-Related Problems

 You come back to your room at the end of the day and notice that the room has not been cleaned. You should call the operator, or *furoNto*. This word is a shortened form of *furoNto desuku*, the front desk. Call him or her and say your room number first. Saying your room number is just like saying telephone numbers—pronounce each digit separately. Make sure that your room number is followed by *-gōshitsu*. If your room number is #423, say:

> *Moshi moshi, yoN ni saN-gōshitsu-desu ga.*   "Hello, this is #423."

Tell him or her that the room is not clean:

> *Heya-ga yogore-te i-masu.*   "The room is not clean."
> (*heya* = "room"; *yogore-te i-masu* = "is dirty")

Or, you can say that there has not been maid service yet:

> *Mēdo sābisu-ga mada-desu ga.*   "There has not been any maid service yet."
> (*mada* = "not yet")

As introduced in Chapters 11 and 16, the phrase *mada* ("not yet") is useful when you want to mention that something is not done or ready.

HUH?

The opposite of *mada* ("not yet") is *mō* ("already"). See these words in action in the following dialogue:

Q: *Mō tabe-mashita ka?*   "Did you eat already?"
A: *Mada-desu.*   "Not yet."

Here is how you ask for maid service. Yes, use the familiar *onegai shimasu:*

> *Mēdo sābisu-o onegai shimasu.*   "Maid service, please."

If something in your room is broken, the following pattern will be useful:

> XYZ-*ga koware-te i-masu.*   "XYZ is broken."

An example would be ...

> *Terebi-ga koware-te i-masu.*   "The TV is broken."

LIFESAVERS

Another expression for "broken" is *koshō shi-te i-masū;* "is out of order."

Here's a list of things that can break in your hotel room:

air conditioner	*eakoN*	lightbulb	*deNkyū*
alarm clock	*arāmu*	lock	*kagi*
bathtub	*basutabu*	radio	*rajio*
bed	*beddo*	refrigerator	*rēzōko*
chair	*isu*	shower	*shawā*
clock	*tokē*	sink	*nagashi*
closet	*kurōzetto*	table	*tēburu*
desk	*tsukue*	toilet	*toire*
door	*doa*	TV	*terebi*
hair dryer	*doraiyā*	water faucet	*jaguchi*
heater	*hītā*	window	*mado*
lamp	*raNpu*		

The word for "fix; repair" is *naoshi-masu.* Say the following when you want someone to come fix it:

Naoshi-ni ki-te kudasai.   "Please come fix it."

Remember that *-te kudasai* is a pattern used when making a request.

In Chapter 12, you learned a more formal pattern, as seen here:

Naoshi-ni ki-te kudasai maseN ka?   "Could you please come fix it?"

Because you're making a complaint here, *-te kudasai maseN ka* would sound too polite. Here is another useful pattern that is less formal than *-te kudasai maseN ka* but more appropriate than *-te kudasai* in this particular circumstance:

-Te kure maseN ka?   "Would you do so-and-so for me?"

With this pattern, "Please come fix it" would be ...

Naoshi-ni ki-te kure maseN ka?   "Would you come fix it for me?"

Let's stick to this pattern for the rest of this section.

Rather than fixing it, you could ask him or her to replace it:

Torikae-te kure maseN ka?   "Would you replace it?"
(torikae-masu = "replace")

What if there is an amenity that is supposed to be in your room but isn't? Here is a list of typical hotel room amenities:

bath towel	*basu taoru*	laundry bag	*seNtakubukuro*
body lotion	*rōshoN*	razor	*kamisori*
comb	*kushi*	sewing set	*saihō setto*
conditioner	*riNsu*	shampoo	*shaNpū*
extra towel	*kae-no taoru*	shaving cream	*shēbu kurīmu*
facial towel	*taoru*	shower cap	*shawā kyappu*
hair brush	*hea burashi*	soap	*sekkeN*
hanger	*haNgā*	toothbrush	*haburashi*
iron	*airoN*	toothpaste	*hamigaki*
ironing board	*airoN dai*		

Tell the front desk operator that you don't have, say, shampoo, and you want some brought to your room:

ShaNpū-ga ari-maseN.   "There is no shampoo."
(ari-masu = "there is")

Mot-te ki-te kure maseN ka?   "Would you bring it to me?"
(mot-te ki-masu = "bring")

Other Problems

Let's look at some other hotel-related complaints. Suppose that you ordered room service for breakfast, and you've been waiting for half an hour. Let's let the front desk operator know:

Rūmu sābisu-o tanomi-mashita ga,   "I requested room service,
mada ki-maseN.   but it hasn't come yet."
(tanomi-masu = "to request")

Notice that the handy *mada* ("not yet") is used here again.

Noises are another common complaint. I remember staying in a cheap hotel once. I realized when I lay down to sleep that my room was sandwiched between groups of high school basketball players! They were partying and playing at all hours of the night! Sound familiar? I think you can easily imagine how irritating that could be. In such a case, you should call the front desk and hope that they can take care of the problem. This might not always solve the problem, but it's worth a try!

> *Tonari-no heya-ga urusa-i-N-desu ga.*   "The (room) next door is noisy."
> (*tonari* = "next door")

HUH?

The adjective *urusa-i* ("noisy") can also be used for "Shut up!" Because the emphasis is placed on *sa*, as in *urusai*, it sounds like *SAi!*

If you want to tell people nicely to be quiet, use the following phrase:

> *SumimaseN ga, shizuka-ni shi-te kure maseN ka?*
> "Excuse me. Would you be quiet?" (*shizuka* = "quietness")

Before leaving this section, let's look at another important matter—an error on the bill. The word for "bill; invoice" is *sēkyūsho.* If you find a discrepancy on your bill, bring it to the appropriate person's attention!

> *Sēkyūsho-ga machigat-te i-maseN ka?*   "Isn't there an error on the bill?"

The verb *machigat-te i-masu* literally means "incorrect." What if you got the bill for a different room?

> *Watashi-no heya-no-jana-idesu.*   "This is not my room's."

For other important hotel-related matters, refer to Chapter 16.

SHORTCUTS TO SUCCESS

Making a complaint is a tough task because you might fear offending people. Try to say the magic word—*sumimaseN*—at the beginning of your sentence. You will be amazed at how effectively this little word softens the tone of your speech.

Inconveniences at a Restaurant

Besides satisfying your appetite, one of the reasons for dining out is convenience: you don't have to go grocery shopping or cook or wash dishes. So you are eating at a restaurant; however, you might occasionally come across a restaurant that does not give you adequate service. In this section, we look at common problems you might experience at a restaurant and learn how to make a complaint. Remember, because you are buying a service, it's perfectly okay to make a complaint! However, let's learn how to do so in a polite way.

I am sure that you have experienced waiting for your food for what seems like an eternity! Here is a useful expression you can say to the waitress or waiter:

> *Watashi-no ryōri-wa mada-desu ka?*   "Is my food coming yet?"

Of course, you can make your complaint more specific:

> *SaN-jup-puN mae-ni chūmoN shi-mashita ga.*   "I ordered 30 minutes
> (*mae-ni* = "ago")   ago."

You are dining with your friends. Everyone is served but you, and you are all waiting for your food to arrive. Even though this is not at all your fault, I'm sure that you feel guilty because it makes your friends uncomfortable to start eating without you! To avoid this, you might want to make the following request when placing an order:

> *MiNna issho-ni mot-te ki-te kudasai.*   "Please bring everything together."
> (*miNna* = "everything"; *issho-ni* = "together")

What if the waitress or waiter brings something you didn't order? Here is how to say "I didn't order this!" The word for "to order" is *chūmoN shi-masu.*

> *SumimaseN, kore-wa chūmoN shi-te*   "Excuse me. I didn't order this,
> *i-maseN ga …*   but …"

 GREEN TEA BREAK

Nowadays—particularly in Western-style restaurants or bars—instead of *chūmoN shi-masu* ("to order"), you can use the loanword *ōdā shi-masu.* This is used mostly among young people.

Just like Western countries, a good, reputable restaurant in Japan (serving Japanese or non-Japanese cuisines) is hard to get into without a reservation. Let's say that you made a reservation on the phone and got there at the specified time: 6 P.M. However, because of their mistake, the restaurant does not have your table ready. How would you convey your frustration to them?

> *Machigainaku, roku-ji-ni yoyaku-o*   "I'm absolutely sure I made a
> *shi-mashita kedo.*   reservation for 6 P.M.!"
> (*machigainaku* = "I'm absolutely sure"; *yotaku* = "reservation")

HUH?

The sentence-final particle *kedo* literally means "but." Use this particle when you are in disagreement with the listener. For example, in *Machigainaku, roku-ji-ni yoyaku-o shi-mashita kedo.* ("I'm absolutely sure I made a reservation for 6 P.M.!"), you are in disagreement with the restaurant receptionist's assumption that you did not make a reservation.

To make your argument even more convincing, mention the name of the person who received your reservation request:

> *Tanaka-saN-ni onegai shi-mashita ga ...*
> "I asked Ms./Mr. Tanaka to take care of my reservation, but ..."

Refer to Chapter 19 for other important restaurant-related matters, such as placing an order.

Although we have looked at several problematic scenarios, it is comforting to know that overall service in Japan is excellent. You will probably not encounter any major problems.

Shopping-Related Problems

The refund-and-return aspect of shopping can be frustrating. Because you are visiting Japan, all such problems related to your purchases must be resolved before leaving the country.

Damaged Items

You've bought a camera. You left the store and opened the box, only to find that the camera is broken. You must return it to the shop and express that it is broken:

> *Kore-o kai-mashita ga, koware-te i-masu.*   "I bought this, but it's broken."
> (*koware-te i-masu* = "is broken")

LIFESAVERS

A warranty on products purchased in Japan, or *hoshōsho*, is usually good only within Japan. If you want your product covered in your home country, I suggest that you go to a designated duty-free shop. You can find duty-free shops in department stores and at the airport as well.

Do you want to buy a camera with a warranty? Then try Shinjuku if you are in Tokyo and Nihonbashi if you are in Osaka. If you are looking for any electronics, try Akihabara in Tokyo. In Osaka, Nihonbashi is also the place for electronics.

Besides *koware-te i-masu* ("is broken"), here are some more words for "defects":

torn (fabric)   *yabure-te i-masu*

does not function/work   *ugoki-maseN*

broken (plates, glasses)   *ware-te i-masu*

manufacturer's defect   *furyōhiN-desu*

spoiled (food)   *itaN-de i-masu*

rotten (food)   *kusat-te i-masu*

HUH?

The phrase for "to return (merchandise)" is *heNpiN shi-masu*. A common expression would be …

HeNPiN shi-tai-N-desu ga.   "I want to return (this)."

To replace the broken camera with a new one, say the following:

Atarashi-i no-to torikae-te   "Would you replace it with a new one?"
kure maseN ka?
(*atarashi-i* = "new", *no* = "one")

Don't forget to take the receipt with you! The word for "receipt" in Japanese is either *ryōshūsho* or *reshīto*.

This Is Not What I Bought!

What if they gave you something you didn't buy?

Kat-ta mono-to chigai-masu!   "This is different from what I bought!"
(*chigai-masu* = "different")

Even if it is the same product, it might be the wrong size:

Saizu-ga chigai-masu!   "Wrong size!"
(*chigai-masu* = "different; wrong")

Let me introduce an important expression here, which means "too [ADJECTIVE]":

[Adjective Stem] + *sugi-masu* = "It is too [ADJECTIVE]."

HUH?

An adjective stem is one *without -i*. For example, the stem for *taka-i* ("expensive") is *taka*.

For example, if the jacket you got is too big, say:

Ōki sugi-masu!   "It is too big!"
(*ōki* = "big" [derived from *ōki-i*])

If, on the other hand, it is too small, say:

Chīsa sugi-masu!   "It is too small!"
(*chīsa* = "small" [derived from *chīsa-i*])

If they don't have a replacement item in stock, ask them to send it to you:

Okut-te kure maseN ka?   "Would you send it to me?"
(*okuri-masu* = "send")

Because competition among retail stores is so fierce, Japanese shops are famous for quality customer service. I am sure that they will send it to you by express delivery at no cost!

GREEN TEA BREAK

The word for "customer service" is *afutā sābisu,* a Japanized loanword ("after service"). I guess this means that the Japanese provide good service to a customer even *after* the purchase.

We have looked at only three situations, but I am sure that you can apply the same principles to other situations. Don't be too hesitant to complain when you believe you are right. You pay for services, and you deserve satisfaction. They will listen to you, I promise. In Japan, the customer is treated as a god. There is a phrase to express this sentiment: *Okyakusama-wa kamisama-desu!* ("Customers are gods!")

So you are almighty!

The Least You Need to Know

- Don't hesitate to complain when the situation requires it. You deserve the best possible customer service.

- X-*ga mada-desu ga* ("*X* hasn't come yet") is a handy phrase to use when you wait too long for the service you requested.

- Know how to make a complaint without offending people. When you must make a request, -*Te kuremaseN ka?* is a useful expression, which is neither too rude nor too polite.

- Be familiar with basic words for problems, such as *Koware-te i-masu* ("It's broken") and *Kat-ta mono-to chigai-masu!* ("This is different from what I bought!").

- Be familiar with the pattern Adjective Stem + *sugi-masu* ("It's too *X*"), as in *Chīsa sugi-masu!* ("It's too small!")

Useful Signs and Symbols for Travelers to Japan

In This Chapter

- Essential signs and symbols around you
- Shopping-related signs and symbols
- Signs and symbols that get you around town

In any town, you will notice that you are surrounded by hundreds of signs and symbols. Each of those is there to help you find something, take you to your destination, or even warn you. However, imagine that those signs and symbols are written in a foreign language like Japanese. You might miss important information, lose your way, or even put yourself in danger.

In this chapter, we get acquainted with some important signs, symbols, and characters that will enable you to safely and pleasantly stay in Japan, as well as save you precious time!

Essential Signs and Symbols

Japanese signs can be composed of simple, universally understood illustrations; illustrations and accompanying Japanese text; or just text. In the following, I've provided examples of signs and symbols you commonly see throughout Japan. Understanding—or at least being familiar with—symbols, whether they contain Japanese characters or not, will definitely make your stay in Japan less stressful.

Emergency Exit:

Wherever you are, it's a relief to know the locations of emergency exits. Most emergency exit signs are pictorial, but some contain only Japanese characters. The *kanji* for an emergency exit is 非常口 (*hijōguchi*).

Entrance:

Exit:

Don't enter a shop from the exit or leave from the entrance and end up setting off the security alarm! 入口 (*iriguchi*) literally means "into the mouth" and 出口 (*deguchi*) "out of the mouth."

Restroom:

The sign for a restroom, which is pronounced *otearai*, contains a combination of *hiragana* characters and *kanji* characters and is written お手洗い.

You might also come across a fancier sign with *kanji* only (also read *otearai*). Such signs are often found in nontourist places or rural parts of Japan.

Push:

Pull:

Isn't it embarrassing when you try to push the door open when there is a "Pull" sign on it? Don't let that happen even when you are in Japan! The word for "push" in Japanese is *osu* and is written as either おす in *hiragana* or 押 in *kanji*. For "pull," the characters are ひく in *hiragana* or 引 in *kanji*, both of which are pronounced *hiku*.

Do Not Enter!:

If you know this sign and its characters, you will be able to avoid unnecessary danger. 立入禁止 or *tachiiri kiNshi* means "off-limits."

Elevator OPEN/CLOSE Buttons:

The *kanji* character for "OPEN" is 開 (*kai*) and "CLOSE" is 閉 (*hē*). Because these characters look alike, even Japanese people who hurriedly get in the elevator sometimes push the wrong button! Because of this, pictographic signs now often accompany these characters.

Telephone:

Although you can take your cell phone abroad with you or rent one at the airport, you might still need to use a public phone. The word for telephone is *deNwa*, written as 電話.

Coin Locker:

Many tourists visiting Japan are surprised by the number of coin lockers in train stations, department stores, and other public places. Look for this sign and the characters コインロッカー (*koiN rokkā*). The fee is usually 300 *yen* per day. A larger locker for a suitcase often costs more, ranging from 400 to 500 *yen* per day.

Police Box or *Koban*:

Police Station:

When you get into trouble—for example, by getting lost or losing your belongings—look for a *koban*, a small houselike building where a couple of police officers are stationed to offer citizens help. The *kanji* for *koban* is 交番, and many *koban* stations have a "KOBAN" sign.

On the other hand, the word for police station is *kēsatsu* 警察 (or けいさつ). When you want to know whether a building is a police station, look for a gold star on the front of the building, as shown in the picture.

LIFESAVERS

Although there are variations from city to city, Information Desks are indicated by either a ⓪ or ⓘ sign. An information desk is an *aNnaijo*, written as 案内所 in *kanji* characters. Keep in mind that not every town has an information center for tourists. I suggest that you do research and plan ahead using useful websites such as that from the *Japan National Tourism Organization* (www.jnto.go.jp/eng/), where you can browse a map of Japan, try virtual tours, or even download tourist guides.

Shops and Facilities

When I first came to the States, I had no idea what the R_X meant. Such a symbol means nothing to a stranger. Similarly, if you don't understand *kanji* characters, you might not know what a shop sells until you actually enter it. Many shops have huge signs or billboards so that you can identify them from a distance—if you know what the characters mean, that is. Here are some signs you might commonly see on the street.

Pharmacy:

Many drugstore signs contain a blue or green cross accompanied by a word referring to medicine: *kusuri*. The characters for medicine are くすり in *hiragana* and 薬 in *kanji*.

Bank:

Currency Exchange:

If you are looking for a bank, or *giNkō* in Japanese, try to find the 銀行 sign.

You can exchange foreign currency at a bank or an airport, but you can also change money at a currency exchange shop. Look for the 両替 sign (*ryōgae*), "currency exchange," or 外貨両替 (*gaika ryōgae*), "foreign currency exchange."

LIFESAVERS

Many convenience stores have ATMs that allow you to withdraw money (Japanese currency, of course) from your bank/credit card. It's also a relief to know that by touching the "English" icon on the ATM screen, you can perform all the transactions in your native language—without guessing!

Post Office:

Post office is *yūbiNkyoku* in Japanese and is written as 郵便局. You can also look for *JP*, which stand for *Japan Post*. As shown in the pictures, post offices have a distinct symbol that looks like a *T* with a bar above it.

Bookstore:

In the United States, bookstores such as Borders or Barnes and Noble are popular. Huge bookstores exist in Japan as well. Such stores usually have a large billboard with the *kanji* character 本 (*hoN*), meaning "books." 書店 (*shoteN*) also refers to "bookstore."

Coffee Shop:

Japanese people are crazy about coffee (Japan is the third-largest coffee-importing country following the United States and Germany), and coffee shops are everywhere. If you want to explore a local coffee shop other than Starbucks or Tully's, look for コーヒー or 珈琲 signs, both of which are pronounced *kōhī*. Remember, English "Coffee" or "Café" signs are also common, so you coffee lovers won't have to suffer from withdrawal symptoms! Caution: If you are a coffee lover but not a smoker, keep in mind that many local coffee shops still allow smoking.

Cigarette Shop:

Japan is no longer a smoker's heaven, and fewer and fewer tobacco shops are found around town. However, if you are a smoker, you should know the sign たばこ, which is pronounced *tabako*.

 GREEN TEA BREAK

Japan is the most advanced country in the world when it comes to vending machines. You can buy almost anything at a vending machine, ranging from soft drinks, beer, and instant noodles to genuine gold coins! Of course, you can buy cigarettes at a vending machine, but you are required to insert a *tasupo* card (タスポ), an age verification card that is used to prevent minors from purchasing cigarettes. To get a *tasupo* card, you need to apply and wait for a few days to receive it. If your stay in Japan is short and you are dying for nicotine, try a local tobacco shop or supermarket where you don't have to verify your age with a *tasupo* card.

Smoking Area and No Smoking:

Many public places are now nonsmoking, so smokers will need to look for a sign indicating a smoking area, 喫煙所 (*kitsueNjo*). "No Smoking" is written as 禁煙 (*kiNeN*).

Cashier:

Finding cashiers in a huge shop like a department store might not be easy because they are scattered around the store and not necessarily located near the exit. Cashiers often have a *yen* symbol (¥) above them accompanied by the *kanji* characters 会計 (*kaikē*).

 GREEN TEA BREAK

Once you land in Japan, you will be surprised by the thousands of signs, billboards, and ads written in English. Because of spelling or grammatical errors, however, some of those signs carry different and sometimes funny connotations. The website www.engrish.com collects thousands of hilarious pictures. (Some pictures in the site might require viewer discretion.)

The reverse is also true! Be careful when you buy a souvenir with Japanese characters on it. I saw a tourist wearing a T-shirt with the Japanese phrase 死に至る病, meaning "(I suffer from) a terminal illness."

Signs and Symbols Around Town

As I said at the beginning of this chapter, the key to success in getting around town efficiently and smoothly is to be familiar with signs and symbols. By becoming visually accustomed to the following signs, you will be able to get to your destination without experiencing an unnecessary delay.

Taxi Stand:

First of all, the Japanese word for taxi is *takushī*, and its characters are タクシー. If you want to use a taxi cab at a busy place such as Main Street or at a train station, simply look for this sign for a taxi stand, タクシーのりば (*takushī noriba*). Keep in mind that cab doors in Japan open automatically, so rather than opening the door with the handle, just wait by the taxi's left-side rear door until the driver activates the door.

Taxi Vacancy:

You might have to catch a cab on the street. At night, this is an easy task—you simply raise your hand when you see a cab with its roof lamp on, meaning the cab is vacant. But in daytime, you need to check the sign behind the passenger-side windshield. If vacant, the sign should be in red with the symbols 空車 (*kūsha*), meaning "available." If the cab is not available, the sign should be in green.

Bus Stand:

The Japanese word for bus is *basu*, and its characters are バス. If you are traveling independently and make your own itinerary, buses are a good means of public transportation. A bus stand sign is commonly round, as shown in the picture, and it often includes the characters バスのりば (*basu noriba*). *Noriba* literally means a "place to get on a vehicle." If you have a good visual memory, you might remember seeing the same characters above, in タクシーのりば, a taxi stand. On a related note, a ferry pier is フェリーのりば (*ferī noriba*).

Subway Sign:

Tokyo Metro Sign:

The word "subway" in Japanese is *chikatetsu*, and the *kanji* is 地下鉄. Simply because the subway runs underground, a subway station is harder to locate than a train station, but you can always look for subway signs on the street. Most subway systems are municipally owned, so their company logos or signs look different from region to region, but many companies have adopted the alphabetic character of Ⓜ, standing for "metro," as shown in the pictures.

Subway Track:

Near a subway track you will find a sign like that in the picture. Once again, the word のりば (*noriba*) is used. By the way, each subway line has its own distinct color for identification. So at a big station where several lines are interconnected, knowing the color of your desired subway line is handy. For example, the *Ginza* Line trains, logos, and tracks are all indicated in yellow; the *Marunouchi* Line in red; and so on.

Transfer:

If you need to transfer to another train at a station, just follow the のりかえ口 (*norikae guchi*) sign, a transfer exit. The *kanji* character 口 literally means "mouth." If you remember that the same character is used for the words "entrance" and "exit" above, excellent! You are getting used to the world of *kanji!* Learning *kanji* can be tough, but visual association is the important first step.

Bullet Train (*Shinkansen*):

A Bullet Train, or *Shinkansen*, is amazingly fast, reliable, and comfortable. Although it is generally easy to find the *Shinkansen* tracks, you can easily get lost at a mega-station like Tokyo's, which has 23 tracks, including local lines! To make sure that you get to the right place, you just need to look for the pictorial sign for the Bullet Train. The *kanji* version of *Shinkansen* is 新幹線.

Ticket Vending Machine:

Train tickets can be purchased at きっぷうりば (*kippu uriba*). きっぷ (*kippu*) means "ticket," and うりば (*uriba*) means "counter."

Ticket Reservation Center:

If you are in a major *JR* (Japan Railways—the nationwide train system) station and want to reserve train tickets or simply prefer to buy tickets from a sales clerk rather than at a vending machine, look for the green sign for a ticket reservation center, which is called *Midori-no Madoguchi*, or みどりの窓口 in *kanji*. *Midori-no Madoguchi* literally means "green counter," even though the counters are not green at all. Because the sign is in vivid green and has a distinct logo (of a reclining seat), you won't miss it.

The Least You Need to Know

- In urban areas, important signs are often written in several languages, but if you plan to explore rural areas, you should get familiar with some basic Japanese signs and symbols.

- Knowing distinct *kanji* characters for shops can get you what you want to buy quickly.

- Many traffic signs are international. However, if you plan to drive in Japan, study local signs beforehand.

Written Japanese: A Brief Introduction

There are two kinds of writing systems in Japanese, *kana* (syllable characters) and *kanji* (Chinese characters). *Kana* represents Japanese syllables. Remember that Japanese has 102 possible syllables (see Chapter 3). Each syllable has its corresponding *kana*. That is, *kana* can represent any Japanese sound. For example, the Japanese word *kawa*, which consists of two syllables (*ka* and *wa*), can be represented by two *kana* characters, as in かわ.

Kana is useful, but the problem with this system is that it only represents syllable sounds, not meanings. For example, *kawa* has two meanings in Japanese, "river" and "skin," but the *kana* representation of this word, namely かわ, does not distinguish the meanings.

Kanji, or Japanized Chinese characters, resolve this shortcoming of *kana*. The *kanji* for *kawa*, "river," is 川, and the *kanji* for *kawa*, "skin," is 皮. *Kanji* provides both sound and meaning.

Japanese speakers mix both *kana* and *kanji* systems in written Japanese. For example, if a Japanese newspaper were written entirely in *kana*, it would be difficult for readers because of the many possible synonyms. However, by using *kanji* characters appropriately, writers can ensure that readers can read the newspaper without ambiguity.

In the sections that follow, I will introduce the complete set of *kana* and briefly discuss the *kanji* system.

Kana

As mentioned, *kana* represents Japanese syllables. *Kana* includes two subsystems, *hiragana* and *katakana*. *Hiragana* characters represent native Japanese words such as *omoshiroi*, "interesting"; *kotoba*, "language"; and so on. On the other hand, *katakana* characters represent (1) foreign words such as *kamera*, "camera"; *waiN*, "wine"; and so on and (2) sound mimics such as *nyānyā*, "meow"; *bataN*, "slam!"; and so on. First, let's look at *hiragana*.

Hiragana: For Native Japanese Words

In Chapter 3, we learned that Japanese has 102 syllables. Here are all of the syllables with their corresponding *hiragana*.

Hiragana

	ø	k	s	t	n	h	m	y	r	w
a	あ	か	さ	た	な	は	ま	や	ら	わ
	a	*ka*	*sa*	*ta*	*na*	*ha*	*ma*	*ya*	*ra*	*wa*
i	い	き	し	ち	に	ひ	み		り	
	i	*ki*	*shi*	*chi*	*ni*	*hi*	*mi*		*ri*	
u	う	く	す	つ	ぬ	ふ	む	ゆ	る	
	u	*ku*	*su*	*tsu*	*nu*	*fu*	*mu*	*yu*	*ru*	
e	え	け	せ	て	ね	へ	め		れ	
	e	*ke*	*se*	*te*	*ne*	*he*	*me*		*re*	
o	お	こ	そ	と	の	ほ	も	よ	ろ	[を]*
	o	*ko*	*so*	*to*	*no*	*ho*	*mo*	*yo*	*ro*	*(o)*

*The character [を] (o) is a special grammatical marker that indicates a direct object. For a full explanation of the grammatical function of this -o, see Chapter 4.

	g	z	d	b	p
a	が	ざ	だ	ば	ぱ
	ga	*za*	*da*	*ba*	*pa*
i	ぎ	じ	(ぢ)*	び	ぴ
	gi	*ji*	*(ji)*	*bi*	*pi*
u	ぐ	ず	(づ)*	ぶ	ぷ
	gu	*zu*	*(zu)*	*bu*	*pu*

	g	z	d		b	p
e	げ	ぜ	で		べ	ぺ
	ge	*ze*	*de*		*be*	*pe*
o	ご	ぞ	ど		ぼ	ぽ
	go	*zo*	*do*		*bo*	*po*

*The characters ち and づ in parentheses are pronounced exactly the same as じ (ji) and ず (zu), respectively. These are classical characters and are hardly used in the contemporary Japanese writing system.

	ky	sh	ch	ny	hy	my	ry
a	きゃ	しゃ	ちゃ	にゃ	ひゃ	みゃ	りゃ
	kya	*sha*	*cha*	*nya*	*hya*	*mya*	*rya*
u	きゅ	しゅ	ちゅ	にゅ	ひゅ	みゅ	りゅ
	kyu	*shu*	*chu*	*nyu*	*hyu*	*myu*	*ryu*
o	きょ	しょ	ちょ	にょ	ひょ	みょ	りょ
	kyo	*sho*	*cho*	*nyo*	*hyo*	*myo*	*ryo*

	gy	j (= zy)	by	py
a	ぎゃ	じゃ	びゃ	ぴゃ
	gya	*ja*	*bya*	*pya*
u	ぎゅ	じゅ	びゅ	ぴゅ
	gyu	*ju*	*byu*	*pyu*
o	ぎょ	じょ	びょ	ぴょ
	gyo	*jo*	*byo*	*pyo*

Stand-Alone Consonants

Double consonant: っ *(smaller than* つ*)*

N: ん

You might have noticed that some characters are a little smaller in size than others. Y sounds such as *kya*, *myo*, and *byu* are written as きゃ, みょ, and びゅ, respectively. Even though these are written as two attached characters, these are all one-syllable sounds. The other small character is the double consonant sound っ (as opposed to つ). For example, *sotto*, "gently," should be written そっと.

It's important to remember that *hiragana* represents ordinary Japanese words—words such as *nihoN*, "Japan" にほん; *sakana*, "fish" さかな; *neko*, "cat" ねこ; and *Fuji-saN*, "Mt. Fuji" ふじさん. *Hiragana* is not used for sound effects or words imported from other languages.

Now let's do a couple of exercises. Using the preceding tables, convert the following words into *hiragana*. Remember, to convert to *hiragana*, you combine the symbols for each syllable. The answers are at the end of this appendix.

Exercise 1

Ex.	"shoulder"	*kata*	かた
1.	"nose"	*hana*	_____
2.	"shoes"	*kutsu*	_____
3.	"kimono"	*kimono*	_____
4.	"head"	*atama*	_____
5.	"teacup"	*chawaN*	_____
6.	"dictionary"	*jisho*	_____
7.	"pencil"	*eNpitsu*	_____
8.	"telephone"	*deNwa*	_____
9.	"stamp"	*kitte*	_____
10.	"meal"	*shokuji*	_____

How about trying it the other way around now? I'll list some well-known Japanese words in *hiragana*. Your task is to figure out what the words are.

Exercise 2

Ex.	きもの	kimono
1.	てんぷら	_____
2.	すきやき	_____
3.	すし	_____
4.	つなみ	_____
5.	さけ	_____
6.	かぶき	_____
7.	からて	_____
8.	ふとん	_____
9.	ぜん	_____
10.	よこはま	_____

Katakana: **For Loanwords and Sound Mimics**

Katakana is the other *kana* system. While *hiragana* is used to represent native Japanese vocabulary, *katakana* is used to represent foreign (particularly Western) words and sound mimics.

First, let's take a look at the *katakana* tables. You will notice that many *katakana* characters, such as カ (*ka*) and セ (*se*), resemble their *hiragana* counterparts, か and せ, respectively.

Katakana

	ø	k	s	t	n	h	m	y	r	w
a	ア	カ	サ	タ	ナ	ハ	マ	ヤ	ラ	ワ
	a	*ka*	*sa*	*ta*	*na*	*ha*	*ma*	*ya*	*ra*	*wa*
i	イ	キ	シ	チ	ニ	ヒ	ミ		リ	
	i	*ki*	*shi*	*chi*	*ni*	*hi*	*mi*		*ri*	
u	ウ	ク	ス	ツ	ヌ	フ	ム	ユ	ル	
	u	*ku*	*su*	*tsu*	*nu*	*fu*	*mu*	*yu*	*ru*	
e	エ	ケ	セ	テ	ネ	ヘ	メ		レ	
	e	*ke*	*se*	*te*	*ne*	*he*	*me*		*re*	
o	オ	コ	ソ	ト	ノ	ホ	モ	ヨ	ロ	
	o	*ko*	*so*	*to*	*no*	*ho*	*mo*	*yo*	*ro*	

	g	z	d	b	p
a	ガ	ザ	ダ	バ	パ
	ga	*za*	*da*	*ba*	*pa*
i	ギ	ジ	(チ)*	ビ	ピ
	gi	*ji*	*(ji)*	*bi*	*pi*
u	グ	ズ	(ツ)*	ブ	プ
	gu	*zu*	*(zu)*	*bu*	*pu*
e	ゲ	ゼ	デ	ベ	ペ
	ge	*ze*	*de*	*be*	*pe*
o	ゴ	ゾ	ド	ボ	ポ
	go	*zo*	*do*	*bo*	*po*

The characters チ and ヅ in parentheses are pronounced exactly the same as ジ (ji) and ズ (zu), respectively. These are classical characters and are hardly used in the contemporary Japanese writing system.

	ky	**sh**	**ch**	**ny**	**hy**	**my**	**ry**
a	キャ	シャ	チャ	ニャ	ヒャ	ミャ	リャ
	kya	*sha*	*cha*	*nya*	*hya*	*mya*	*rya*
u	キュ	シュ	チュ	ニュ	ヒュ	ミュ	リュ
	kyu	*shu*	*chu*	*nyu*	*hyu*	*myu*	*ryu*
o	キョ	ショ	チョ	ニョ	ヒョ	ミョ	リョ
	kyo	*sho*	*cho*	*nyo*	*hyo*	*myo*	*ryo*

	gy	**j (= zy)**	**by**	**py**
a	ギャ	ジャ	ビャ	ピャ
	gya	*ja*	*bya*	*pya*
u	ギュ	ジュ	ビュ	ピュ
	gyu	*ju*	*byu*	*pyu*
o	ギョ	ジョ	ビョ	ピョ
	gyo	*jo*	*byo*	*pyo*

Stand-Alone Consonants

Double consonant: ッ *(smaller than* ツ*)*

N: ン

We find frequent use of loanwords in Japanese daily life in areas like fashion, information technology, and entertainment such as movies and music. But don't forget food! Japanese people are crazy about eating foods from all over the world. They Japanize not only the tastes but also the names of foods.

In the following exercise, 10 international foods are given in *katakana*. Using the preceding tables, pronounce the words and try to figure out what they are. This may be a bit challenging, so I will give you a hint for each question by adding the name of the country the food comes from. The answers are at the end of this appendix.

In questions 8, 9, and 10, you'll see a new symbol, ー. This is the character for a long vowel, a convention seen only in *katakana*.

Exercise 3

Ex. カラマリ (Spain) "calamari"

1. エスカルゴ (France) _____

2. エンチラダ (Mexico) _____

3. ペキンダック (China) _____

4. サンドイッチ (United Kingdom) _____

5. リングイニ (Italy) _____

6. パエリア (Spain) _____

7. キムチ (Korea) _____

8. メープルシロップ (Canada) _____

9. カレー (India) _____

10. ハンバーガー (United States) _____

Now, try the opposite. Can you convert the following place names into *katakana*? This is a more challenging task than the transcription you did in the *hiragana* section, because first you need to Japanize these loanwords. For example, if you wanted to transcribe "France" into *katakana*, you would first need to Japanize it (*furaNsu*), then transcribe each syllable into *katakana*, as in フランス. The words used in the exercise are all relatively simple words, so you can transcribe them as they are pronounced in English.

Exercise 4

Ex. France   *furaNsu*   フランス

1. America   _____   _____

2. Canada   _____   _____

3. Poland   _____   _____

4. Morocco   _____   _____

5. Brazil   _____   _____

6. Florida   _____   _____

7. Spain   _____   _____

8. Monaco   _____   _____

9. Panama   _____   _____

10. Africa   _____   _____

Foreign words are written in *katakana*. You're now familiar with *katakana*, so why not try to write your name? Remember the steps: First Japanize your name, then transcribe it using *katakana*. Following are some common English names in *katakana*. I hope you find yours here!

Names in *Katakana*

Female Names

Alice	アリス	(*Arisu*)
Amy	エイミー	(*Eimī*)
Angela	アンジェラ	(*ANjera*)
Anne	アン	(*AN*)
Barbara	バーバラ	(*Bārbara*)
Carol	キャロル	(*Kyaroru*)
Christy	クリスティ	(*Kurisuti*)
Cindy	シンディ	(*ShiNdi*)
Diana	ダイアナ	(*Daiana*)
Ellen	エレン	(*EreN*)
Hanna	ハンナ	(*HaNna*)
Julie	ジュリー	(*Jurī*)
Kate	ケイト	(*Keito*)
Kathy	キャシー	(*Kyashī*)
Laurie	ローリー	(*Rōrī*)
Lisa	リサ	(*Risa*)
Mary	メアリー	(*Mearī*)
Meg	メグ	(*Megu*)
Melissa	メリッサ	(*Merissa*)
Paula	ポーラ	(*Pōra*)
Rebecca	レベッカ	(*Rebekka*)
Sammy	サミー	(*Samī*)
Sandy	サンディ	(*SaNdi*)
Sara	サラ	(*Sara*)
Vanessa	バネッサ	(*Banessa*)

Male Names

Alex	アレックス	(*Arekkusu*)
Andy	アンディー	(*ANdi*)
Ben	ベン	(*BeN*)
Bill	ビル	(*Biru*)
Bob	ボブ	(*Bobu*)
Chris	クリス	(*Kurisu*)
Colin	コリン	(*KoriN*)
David	デービッド	(*Dēbiddo*)
Derek	デレク	(*Dereku*)
Ed	エド	(*Edo*)
Eric	エリック	(*Erikku*)
George	ジョージ	(*Jōji*)
Jack	ジャック	(*Jakku*)
Jim	ジム	(*Jimu*)
John	ジョン	(*JoN*)
Ken	ケン	(*KeN*)
Mark	マーク	(*Māku*)
Mike	マイク	(*Maiku*)
Pete	ピート	(*Pīto*)
Phil	フィル	(*Firu*)
Robert	ロバート	(*Robāto*)
Sam	サム	(*Samu*)
Sean	ショーン	(*ShōN*)
Tim	ティム	(*Timu*)
Tom	トム	(*Tomu*)

In native Japanese vocabulary, the following sounds do not exist:

ti as in "<u>Ti</u>m"	*fo* as in "<u>Fo</u>rd"
di as in "San<u>dy</u>"	*she* as in "<u>She</u>lly"
fa as in "<u>Fa</u>ust"	*che* as in "<u>Che</u>lsea"
fi as in "<u>Phi</u>l"	*je* as in "<u>Je</u>n"
fe as in "<u>Fe</u>llini"	

To transcribe these foreign sounds as accurately as possible, special notations are used in *katakana*:

ti	ティ	as in ティム "Tim"
di	ディ	as in サンディ "Sandy"
fa	ファ	as in ファウスト "Faust"
fi	フィ	as in フィル "Phil"
fe	フェ	as in フェリーニ "Fellini"
fo	フォ	as in フォード "Ford"
she	シェ	as in シェリー "Shelly"
che	チェ	as in チェルシー "Chelsea"
je	ジェ	as in ジェン "Jen"

There are two characters combined to make one syllable. Note that the companion vowel such as イ should be written smaller, as in ィ.

Katakana also represents sound mimics. It's interesting to compare English sound mimics with their Japanese counterparts. You may be surprised how different the Japanese mimic sounds are.

English Sound Mimics	Japanese Sound Mimics
slam!	バタン！ (*bataN*)
tap tap	トントン (*toNtoN*)
ding-dong	ピンポーン (*piNpōN*)
cock-a-doodle-doo	コケコッコー (*kokekokkō*)
moo	モー (*mō*)
bowwow	ワンワン (*waNwaN*)
meow	ニャーニャー (*nyānyā*)
oink oink	ブーブー (*būbū*)

Kanji

There is one last writing convention in Japanese, called *kanji*, or Japanized Chinese characters. As mentioned earlier, unlike *kana*, each *kanji* character represents not only a sound, but also a word meaning. For example, the character 山 is pronounced *ya-ma* and means "mountain." The beauty of *kanji* is that it is so visual that you get the word meaning at first glance.

Kana actually evolved as a simplification of Chinese characters. This invention was brilliant, but the Japanese didn't abandon Chinese *kanji* characters even after the invention of *kana*; *kanji* were important to keep because of their convenience. As a result of not discarding *kanji*, written Japanese can express highly abstract ideas. This is great unless you're one of many young Japanese students having to memorize all the basic *kanji!* I remember taking hundreds and thousands of *kanji* quizzes when I was in school.

The Japanese Ministry of Education and Science says the mastery of a little fewer than 2,000 *kanji* characters would be sufficient to read more than 90 percent of daily Japanese words. Japanese publications, except children's books, are written in a combination of both *kana* and *kanji*. For example, with the recommended number of *kanji*, you will be able to read a Japanese newspaper without any difficulty.

Comprehensive coverage of *kanji* is beyond the scope of this book. Interested readers should refer to textbooks or exercise books available in bookstores. I recommend the following books for beginning learners of the Japanese writing system:

> Henshall, K., and T. Takagaki. *A Guide to Learning Hiragana and Katakana.* Rutland, VT: Charles E. Tuttle Company, 1990.
>
> Association for Japanese-Language Teaching, ed. *Japanese for Busy People—Kana Workbook.* New York: Kodansha International, 1996.
>
> Henshall, K. *A Guide to Remembering Japanese Characters.* Rutland, VT: Charles E. Tuttle Company, 1988.
>
> Foerster, A., and N. Tamura. *Kanji ABC: A Systematic Approach to Japanese Characters.* Rutland, VT: Charles E. Tuttle Company, 1994.

Answers

Exercise 1

1.	"nose"	*hana*	はな
2.	"shoes"	*kutsu*	くつ
3.	"kimono"	*kimono*	きもの
4.	"head"	*atama*	あたま
5.	"teacup"	*chawaN*	ちゃわん
6.	"dictionary"	*jisho*	じしょ
7.	"pencil"	*eNpitsu*	えんぴつ
8.	"telephone"	*deNwa*	でんわ
9.	"stamp"	*kitte*	きって
10.	"meal"	*shokuji*	しょくじ

Exercise 2

1.	てんぷら	*teNpura* ("tempura")
2.	すきやき	*sukiyaki*
3.	すし	*sushi*
4.	つなみ	*tsunami* ("tidal wave")
5.	さけ	*sake*
6.	かぶき	*kabuki*
7.	からて	*karate*
8.	ふとん	*futoN* ("futon")
9.	ぜん	*zeN* ("zen")
10.	よこはま	*Yokohama*

Exercise 3

1. エスカルゴ	(France)	escargot
2. エンチラダ	(Mexico)	enchilada
3. ペキンダック	(China)	Peking duck
4. サンドイッチ	(United Kingdom)	sandwich
5. リングイニ	(Italy)	linguine
6. パエリア	(Spain)	paella
7. キムチ	(Korea)	kim chee
8. メープルシロップ	(Canada)	maple syrup
9. カレー	(India)	curry
10. ハンバーガー	(United States)	hamburger

Exercise 4

1. America	*Amerika*	アメリカ
2. Canada	*Kanada*	カナダ
3. Poland	*PōraNdo*	ポーランド
4. Morocco	*Morokko*	モロッコ
5. Brazil	*Burajiru*	ブラジル
6. Florida	*Furorida*	フロリダ
7. Spain	*SupeiN*	スペイン
8. Monaco	*Monako*	モナコ
9. Panama	*Panama*	パナマ
10. Africa	*Afurika*	アフリカ

English to Japanese Dictionary

This mini English-Japanese dictionary contains most of the words introduced in this book, as well as other frequently used basic words.

The English entries are listed in alphabetical order in the leftmost column. For each entry, its Japanese corresponding word or words are provided in romanized characters in the second column. When there are two Japanese words, they are divided by a semicolon (;).

The Japanese word or words in each entry are transcribed into Japanese *kana* characters in the rightmost column. For a more detailed explanation of *kana* characters, see Appendix A.

The *kanji* (Chinese characters) counterpart of a Japanese word is provided in square brackets [ ]. Note that not every Japanese word has a *kanji* counterpart. (For example, see the entry for "able.")

The Japanese characters in the rightmost column may be helpful when you need to let a Japanese speaker know which word you are referring to.

A

able	*deki-masu*	できます
above	*ue*	うえ［上］
absence	*yasumi*	やすみ［休み］
absent	*yasumi-masu*	やすみます［休みます］
accident	*jiko*	じこ［事故］
across	*mukō*	むこう［向こう］
address	*jūsho*	じゅうしょ［住所］
adult	*otona*	おとな［大人］
afraid	*kowa-i*	こわい［怖い］
after	*ato(de)*	あと（で）［後（で）］
afternoon	*gogo*	ごご［午後］
again	*mō ichido*	もう いちど［もう一度］
age	*toshi; neNrē*	とし［年］；ねんれい［年齢］
ago	*mae*	まえ［前］
ahead	*saki*	さき［先］
airplane	*hikōki*	ひこうき［飛行機］
airport	*kūkō*	くうこう［空港］
all	*zeNbu*	ぜんぶ［全部］
all day	*ichinichijū*	いちにちじゅう［一日中］
all night	*hitobaNjū*	ひとばんじゅう［一晩中］
all right	*i-i*	いい
almost	*hotoNdo*	ほとんど
already	*mō*	もう
although -	*- kedo*	〜けど
always	*itsumo*	いつも
A.M.	*gozeN*	ごぜん［午前］
ambulance	*kyūkyūsha*	きゅうきゅうしゃ［救急車］
American people	*AmerikajiN*	アメリカじん［アメリカ人］
among -	*- no nakade*	〜の なかで［〜の中で］
animal	*dōbutsu*	どうぶつ［動物］

another	*betsu(no)*	べつ（の）［別（の）］
answer (verb)	*kotae-masu*	こたえます［答えます］
apple	*riNgo*	りんご
appointment	*yakusoku*	やくそく［約束］
April	*Shi-gatsu*	しがつ［四月］
arm	*ude*	うで［腕］
around	*mawari*	まわり
arrive	*tsuki-masu*	つきます［着きます］
ask	*kiki-masu*	ききます［聞きます］
August	*Hachi-gatsu*	はちがつ［八月］
aunt	*obasaN*	おばさん
autumn	*aki*	あき［秋］

B

baby	*akachaN*	あかちゃん［赤ちゃん］
back	*ushiro*	うしろ［後ろ］
back (body part)	*senaka*	せなか［背中］
bad	*waru-i*	わるい［悪い］
bag	*baggu; kabaN*	バッグ；かばん
bake	*yaki-masu*	やきます［焼きます］
bank	*giNkō*	ぎんこう［銀行］
barber shop	*tokoya*	とこや［床屋］
bath (tub)	*ofuro*	おふろ［お風呂］
bathroom (toilet)	*toire; otearai*	トイレ；おてあらい［お手洗い］
beard	*hige*	ひげ
beautiful	*utsukushi-i*	うつくしい［美しい］
beauty salon	*biyōiN*	びよういん［美容院］
become	*nari-masu*	なります
beer	*bīru*	ビール
before	*mae*	まえ［前］
begin	*hajime-masu*	はじめます［始めます］

behind	*ushiro*	うしろ［後ろ］
bend	*mage-masu*	まげます［曲げます］
best	*ichibaN*	いちばん［一番］
between - and -	*- to - no aida*	〜と〜の あいだ［〜と〜の間］
beverage	*nomimono*	のみもの［飲み物］
big	*ōki-i*	おおきい［大きい］
bill (invoice)	*sēkyūsho*	せいきゅうしょ［請求書］
bird	*tori*	とり［鳥］
birth date	*sēneNgappi*	せいねんがっぴ［生年月日］
birthday	*taNjōbi*	たんじょうび［誕生日］
black	*kuro-i*	くろい［黒い］
blanket	*mōfu*	もうふ［毛布］
blood	*chi*	ち［血］
blue	*ao-i*	あおい［青い］
body	*karada*	からだ［体］
book	*hoN*	ほん［本］
bookstore	*hoNya*	ほんや［本屋］
boring	*taikutsu(na)*	たいくつ（な）［退屈（な）］
born	*umare-masu*	うまれます［生まれます］
box	*hako*	はこ［箱］
boy	*otokonoko*	おとこのこ［男の子］
bread	*paN*	パン
break (destroy)	*kowashi-masu*	こわします［壊します］
breakfast	*asagohaN; chōshoku*	あさごはん［朝ご飯］；ちょうしょく［朝食］
bridge	*hashi*	はし［橋］
bright	*akaru-i*	あかるい［明るい］
bring (person)	*tsure-te ki-masu*	つれて きます［連れてきます］
bring (thing)	*mot-te ki-masu*	もって きます［持ってきます］
British people	*IgirisujiN*	イギリスじん［イギリス人］
broken (machine, etc.)	*koware-te i-masu; koshō shi-te i-masu*	こわれて います［壊れています］；こしょう して います［故障しています］

broken (plate, etc.)	*ware-te i-masu*	われて います［割れています］
brother (older)	*onīsaN*	おにいさん［お兄さん］
brother (younger)	*otōto*	おとうと［弟］
brown	*chairo-i*	ちゃいろい［茶色い］
Buddhism	*Bukkyō*	ぶっきょう［仏教］
build	*tate-masu*	たてます［建てます］
building	*biru*	ビル
Bullet Train	*ShiNkaNseN*	しんかんせん［新幹線］
bus stop	*basutē*	バスてい［バス停］
business	*shigoto*	しごと［仕事］
business card	*mēshi*	めいし［名刺］
business trip	*shucchō*	しゅっちょう［出張］
busy	*isogashi-i*	いそがしい［忙しい］
but	*demo*	でも
buttocks	*oshiri*	おしり［お尻］
buy	*kai-masu*	かいます［買います］
by - (time)	*- madeni*	～までに

C

cake	*kēki*	ケーキ
call (to address; to invite)	*yobi-masu*	よびます［呼びます］
call (telephone)	*deNwa shi-masu*	でんわ します［電話します］
can (do)	*deki-masu*	できます
Canadian people	*KanadajiN*	カナダじん［カナダ人］
car	*kuruma*	くるま［車］
cat	*neko*	ねこ［猫］
cellular phone	*kētai (deNwa)*	けいたい（でんわ）［携帯（電話）］
center	*maNnaka*	まんなか［真ん中］
chair	*isu*	いす
change (verb)	*kae-masu*	かえます
change (money)	*otsuri*	おつり［お釣り］

cheap	*yasu-i*	やすい［安い］
child	*kodomo*	こども［子供］
China	*Chūgoku*	ちゅうごく［中国］
Chinese language	*Chūgokugo*	ちゅうごくご［中国語］
choose	*erabi-masu*	えらびます［選びます］
chopsticks	*hashi*	はし［箸］
Christ	*Kirisuto*	キリスト
Christian	*KurisuchaN*	クリスチャン
Christianity	*Kirisutokyō*	キリストきょう［キリスト教］
church	*kyōkai*	きょうかい［教会］
cigarette	*tabako*	タバコ
city	*machi*	まち［町 or 街］
clean (adjective)	*kirē(na)*	きれい（な）
clean up (verb)	*sōji shi-masu*	そうじ します［掃除します］
climb	*nobori-masu*	のぼります［登ります］
clock	*tokē*	とけい［時計］
close	*shime-masu*	しめます［閉めます］
clothes	*fuku*	ふく［服］
cloudy	*kumori*	くもり［曇］
coffee	*kōhī*	コーヒー
coffee shop	*kissateN*	きっさてん［喫茶店］
cold	*samu-i*	さむい［寒い］
cold (illness)	*kaze*	かぜ［風邪］
color	*iro*	いろ［色］
come	*ki-masu*	きます［来ます］
company	*kaisha*	かいしゃ［会社］
company employee	*kaishaiN*	かいしゃいん［会社員］
conference	*kaigi*	かいぎ［会議］
consulate	*ryōjikaN*	りょうじかん［領事館］
continue	*tsuzuke-masu*	つづけます［続けます］
convenience store	*koNbini*	コンビニ
convenient	*beNri(na)*	べんり（な）［便利（な）］

conversation	*kaiwa*	かいわ［会話］
cooking	*ryōri*	りょうり［料理］
cool	*suzushi-i*	すずしい［涼しい］
count	*kazoe-masu*	かぞえます［数えます］
country	*kuni*	くに［国］
cousin	*itoko*	いとこ
cry	*naki-masu*	なきます［泣きます］
Customs (office)	*zēkaN*	ぜいかん［税関］
cut	*kiri-masu*	きります［切ります］

D

dance (verb)	*odori-masu*	おどります［踊ります］
dangerous	*abuna-i*	あぶない［危ない］
dark	*kura-i*	くらい［暗い］
date (going out)	*dēto*	デート
date (on a calendar)	*hizuke*	ひづけ［日付］
daughter	*musume*	むすめ［娘］
day off	*yasumi*	やすみ［休み］
day planner	*techō*	てちょう［手帳］
December	*Jū ni-gatsu*	じゅう にがつ［十二月］
decide	*kime-masu*	きめます［決めます］
deep	*fuka-i*	ふかい［深い］
delicious	*oishi-i*	おいしい
depart (leave)	*de-masu*	でます［出ます］
department store	*depāto*	デパート
desk	*tsukue*	つくえ［机］
dictionary	*jisho*	じしょ［辞書］
die	*shini-masu*	しにます［死にます］
different	*chigai-masu*	ちがいます［違います］
difficult	*muzukashi-i*	むずかしい
dining	*shokuji*	しょくじ［食事］

dinner	*baNgohaN; yūshoku*	ばんごはん［晩ご飯］; ゆうしょく［夕食］
dirty	*kitana-i*	きたない［汚い］
dislike	*kirai(na)*	きらい（な）［嫌い（な）］
do	*shi-masu; yari-masu*	します; やります
doctor; doctor's office	*isha*	いしゃ［医者］
dog	*inu*	いぬ［犬］
dollar	*doru*	ドル
down	*shita*	した［下］
draw	*kaki-masu*	かきます［描きます］
drink	*nomi-masu*	のみます［飲みます］
drive	*uNteN shi-masu*	うんてん します［運転します］
driver's license	*meNkyoshō*	めんきょしょう［免許証］
drop	*otoshi-masu*	おとします［落とします］
drugstore	*kusuriya; yakkyoku*	くすりや［薬屋］; やっきょく［薬局］
dry (verb)	*kawakashi-masu*	かわかします［乾かします］
during -	*- no aida*	〜の あいだ［〜の間］
duty-free merchandise	*meNzēhiN*	めんぜいひん［免税品］

E

ear	*mimi*	みみ［耳］
early	*haya-i*	はやい［早い］
east	*higashi*	ひがし［東］
easy	*yasashi-i*	やさしい
eat	*tabe-masu*	たべます［食べます］
egg	*tamago*	たまご［卵 *or* 玉子］
eight	*hachi*	はち［八］
elbow	*hiji*	ひじ
electricity	*deNki*	でんき［電気］
elementary school	*shōgakkō*	しょうがっこう［小学校］

embassy	taishikaN	たいしかん［大使館］
employed	tsutome-te i-masu	つとめて います［勤めています］
English language	Ēgo	えいご［英語］
enjoy	tanoshimi-masu	たのしみます［楽しみます］
enjoyable	tanoshi-i	たのしい［楽しい］
enter	hairi-masu	はいります［入ります］
entrance	iriguchi	いりぐち［入口］
errand	yōji	ようじ［用事］
evening	baN	ばん［晩］
everybody	miNna	みんな
everything	zeNbu	ぜんぶ［全部］
exchange (money)	ryōgae	りょうがえ［両替］
exit	deguchi	でぐち［出口］
expensive	taka-i	たかい［高い］
eye	me	め［目］

F

face	kao	かお［顔］
family	kazoku	かぞく［家族］
far away	tō-i	とおい［遠い］
father	otōsaN	おとうさん［お父さん］
favorite	daisuki(na)	だいすき（な）［大好き（な）］
February	Ni-gatsu	にがつ［二月］
feel	kaNji-masu	かんじます［感じます］
festival	matsuri	まつり［祭］
few	sukoshi	すこし［少し］
find	mitsuke-masu	みつけます
finger	yubi	ゆび［指］
finish	owarase-masu	おわらせます［終わらせます］
fire (flame; blaze)	hi	ひ［火］
fire (a fire; on fire)	kaji	かじ［火事］

firework	*hanabi*	はなび［花火］
first	*hajime*	はじめ
fishing	*tsuri*	つり［釣り］
five	*go*	ご［五］
fix	*naoshi-masu*	なおします［直します］
flower	*hana*	はな［花］
follow (someone)	*tsui-te iki-masu*	ついて いきます
food	*tabemono*	たべもの［食べ物］
foot	*ashi*	あし［足］
for the sake of -	*- no tameni*	〜の ために
forest	*mori*	もり［森］
forget	*wasure-masu*	わすれます［忘れます］
four	*yoN; shi*	よん; し［四］
free (of charge)	*tada*	ただ
freezer	*rētōko*	れいとうこ［冷凍庫］
Friday	*KiN-yōbi*	きんようび［金曜日］
friend	*tomodachi*	ともだち［友達］
from -	*- kara*	〜から
front	*mae*	まえ［前］
fun	*tanoshi-i*	たのしい［楽しい］
function (verb)	*ugoki-masu*	うごきます［動きます］

G

get (obtain)	*morai-masu*	もらいます
get off (vehicle)	*ori-masu*	おります［降ります］
get on (vehicle)	*nori-masu*	のります［乗ります］
girl	*oNnanoko*	おんなのこ［女の子］
give	*age-masu*	あげます
give birth	*umi-masu*	うみます［産みます］
glass	*garasu*	ガラス
go	*iki-masu*	いきます［行きます］

go home	*kaeri-masu*	かえります ［帰ります］
God	*Kamisama*	かみさま ［神様］
gold	*kiN*	きん ［金］
good	*i-i*	いい
graduate school	*daigakuiN*	だいがくいん ［大学院］
grandchild	*mago*	まご ［孫］
grandfather	*ojīsaN*	おじいさん
grandmother	*obāsaN*	おばあさん

H

half	*haNbuN*	はんぶん ［半分］
hand	*te*	て ［手］
happy	*ureshi-i*	うれしい
hard (difficult)	*muzukashi-i*	むずかしい
hard (stiff)	*kata-i*	かたい ［堅い］
hat	*bōshi*	ぼうし ［帽子］
have	*mot-te i-masu*	もって います ［持っています］
he	*kare*	かれ ［彼］
head	*atama*	あたま ［頭］
health insurance	*keNkō hokeN*	けんこう ほけん ［健康保険］
healthy	*geNki(na);keNkō(na)*	げんき（な）［元気（な）］；けんこう（な）［健康（な）］
hear	*kikoe-masu*	きこえます ［聞こえます］
heavy	*omo-i*	おもい ［重い］
help (assist)	*tetsudai-masu*	てつだいます ［手伝います］
help (rescue)	*tasuke-masu*	たすけます ［助けます］
here	*koko*	ここ
high	*taka-i*	たかい ［高い］
high school	*kōkō*	こうこう ［高校］
hobby	*shumi*	しゅみ ［趣味］
home	*uchi*	うち ［家］

homemaker	*shufu*	しゅふ［主婦］
hospital	*byōiN*	びょういん［病院］
hospitalization	*nyūiN*	にゅういん［入院］
hot (spicy)	*kara-i*	からい［辛い］
hot (temperature)	*atsu-i*	あつい［暑い *or* 熱い］
hot water	*oyu*	おゆ［お湯］
hour	*jikaN*	じかん［時間］
house	*ie; uchi*	いえ［家］；うち［家］
how	*dōyatte*	どうやって
how long	*donogurai*	どのぐらい
how many	*ikutsu*	いくつ
how much (money)	*ikura*	いくら
how much (quantity)	*donogurai*	どのぐらい
how old (age)	*ikutsu; naNsai*	いくつ；なんさい［何歳］
humid	*mushiatsu-i*	むしあつい［むし暑い］
hundred	*hyaku*	ひゃく［百］
hurt (painful)	*ita-i*	いたい［痛い］
husband (my husband)	*shujiN; otto*	しゅじん［主人］；おっと［夫］
husband (someone's husband)	*goshujiN*	ごしゅじん［ご主人］

I

I	*watashi*	わたし［私］
ice	*kōri*	こおり［氷］
idea	*kaNgae*	かんがえ［考え］
illness	*byōki*	びょうき［病気］
important	*taisetsu(na)*	たいせつ（な）［大切（な）］
in what way	*dōyatte*	どうやって
inconvenient	*fubeN(na)*	ふべん（な）［不便（な）］
information booth	*aNnaijo*	あんないじょ［案内所］
injury	*kega*	けが

inn (Japanese style)	*ryokaN*	りょかん［旅館］
inside	*naka*	なか［中］
insurance	*hokeN*	ほけん［保険］
interesting	*omoshiro-i*	おもしろい
international driver's license	*kokusai meNkyoshō*	こくさい めんきょしょう ［国際免許証］
intersection	*kōsateN*	こうさてん［交差点］
it	*sore*	それ
itchy	*kayu-i*	かゆい

J

January	*Ichi-gatsu*	いちがつ［一月］
Japan	*NihoN; NippoN*	にほん［日本］；にっぽん［日本］
Japanese language	*NihoNgo*	にほんご［日本語］
Japanese people	*NihoNjiN*	にほんじん［日本人］
Jesus Christ	*Iesu Kirisuto*	イエス キリスト
job	*shigoto*	しごと［仕事］
July	*Shichi-gatsu*	しちがつ［七月］
June	*Roku-gatsu*	ろくがつ［六月］

K

keep	*tot-te oki-masu*	とって おきます
kind (gentle)	*shiNsetsu(na); yasashi-i*	しんせつ（な）［親切（な）］； やさしい［優しい］
kindergarten	*yōchieN*	ようちえん［幼稚園］
knee	*hiza*	ひざ［膝］
know	*shitte i-masu*	しって います［知って います］
Korea	*KaNkoku*	かんこく［韓国］

L

lake	*mizūmi*	みずうみ［湖］
language	*kotoba*	ことば［言葉］
laptop computer	*nōto pasokoN*	ノート パソコン
large	*ōki-i*	おおきい［大きい］
last	*saigo*	さいご［最後］
last month	*seNgetsu*	せんげつ［先月］
last week	*seNshū*	せんしゅう［先週］
last year	*kyoneN*	きょねん［去年］
late	*oso-i*	おそい［遅い］
later	*atode*	あとで［後で］
laugh	*warai-masu*	わらいます［笑います］
laundry	*seNtaku*	せんたく［洗濯］
lawyer	*beNgoshi*	べんごし［弁護士］
learn	*narai-masu*	ならいます［習います］
leave (depart)	*de-masu*	でます［出ます］
leave (something)	*nokoshi-masu*	のこします［残します］
left (direction)	*hidari*	ひだり［左］
leg	*ashi*	あし［足］
letter	*tegami*	てがみ［手紙］
library	*toshokaN*	としょかん［図書館］
light (electric)	*deNki*	でんき［電気］
light (weight)	*karu-i*	かるい［軽い］
like	*suki-desu*	すきです［好きです］
lip	*kuchibiru*	くちびる［唇］
liquor	*sake*	さけ［酒］
listen	*kiki-masu*	ききます［聞きます］
little (amount)	*sukoshi*	すこし［少し］
live (reside)	*sumi-masu*	すみます［住みます］
lock	*kagi*	かぎ［鍵］
lonely	*sabishi-i*	さびしい［寂しい］

long	*naga-i*	ながい［長い］
look	*mi-masu*	みます［見ます］
look for	*sagashi-masu*	さがします［探します］
lose	*nakushi-masu*	なくします
lost article	*otoshimono*	おとしもの［落とし物］
love (noun)	*ai*	あい［愛］
love (verb)	*aishi-te i-masu*	あいして います［愛しています］
low	*hiku-i*	ひくい［低い］
luggage	*nimotsu*	にもつ［荷物］
lunch	*hirugohaN; chūshoku*	ひるごはん［昼ご飯］; ちゅうしょく［昼食］

M

make	*tsukuri-masu*	つくります［作ります］
man	*otoko; otoko-no hito*	おとこ［男］; おとこの ひと［男の人］
many	*takusaN*	たくさん
map	*chizu*	ちず［地図］
March	*SaN-gatsu*	さんがつ［三月］
marriage	*kekkoN*	けっこん［結婚］
May	*Go-gatsu*	ごがつ［五月］
mean (attitude)	*ijiwaru(na)*	いじわる（な）
meaning	*imi*	いみ［意味］
meat	*niku*	にく［肉］
medicine	*kusuri*	くすり［薬］
meet	*ai-masu*	あいます［会います］
meeting	*kaigi*	かいぎ［会議］
menstruation	*sēri*	せいり［生理］
messy	*yogore-te i-masu*	よごれて います［汚れています］
microwave oven	*deNshi reNji*	でんし レンジ［電子レンジ］
middle	*maNnaka*	まんなか［真ん中］
middle school	*chūgakkō*	ちゅうがっこう［中学校］

mind	*kokoro*	こころ［心］
mirror	*kagami*	かがみ［鏡］
missionary	*seNkyōshi*	せんきょうし［宣教師］
mistake	*machigae-masu*	まちがえます［間違えます］
Monday	*Getsu-yōbi*	げつようび［月曜日］
money	*okane*	おかね［お金］
month	*tsuki*	つき［月］
moon	*tsuki*	つき［月］
morning	*asa*	あさ［朝］
mother	*okāsaN*	おかあさん［お母さん］
mountain	*yama*	やま［山］
mouth	*kuchi*	くち［口］
move	*ugoki-masu*	うごきます［動きます］
movie	*ēga*	えいが［映画］
movie theater	*ēgakaN*	えいがかん［映画館］
music	*oNgaku*	おんがく［音楽］
mustache	*hige*	ひげ

N

name	*namae; shimē*	なまえ［名前］；しめい［氏名］
near	*chika-i*	ちかい［近い］
nearby (location)	*chikaku*	ちかく［近く］
neck	*kubi*	くび［首］
need	*iri-masu*	います
nephew	*oi*	おい［甥］
new	*atarashi-i*	あたらしい［新しい］
newspaper	*shiNbun*	しんぶん［新聞］
New Year	*Shōgatsu*	しょうがつ［正月］
New Year's Eve	*ōmisoka*	おおみそか［大みそか］
next	*tsugi*	つぎ［次］
next door	*tonari*	となり［隣］
next month	*raigetsu*	らいげつ［来月］

next week	*raishū*	らいしゅう［来週］
next year	*raineN*	らいねん［来年］
nice	*i-i*	いい
niece	*mei*	めい［姪］
night	*yoru*	よる［夜］
nine	*kyū; ku*	きゅう；く［九］
no	*īe*	いいえ
no smoking	*kiNeN*	きんえん［禁煙］
noisy	*urusa-i*	うるさい
north	*kita*	きた［北］
nose	*hana*	はな［鼻］
not yet	*mada*	まだ
notebook	*nōto*	ノート
November	*Jū ichi-gatsu*	じゅう いちがつ［十一月］
now	*ima*	いま［今］
number	*baNgō*	ばんごう［番号］
nurse	*kaNgofu*	かんごふ［看護婦］

O

October	*Jū-gatsu*	じゅうがつ［十月］
of course	*mochiroN*	もちろん
okay	*i-i*	いい
old	*furu-i*	ふるい［古い］
old (age)	*toshi-o totta*	としを とった［年をとった］
one	*ichi*	いち［一］
only -	*- dake*	〜だけ
open	*ake-masu*	あけます［開けます］
order (food)	*chūmoN shi-masu*	ちゅうもん します［注文します］
other	*hoka(no)*	ほか（の）［他（の）］
out of order	*koshōchū*	こしょうちゅう［故障中］
outside	*soto*	そと［外］

P

pain	*itami*	いたみ［痛み］
painful	*ita-i*	いたい［痛い］
paper	*kami*	かみ［紙］
parcel	*kozutsumi*	こづつみ［小包み］
parent	*oya*	おや［親］
parents	*ryōshiN*	りょうしん［両親］
park	*kōeN*	こうえん［公園］
pass (through)	*tōri-masu*	とおります［通ります］
passport	*pasupōto*	パスポート
pastor	*bokushi*	ぼくし［牧師］
pay	*harai-masu*	はらいます［払います］
peach	*momo*	もも［桃］
pencil	*eNpitsu*	えんぴつ［鉛筆］
people	*hito*	ひと［人］
pepper	*koshō*	こしょう
period (menstruation)	*sēri*	せいり［生理］
person	*hito*	ひと［人］
pharmacy	*kusuriya; yakkyoku*	くすりや［薬屋］；やっきょく［薬局］
phone book	*deNwachō*	でんわちょう［電話帳］
photograph	*shashiN*	しゃしん［写真］
picture	*e*	え［絵］
pillow	*makura*	まくら［枕］
place	*basho; tokoro*	ばしょ［場所］；ところ［所］
plate	*osara*	おさら［お皿］
platform (station)	*hōmu*	ホーム
play (have fun)	*asobi-masu*	あそびます［遊びます］
play (sports)	*shi-masu; yari-masu*	します；やります
plenty	*takusaN*	たくさん

P.M.	*gogo*	ごご［午後］
police	*kēsatsu*	けいさつ［警察］
police car	*patokā*	パトカー
police officer	*omawarisaN; kēkaN*	おまわりさん; けいかん［警官］
police station	*kēsatsusho*	けいさつしょ［警察署］
pond	*ike*	いけ［池］
poor (poverty)	*biNbō(na)*	びんぼう（な）［貧乏（な）］
poor (unskilled)	*heta(na)*	へた（な）［下手（な）］
post office	*yūbiNkyoku*	ゆうびんきょく［郵便局］
postcard	*ehagaki*	えはがき［絵はがき］
practice	*reNshū*	れんしゅう［練習］
president (company)	*shachō*	しゃちょう［社長］
pretty	*kirē(na)*	きれい（な）
price	*nedaN*	ねだん［値段］
problem	*moNdai*	もんだい［問題］
professor	*kyōju*	きょうじゅ［教授］
promise	*yakusoku*	やくそく［約束］
province	*shū*	しゅう［州］
public telephone	*kōshū deNwa*	こうしゅう でんわ［公衆電話］
pull	*hippari-masu*	ひっぱります［引っぱります］
push	*oshi-masu*	おします［押します］
put (place)	*oki-masu*	おきます［置きます］

Q

question	*shitsumoN*	しつもん［質問］
quick	*haya-i*	はやい［速い］
quickly	*hayaku*	はやく［速く］
quiet	*shizuka(na)*	しずか（な）［静か（な）］

R

radio	*rajio*	ラジオ
rain (noun)	*ame*	あめ［雨］
rain (verb)	*ame-ga furi-masu*	あめが ふります［雨が 降ります］
read	*yomi-masu*	よみます［読みます］
real	*hoNtō(no)*	ほんとう（の）［本当（の）］
really	*hoNtō(ni)*	ほんとうに［本当に］
receive	*morai-masu*	もらいます
receptionist	*uketsuke*	うけつけ［受付］
red	*aka-i*	あかい［赤い］
refrigerator	*rēzōko*	れいぞうこ［冷蔵庫］
remember (memorize)	*oboe-masu*	おぼえます［覚えます］
remember (recall)	*omoidashi-masu*	おもいだします［思い出します］
remove	*tori-masu*	とります［取ります］
repair	*naoshi-masu*	なおします［直します］
replace	*torikae-masu*	とりかえます［取り換えます］
request	*tanomi-masu*	たのみます［頼みます］
reservation	*yoyaku*	よやく［予約］
rest (relax)	*yasumi-masu*	やすみます［休みます］
restaurant (Asian)	*ryōriya; ryōriteN*	りょうりや［料理屋］； りょうりてん［料理店］
restaurant (Western)	*resutoraN*	レストラン
restroom	*toire; otearai*	トイレ；おてあらい［お手洗い］
return	*kaeshi-masu*	かえします［返します］
rice (steamed)	*gohaN*	ごはん［ご飯］
rice bowl	*chawaN*	ちゃわん［茶碗］
rich	*okanemochi(no)*	おかねもち（の）［お金持（の）］
ride	*nori-masu*	のります［乗ります］
right (correct)	*tadashi-i*	ただしい［正しい］
right (direction)	*migi*	みぎ［右］
ring	*yubiwa*	ゆびわ［指輪］

river	*kawa*	かわ［川］
room	*heya*	へや［部屋］
run	*hashiri-masu*	はしります［走ります］

S

sad	*kanashi-i*	かなしい［悲しい］
safe	*aNzeN(na)*	あんぜん（な）［安全（な）］
sake (rice wine)	*sake*	さけ［酒］
sales tax	*shōhizē*	しょうひぜい［消費税］
salt	*shio*	しお［塩］
same	*onaji*	おなじ［同じ］
sanitary product (for women)	*sēri yōhiN*	せいり ようひん［生理用品］
Saturday	*Do-yōbi*	どようび［土曜日］
say	*ī-masu*	いいます［言います］
scary	*kowa-i*	こわい［怖い］
school	*gakkō*	がっこう［学校］
sea	*umi*	うみ［海］
search	*sagashi-masu*	さがします［探します］
season	*kisetsu*	きせつ［季節］
seat	*seki*	せき［席］
see	*mi-masu*	みます［見ます］
sell	*uri-masu*	うります［売ります］
send	*okuri-masu*	おくります［送ります］
September	*Ku-gatsu*	くがつ［九月］
seven	*nana; shichi*	なな; しち［七］
she	*kanojo*	かのじょ［彼女］
Shintoism	*ShiNtō*	しんとう［神道］
ship	*fune*	ふね［船］
ship (send)	*okuri-masu*	おくります［送ります］
shoe	*kutsu*	くつ［靴］

shop (store)	*mise*	みせ［店］
shopping	*kaimono*	かいもの［買い物］
short	*mijika-i*	みじかい［短い］
short (person's height)	*se-ga hiku-i*	せがひくい［背が低い］
shoulder	*kata*	かた［肩］
show (verb)	*mise-masu*	みせます［見せます］
shrimp	*ebi*	えび
shrine (Shinto)	*jiNja*	じんじゃ［神社］
sibling	*kyōdai*	きょうだい
sickness	*byōki*	びょうき［病気］
side	*yoko*	よこ［横］
sightseeing	*kaNkō*	かんこう［観光］
silver	*giN*	ぎん［銀］
since -	*- kara*	〜から
sing	*utai-masu*	うたいます［歌います］
sister (older)	*onēsaN*	おねえさん［お姉さん］
sister (younger)	*imōto*	いもうと［妹］
sit	*suwari-masu*	すわります［座ります］
six	*roku*	ろく［六］
skillful	*jōzu(na)*	じょうず（な）［上手（な）］
sky	*sora*	そら［空］
sleep	*ne-masu*	ねます［寝ます］
sleepy	*nemu-i*	ねむい［眠い］
small	*chīsa-i*	ちいさい［小さい］
smell	*nioi*	におい［匂い］
smelly	*kusa-i*	くさい［臭い］
smoke	*tabako-o sui-masu*	タバコを すいます
snow (noun)	*yuki*	ゆき［雪］
snow (verb)	*yuki-ga furi-masu*	ゆきが ふります［雪が降ります］
soap	*sekkeN*	せっけん
soft	*yawaraka-i*	やわらかい［柔らかい］
someone	*dareka*	だれか

something	*nanika*	なにか
sometime	*itsuka*	いつか
somewhere	*dokoka*	どこか
son	*musuko*	むすこ［息子］
song	*uta*	うた［歌］
so-so	*māmā*	まあまあ
sound	*oto*	おと［音］
sour	*suppa-i*	すっぱい
south	*minami*	みなみ［南］
souvenir	*omiyage*	おみやげ
soy sauce	*shōyu*	しょうゆ
speak	*hanashi-masu*	はなします［話します］
spend (money)	*okane-o tsukai-masu*	おかねを つかいます ［お金を使います］
spicy	*kara-i*	からい［辛い］
spring	*haru*	はる［春］
stairs	*kaidaN*	かいだん［階段］
stamp	*kitte*	きって［切手］
stand (up)	*tachi-masu*	たちます［立ちます］
start	*hajime-masu*	はじめます［始めます］
state	*shū*	しゅう［州］
station	*eki*	えき［駅］
stay	*i-masu*	います
stay (overnight)	*tomari-masu*	とまります［泊まります］
still	*mada*	まだ
stop (halt)	*tome-masu*	とめます［止めます］
stop (quit)	*yame-masu*	やめます
store (shop)	*mise*	みせ［店］
story (tale)	*hanashi*	はなし［話］
straight	*massugu*	まっすぐ
street	*tōri*	とおり［通り］
strong	*tsuyo-i*	つよい［強い］

student	*gakusē*	がくせい［学生］
study	*beNkyō shi-masu*	べんきょう します［勉強します］
study abroad	*ryūgaku*	りゅうがく［留学］
subway	*chikatetsu*	ちかてつ［地下鉄］
sugar	*satō*	さとう［砂糖］
summer	*natsu*	なつ［夏］
sun	*taiyō*	たいよう［太陽］
Sunday	*Nichi-yōbi*	にちようび［日曜日］
sunny	*hare*	はれ［晴］
supermarket	*sūpā*	スーパー
sushi bar	*sushiya*	すしや［寿司屋］
sweet	*ama-i*	あまい［甘い］
swim	*oyogi-masu*	およぎます［泳ぎます］

T

take (obtain)	*tori-masu*	とります［取ります］
take (someone) to somewhere	*tsure-te iki-masu*	つれて いきます［連れて いきます］
take (something) to somewhere	*mot-te iki-masu*	もって いきます［持って いきます］
take a bath	*ofuro-ni hairi-masu*	おふろにはいります［お風呂に入ります］
take a picture	*shashiN-o tori-masu*	しゃしんを とります［写真を撮ります］
take a shower	*shawā-o abi-masu*	シャワーを あびます
take medicine	*kusuri-o nomi-masu*	くすりを のみます［薬を飲みます］
take off (clothes)	*nugi-masu*	ぬぎます［脱ぎます］
talk	*hanashi-masu*	はなします［話します］
tall	*taka-i*	たかい［高い］
tall (person's height)	*se-ga taka-i*	せがたかい［背が高い］
taste	*aji*	あじ［味］
taxi stand	*takushī noriba*	タクシー のりば［タクシー乗り場］
tea (British)	*kōcha*	こうちゃ［紅茶］

tea (Japanese)	*ocha*	おちゃ［お茶］
tea cup (green tea)	*chawaN*	ちゃわん［茶碗］
teach	*oshie-masu*	おしえます［教えます］
teacher	*kyōshi; seNsē*	きょうし［教師］；せんせい［先生］
telephone	*deNwa*	でんわ［電話］
telephone number	*deNwa baNgō*	でんわ ばんごう［電話番号］
television	*terebi*	テレビ
tell	*ī-masu*	いいます［言います］
temple (Buddhist)	*otera*	おてら［お寺］
ten	*jū*	じゅう［十］
than -	*- yori*	～より
that (adjective; near listener)	*sono*	その
that (adjective; over there)	*ano*	あの
that one (near listener)	*sore*	それ
that one over there	*are*	あれ
there (away from speaker and listener)	*asoko*	あそこ
there (near listener)	*soko*	そこ
there is (a person)	*i-masu*	います
there is (a thing)	*ari-masu*	あります
they	*karera*	かれら
thick	*atsu-i*	あつい［厚い］
thin	*usu-i*	うすい［薄い］
thing (intangible)	*koto*	こと［事］
thing (tangible)	*mono*	もの［物］
think (contemplate)	*kaNgae-masu*	かんがえます［考えます］
think (suppose)	*omoi-masu*	おもいます［思います］
this (adjective)	*kono*	この
this month	*koNgetsu*	こんげつ［今月］
this one	*kore*	これ
this week	*koNshū*	こんしゅう［今週］

this year	*kotoshi*	ことし［今年］
thousand	*seN*	せん［千］
three	*saN*	さん［三］
throat	*nodo*	のど
throw away	*sute-masu*	すてます［捨てます］
Thursday	*Moku-yōbi*	もくようび［木曜日］
ticket (for admission)	*chiketto*	チケット
ticket (for transportation)	*kippu; jōshakeN*	きっぷ［切符］；じょうしゃけん［乗車券］
time	*jikaN*	じかん［時間］
tip	*chippu*	チップ
tired	*tsukare-masu*	つかれます［疲れます］
to -	*- ni*	〜に
today	*kyō*	きょう［今日］
together	*isshoni*	いっしょに［一緒に］
tomorrow	*ashita*	あした［明日］
tongue	*shita*	した［舌］
tonight	*koNya*	こんや［今夜］
tooth	*ha*	は［歯］
toothbrush	*haburashi*	ハブラシ
toothpaste	*hamigaki*	ハミガキ
top	*ue*	うえ［上］
traffic signal	*shiNgō*	しんごう［信号］
train	*deNsha*	でんしゃ［電車］
transfer (train, bus)	*norikae-masu*	のりかえます［乗り換えます］
trash	*gomi*	ごみ
trash can	*gomibako*	ごみばこ［ごみ箱］
travel/trip	*ryokō*	りょこう［旅行］
tree	*ki*	き［木］
true	*hoNtō(no)*	ほんとう（の）［本当（の）］
Tuesday	*Ka-yōbi*	かようび［火曜日］

turn	*magari-masu*	まがります［曲がります］
two	*ni*	に［二］
typhoon	*taifu*	たいふう［台風］

U

unappetizing	*mazu-i*	まずい
uncle	*ojisaN*	おじさん
under	*shita*	した［下］
understand	*wakari-masu*	わかります
underwear	*shitagi*	したぎ［下着］
United Kingdom	*Igirisu*	イギリス
university	*daigaku*	だいがく［大学］
until -	*- made*	〜まで
up	*ue*	うえ［上］
use	*tsukai-masu*	つかいます［使います］

V

various	*iroiro(na)*	いろいろ(な)
vegetable	*yasai*	やさい［野菜］
vinegar	*osu*	おす［お酢］
visit	*tazune-masu*	たずねます［訪ねます］
voice	*koe*	こえ［声］
vomit	*haki-masu*	はきます［吐きます］

W

waist	*koshi*	こし［腰］
wait	*machi-masu*	まちます［待ちます］
wake up	*oki-masu*	おきます［起きます］
walk	*aruki-masu*	あるきます［歩きます］
wallet	*saifu*	さいふ［財布］

want (something)	*hoshi-i*	ほしい ［欲しい］
war	*seNsō*	せんそう ［戦争］
warm	*atatakai*	あたたかい ［暖かい］
warranty (product)	*hoshōsho*	ほしょうしょ ［保証書］
wash	*arai-masu*	あらいます ［洗います］
washing machine	*seNtakuki*	せんたくき ［洗濯機］
watch (clock)	*tokē*	とけい ［時計］
watch (look)	*mi-masu*	みます ［見ます］
water	*mizu*	みず ［水］
water faucet	*jaguchi*	じゃぐち ［蛇口］
water heater	*yuwakashiki*	ゆわかしき ［湯沸かし器］
we	*watashitachi*	わたしたち ［私達］
weak	*yowa-i*	よわい ［弱い］
wear (above waist line)	*ki-masu*	きます ［着ます］
wear (below waist line)	*haki-masu*	はきます
weather	*teNki*	てんき ［天気］
wedding (ceremony)	*kekkoNshiki*	けっこんしき ［結婚式］
Wednesday	*Sui-yōbi*	すいようび ［水曜日］
week	*shū*	しゅう ［週］
west	*nishi*	にし ［西］
when	*itsu*	いつ
where	*doko; dochira*	どこ; どちら
which (adjective)	*dono; dochira*	どの; どちら
which one	*dore*	どれ
white	*shiro-i*	しろい ［白い］
why	*dōshite*	どうして
wife (my wife)	*kanai; tsuma*	かない ［家内］; つま ［妻］
wife (someone's wife)	*okusaN*	おくさん ［奥さん］
wind	*kaze*	かぜ ［風］
window	*mado*	まど ［窓］
winter	*fuyu*	ふゆ ［冬］
with - (person)	*- to*	〜と

with - (thing)	*- de*	～で
woman	*oNna; oNna-no hito*	おんな [女] ; おんなの ひと [女の人]
word	*kotoba; taNgo*	ことば [言葉] ; たんご [単語]
work (noun)	*shigoto*	しごと [仕事]
work (verb)	*shigoto-o shi-masu; hataraki-masu*	しごとを します [仕事をします] ; はたらきます [働きます]
write	*kaki-masu*	かきます [書きます]
wrong	*machigat-te i-masu*	まちがって います [間違っています]

X-Y

year	*neN; toshi*	ねん; とし [年]
yellow	*kīro-i*	きいろい [黄色い]
yen (currency)	*eN*	えん [円]
yes	*hai; ē*	はい; ええ
yesterday	*kinō*	きのう [昨日]
you	*anata*	あなた
young	*waka-i*	わかい [若い]

Z

zero	*zero; rei*	ゼロ; れい [零]
zip code	*yūbiN baNgō*	ゆうびん ばんごう [郵便番号]
zoo	*dōbutsueN*	どうぶつえん [動物園]

Japanese to English Dictionary

This mini Japanese-English dictionary contains most of the words introduced in this book, as well as other frequently used basic words.

The Japanese entries are listed in alphabetical order in the leftmost column. They are written in romanized characters. In the second column, each entry is transcribed into Japanese *kana* characters. The *kanji* (Chinese characters) counterpart of a Japanese word is provided in square brackets [ ]. Note that not every Japanese word has a *kanji* counterpart. (For example, see the entry for *age-masu*, "give.")

The English meaning of each Japanese entry is listed in the rightmost column.

There are numerous words whose pronunciations are identical, such as *hashi*, "bridge," and *hashi*, "chopsticks." Since these words are totally different in meaning, they are listed as separate entries. The difference is indicated by their *kanji* (Chinese characters) representations.

A

abuna-i	あぶない ［危ない］	dangerous
age-masu	あげます	give
ai	あい ［愛］	love (noun)
ai-masu	あいます ［会います］	meet
aishi-te i-masu	あいして います ［愛しています］	love (verb)
aji	あじ ［味］	taste
akachaN	あかちゃん ［赤ちゃん］	baby
akaru-i	あかるい ［明るい］	bright
ake-masu	あけます ［開けます］	open
aki	あき ［秋］	autumn
ama-i	あまい ［甘い］	sweet
ame	あめ ［雨］	rain (noun)
ame-ga furi-masu	あめが ふります ［雨が降ります］	rain (verb)
AmerikajiN	アメリカじん ［アメリカ人］	American people
anata	あなた	you
aNnaijo	あんないじょ ［案内所］	information booth
ano	あの	that (adjective; over there)
aNzeN(na)	あんぜん（な） ［安全（な）］	safe
ao-i	あおい ［青い］	blue
arai-masu	あらいます ［洗います］	wash
are	あれ	that one (over there)
ari-masu	あります	there is (a thing)
aruki-masu	あるきます ［歩きます］	walk
asa	あさ ［朝］	morning
asagohaN	あさごはん ［朝ご飯］	breakfast
ashi	あし ［足］	foot; leg
ashita	あした ［明日］	tomorrow
asobi-masu	あそびます ［遊びます］	play (have fun)
asoko	あそこ	there (away from speaker and listener)

atama	あたま ［頭］	head
atarashi-i	あたらしい ［新しい］	new
atatakai	あたたかい ［暖かい］	warm
ato(de)	あと（で）［後（で）］	after; later
atsu-i	あつい ［暑い *or* 熱い］	hot (temperature)
atsu-i	あつい ［厚い］	thick

B

baggu	バッグ	bag
baN	ばん ［晩］	evening
baNgō	ばんごう ［番号］	number
baNgohaN	ばんごはん ［晩ご飯］	supper
basho	ばしょ ［場所］	place
basutē	バスてい ［バス停］	bus stop
beNgoshi	べんごし ［弁護士］	lawyer
beNkyō shi-masu	べんきょうします ［勉強します］	study
beNri(na)	べんり（な）［便利（な）］	convenient
betsu(no)	べつ（の）［別（の）］	another
biNbō(na)	びんぼう（な）［貧乏（な）］	poor (poverty)
biru	ビル	building
bīru	ビール	beer
biyōiN	びょういん ［美容院］	beauty salon
biza	ビザ	visa
bokushi	ぼくし ［牧師］	pastor
bōshi	ぼうし ［帽子］	hat
Budda	ブッダ	Buddha
Bukkyō	ぶっきょう ［仏教］	Buddhism
byōiN	びょういん ［病院］	hospital
byōki	びょうき ［病気］	sickness

C

chairo-i	ちゃいろい［茶色い］	brown
chawaN	ちゃわん［茶碗］	rice bowl; tea cup (green tea)
chi	ち［血］	blood
chigai-masu	ちがいます［違います］	different; wrong
chika-i	ちかい［近い］	near
chikaku	ちかく［近く］	nearby (location)
chikatetsu	ちかてつ［地下鉄］	subway
chiketto	チケット	ticket (for admission)
chippu	チップ	tip
chīsa-i	ちいさい［小さい］	little; small
chizu	ちず［地図］	map
chōshoku	ちょうしょく［朝食］	breakfast
chūgakkō	ちゅうがっこう［中学校］	middle school
Chūgoku	ちゅうごく［中国］	China
Chūgokugo	ちゅうごくご［中国語］	Chinese language
chūmoN shi-masu	ちゅうもん します［注文します］	order (food)
chūshoku	ちゅうしょく［昼食］	lunch

D

daidokoro	だいどころ［台所］	kitchen
daigaku	だいがく［大学］	university
daigakuiN	だいがくいん［大学院］	graduate school
daisuki(na)	だいすき（な）［大好き（な）］	favorite
- dake	～だけ	only -
dareka	だれか	someone
- de	～で	at -; with - (thing)
deguchi	でぐち［出口］	exit
deki-masu	できます	able; can (do)
de-masu	でます［出ます］	leave; depart

demo	でも	but
deNki	でんき［電気］	electricity; light
deNsha	でんしゃ［電車］	train
deNshi reNji	でんし レンジ［電子レンジ］	microwave oven
deNwa	でんわ［電話］	telephone
deNwa baNgō	でんわ ばんごう［電話番号］	telephone
deNwa shi-masu	でんわ します［電話します］	make a phone call
deNwachō	でんわちょう［電話帳］	phone book
depāto	デパート	department store
dēto	デート	date (going out)
dōbutsu	どうぶつ［動物］	animal
dōbutsueN	どうぶつえん［動物園］	zoo
dochira	どちら	where; which
doko	どこ	where
dokoka	どこか	somewhere
dono	どの	which (adjective)
donogurai	どのぐらい	how long; how much (quantity)
dore	どれ	which one
doru	ドル	dollar
dōshite	どうして	why
dōyatte	どうやって	how; in what way
Do-yōbi	どようび［土曜日］	Saturday

E

e	え［絵］	picture
ē	ええ	yes
ebi	えび	shrimp/prawn
ēga	えいが［映画］	movie
ēgakaN	えいがかん［映画館］	movie theater
Ēgo	えいご［英語］	English language

ehagaki	えはがき［絵はがき］	postcard
eki	えき［駅］	station
eN	えん［円］	yen (currency)
eNpitsu	えんぴつ［鉛筆］	pencil
erabi-masu	えらびます［選びます］	choose

F

fubeN(na)	ふべん（な）［不便（な）］	inconvenient
fuka-i	ふかい［深い］	deep
fuku	ふく［服］	clothes
fune	ふね［船］	ship
furu-i	ふるい［古い］	old
fuyu	ふゆ［冬］	winter

G

gakkō	がっこう［学校］	school
gakusē	がくせい［学生］	student
garasu	ガラス	glass
geNki(na)	げんき（な）［元気（な）］	healthy
Getsu-yōbi	げつようび［月曜日］	Monday
giN	ぎん［銀］	silver
giNkō	ぎんこう［銀行］	bank
go	ご［五］	five
Go-gatsu	ごがつ［五月］	May
gogo	ごご［午後］	P.M.; afternoon
gohaN	ごはん［ご飯］	rice (steamed)
gomi	ごみ	trash
gomibako	ごみばこ［ごみ箱］	trash can
goshujiN	ごしゅじん［ご主人］	someone's husband
gozeN	ごぜん［午前］	A.M.
gyūnyū	ぎゅうにゅう［牛乳］	milk

H

ha	は ［歯］	tooth
haburashi	ハブラシ	toothbrush
hachi	はち ［八］	eight
Hachi-gatsu	はちがつ ［八月］	August
hai	はい	yes
hairi-masu	はいります ［入ります］	enter
haisha	はいしゃ ［歯医者］	dentist
hajime	はじめ	first
hajime-masu	はじめます ［始めます］	begin; start
haki-masu	はきます ［吐きます］	vomit
haki-masu	はきます	wear (below waist line)
hako	はこ ［箱］	box
hamigaki	ハミガキ	toothpaste
hana	はな ［花］	flower
hana	はな ［鼻］	nose
hanabi	はなび ［花火］	firework
hanashi	はなし ［話］	story (tale)
hanashi-masu	はなします ［話します］	speak; talk
haNbuN	はんぶん ［半分］	half
harai-masu	はらいます ［払います］	pay
hare	はれ ［晴］	sunny
haru	はる ［春］	spring
hashi	はし ［橋］	bridge
hashi	はし ［箸］	chopsticks
hashiri-masu	はしります ［走ります］	run
hataraki-masu	はたらきます ［働きます］	work (verb)
haya-i	はやい ［早い；速い］	early; quick
hayaku	はやく ［速く］	quickly
heta(na)	へた（な） ［下手（な）］	poor (unskilled)
heya	へや ［部屋］	room

hi	ひ〔火〕	fire (flame; blaze)
hidari	ひだり〔左〕	left (direction)
higashi	ひがし〔東〕	east
hige	ひげ	mustache; beard
hiji	ひじ	elbow
hikōki	ひこうき〔飛行機〕	airplane
hiku-i	ひくい〔低い〕	low
hippari-masu	ひっぱります〔引っぱります〕	pull
hirugohaN	ひるごはん〔昼ご飯〕	lunch
hito	ひと〔人〕	people/person
hitobaNjū	ひとばんじゅう〔一晩中〕	all night
hiza	ひざ〔膝〕	knee
hizuke	ひづけ〔日付〕	date (on a calendar)
hoka(no)	ほか（の）〔他（の）〕	other
hokeN	ほけん〔保険〕	insurance
hōmu	ホーム	platform (station)
hoN	ほん〔本〕	book
hoNtō(ni)	ほんとうに〔本当に〕	really
hoNtō(no)	ほんとう（の）〔本当（の）〕	true; real
hoNya	ほんや〔本屋〕	bookstore
hoshi-i	ほしい〔欲しい〕	want (something)
hotoNdo	ほとんど	almost
hyaku	ひゃく〔百〕	hundred

I

ichi	いち〔一〕	one
ichibaN	いちばん〔一番〕	best
Ichi-gatsu	いちがつ〔一月〕	January
ichinichijū	いちにちじゅう〔一日中〕	all day
ie	いえ〔家〕	house
īe	いいえ	no

Iesu Kirisuto	イエス キリスト	Jesus Christ
Igirisu	イギリス	United Kingdom
IgirisujiN	イギリスじん ［イギリス人］	British people
i-i	いい	all right; good; nice; okay
ijiwaru(na)	いじわる （な）	mean (attitude)
ike	いけ ［池］	pond
iki-masu	いきます ［行きます］	go
ikura	いくら	how much (money)
ikutsu	いくつ	how many; how old (age)
ima	いま ［今］	now
i-masu	います	there is (a person)
ī-masu	いいます ［言います］	say; tell
imi	いみ ［意味］	meaning
imōto	いもうと ［妹］	sister (younger)
inu	いぬ ［犬］	dog
iriguchi	いりぐち ［入口］	entrance
iri-masu	いります	need
iro	いろ ［色］	color
iroiro(na)	いろいろ （な）	various
isha	いしゃ ［医者］	doctor; doctor's office
isogashi-i	いそがしい ［忙しい］	busy
isshoni	いっしょに ［一緒に］	together
isu	いす	chair
ita-i	いたい ［痛い］	painful; hurts
itami	いたみ ［痛み］	pain
itoko	いとこ	cousin
itsu	いつ	when
itsuka	いつか	sometime
itsumo	いつも	always

J

jikaN	じかん［時間］	time; hour
jiko	じこ［事故］	accident
jiNja	じんじゃ［神社］	shrine (Shinto)
jisho	じしょ［辞書］	dictionary
jōshakeN	じょうしゃけん［乗車券］	ticket (for transportation)
jōzu(na)	じょうず（な）［上手（な）］	skillful
jū	じゅう［十］	ten
jū ichi-gatsu	じゅう いちがつ［十一月］	November
jū ni-gatsu	じゅう にがつ［十二月］	December
jū-gatsu	じゅうがつ［十月］	October
jūsho	じゅうしょ［住所］	address

K

kabaN	かばん	bag
kae-masu	かえます	change (verb)
kaeri-masu	かえります［帰ります］	go home
kaeshi-masu	かえします［返します］	return
kagami	かがみ［鏡］	mirror
kagi	かぎ［鍵］	lock; key
kaidaN	かいだん［階段］	stairs
kaigi	かいぎ［会議］	meeting; conference
kai-masu	かいます［買います］	buy
kaimono	かいもの［買い物］	shopping
kaisha	かいしゃ［会社］	company
kaishaiN	かいしゃいん［会社員］	company employee
kaiwa	かいわ［会話］	conversation
kaji	かじ［火事］	fire (a fire; on fire)
kami	かみ［紙］	paper
Kamisama	かみさま［神様］	God
KanadajiN	カナダじん［カナダ人］	Canadian people

kanai	かない ［家内］	my wife
kanashi-i	かなしい ［悲しい］	sad
kaNgae	かんがえ ［考え］	idea
kaNgae-masu	かんがえます ［考えます］	think (contemplate)
kaNgofu	かんごふ ［看護婦］	nurse
kaNji-masu	かんじます ［感じます］	feel
kaNkō	かんこう ［観光］	sightseeing
KaNkoku	かんこく ［韓国］	Korea
kanojo	かのじょ ［彼女］	she
kao	かお ［顔］	face
- kara	～から	since -; from -
karada	からだ ［体］	body
kara-i	からい ［辛い］	spicy; hot (taste)
kare	かれ ［彼］	he
karera	かれら	they
karu-i	かるい ［軽い］	light (weight)
kata	かた ［肩］	shoulder
kata-i	かたい ［堅い］	hard; stiff
kawa	かわ ［川］	river
kawakashi-masu	かわかします ［乾かします］	dry (verb)
Ka-yōbi	かようび ［火曜日］	Tuesday
kayu-i	かゆい	itchy
kaze	かぜ ［風邪］	cold (illness)
kaze	かぜ ［風］	wind
kazoe-masu	かぞえます ［数えます］	count
kazoku	かぞく ［家族］	family
kega	けが	injury
kēkaN	けいかん ［警官］	police officer
kēki	ケーキ	cake
kekkoN	けっこん ［結婚］	marriage
kekkoNshiki	けっこんしき ［結婚式］	wedding (ceremony)
keNkō hokeN	けんこう ほけん ［健康保険］	health insurance

keNkō(na)	けんこう（な）［健康（な）］	healthy
kēsatsu	けいさつ［警察］	police
kēsatsusho	けいさつしょ［警察署］	police station
kētai (deNwa)	けいたい（でんわ） ［携帯（電話）］	cellular phone
ki	き［木］	tree
kiki-masu	ききます［聞きます］	listen; ask
kikoe-masu	きこえます［聞こえます］	hear
ki-masu	きます［来ます］	come
ki-masu	きます［着ます］	wear (above waist line)
kime-masu	きめます［決めます］	decide
kinō	きのう［昨日］	yesterday
kiN	きん［金］	gold
kiNeN	きんえん［禁煙］	no smoking
KiN-yōbi	きんようび［金曜日］	Friday
kippu	きっぷ［切符］	ticket (for transportation)
kirai(na)	きらい（な）［嫌い（な）］	dislike
kirē(na)	きれい（な）	clean; pretty
kiri-masu	きります［切ります］	cut
Kirisuto	キリスト	Jesus Christ
Kirisutokyō	キリストきょう［キリスト教］	Christianity
kīro-i	きいろい［黄色い］	yellow
kisetsu	きせつ［季節］	season
kissateN	きっさてん［喫茶店］	coffee shop
kita	きた［北］	north
kitana-i	きたない［汚い］	dirty
kitte	きって［切手］	stamp
kōcha	こうちゃ［紅茶］	tea (British)
kodomo	こども［子供］	child
koe	こえ［声］	voice
kōeN	こうえん［公園］	park
kōhī	コーヒー	coffee

koko	ここ	here
kōkō	こうこう［高校］	high school
kokoro	こころ［心］	mind
kokusai meNkyoshō	こくさい めんきょしょう ［国際免許証］	international driver's license
koNbini	コンビニ	convenience store
koNgetsu	こんげつ［今月］	this month
kono	この	this (adjective)
koNshū	こんしゅう［今週］	this week
koNya	こんや［今夜］	tonight
kore	これ	this one
kōri	こおり［氷］	ice
kōsateN	こうさてん［交差点］	intersection
koshi	こし［腰］	waist
koshō	こしょう	pepper
koshō shi-te i-masu	こしょう しています ［故障しています］	broken (machine, etc.)
koshōchū	こしょうちゅう［故障中］	out of order
kōshū deNwa	こうしゅう でんわ［公衆電話］	public telephone
kotae-masu	こたえます［答えます］	answer (verb)
koto	こと［事］	thing (intangible)
kotoba	ことば［言葉］	language; word
kotoshi	ことし［今年］	this year
kowa-i	こわい［怖い］	afraid; scary
koware-te i-masu	こわれて います［壊れています］	broken (machine, etc.)
kowashi-masu	こわします［壊します］	break (destroy)
ku	く［九］	nine
kubi	くび［首］	neck
kuchi	くち［口］	mouth
kuchibiru	くちびる［唇］	lip
Ku-gatsu	くがつ［九月］	September
kūkō	くうこう［空港］	airport

kumori	くもり［曇］	cloudy
kuni	くに［国］	country
kura-i	くらい［暗い］	dark
KurisuchaN	クリスチャン	Christian
kuro-i	くろい［黒い］	black
kuruma	くるま［車］	car
kusa-i	くさい［臭い］	smelly
kusuri	くすり［薬］	medicine
kusuri-o nomi-masu	くすりを のみます ［薬を飲みます］	take medicine
kusuriya	くすりや［薬屋］	drugstore; pharmacy
kutsu	くつ［靴］	shoe
kutsushita	くつした［靴下］	socks
kyō	きょう［今日］	today
kyōdai	きょうだい	sibling
kyōju	きょうじゅ［教授］	professor
kyōkai	きょうかい［教会］	church
kyoneN	きょねん［去年］	last year
kyōshi	きょうし［教師］	teacher
kyū	きゅう［九］	nine
kyūkyūsha	きゅうきゅうしゃ［救急車］	ambulance

M

machi	まち［町 *or* 街］	city
machigae-masu	まちがえます［間違えます］	mistake
machigat-te i-masu	まちがって います ［間違っています］	wrong
machi-masu	まちます［待ちます］	wait
mada	まだ	not yet; still
- made	〜まで	until -
- madeni	〜までに	by - (time)
mado	まど［窓］	window

mae	まえ［前］	ago; before; front
magari-masu	まがります［曲がります］	turn
mage-masu	まげます［曲げます］	bend
mago	まご［孫］	grandchild; grandson
Mahometto	マホメット	Muhammad
makura	まくら［枕］	pillow
māmā	まあまあ	so-so
maNnaka	まんなか［真ん中］	center; middle
massugu	まっすぐ	straight
matsuri	まつり［祭］	festival
mawari	まわり	around
mazu-i	まずい	unappetizing
me	め［目］	eye
mei	めい［姪］	niece
meNkyoshō	めんきょしょう［免許証］	driver's license
meNzēhiN	めんぜいひん［免税品］	duty-free merchandise
mēshi	めいし［名刺］	business card
michi	みち［道］	road
midori	みどり［緑］	green
migi	みぎ［右］	right (direction)
mijika-i	みじかい［短い］	short
mi-masu	みます［見ます］	look; see; watch
mimi	みみ［耳］	ear
minami	みなみ［南］	south
miNna	みんな	everybody
mise	みせ［店］	shop (store)
mise-masu	みせます［見せます］	show (verb)
mitsuke-masu	みつけます	find
mizu	みず［水］	water
mizūmi	みずうみ［湖］	lake
mō	もう	already
mō ichido	もういちど［もう一度］	again

mochiroN	もちろん	of course
mōfu	もうふ［毛布］	blanket
Moku-yōbi	もくようび［木曜日］	Thursday
moNdai	もんだい［問題］	problem; trouble
mono	もの［物］	thing (tangible)
morai-masu	もらいます	receive; get; obtain
mori	もり［森］	forest
mot-te i-masu	もっています［持っています］	have; possess
mot-te iki-masu	もっていきます ［持っていきます］	take (something) somewhere
mot-te ki-masu	もってきます［持ってきます］	bring (thing)
mukō	むこう［向こう］	across
mushiatsu-i	むしあつい［むし暑い］	humid
musuko	むすこ［息子］	son
musume	むすめ［娘］	daughter
muzukashi-i	むずかしい	difficult; hard

N

naga-i	ながい［長い］	long
naka	なか［中］	inside
naki-masu	なきます［泣きます］	cry
nakushi-masu	なくします	lose
namae	なまえ［名前］	name
nana	なな［七］	seven
nanika	なにか	something
naNsai	なんさい［何歳］	how old (age)
naoshi-masu	なおします［直します］	fix; repair
narai-masu	ならいます［習います］	learn
nari-masu	なります	become
natsu	なつ［夏］	summer
nedaN	ねだん［値段］	price

neko	ねこ［猫］	cat
ne-masu	ねます［寝ます］	sleep
nemu-i	ねむい［眠い］	sleepy
neN	ねん［年］	year
neNrē	ねんれい［年齢］	age
ni	に［二］	two
- ni	〜に	to -
Nichi-yōbi	にちようび［日曜日］	Sunday
Ni-gatsu	にがつ［二月］	February
NihoN	にほん［日本］	Japan
NihoNgo	にほんご［日本語］	Japanese language
NihoNjiN	にほんじん［日本人］	Japanese people
niku	にく［肉］	meat
nimotsu	にもつ［荷物］	luggage
nioi	におい［匂い］	smell
NippoN	にっぽん［日本］	Japan
nishi	にし［西］	west
- no aida	〜の あいだ［〜の間］	during -
- no nakade	〜のなかで［〜の中で］	among -
- no tameni	〜の ために	for the sake of -
nobori-masu	のぼります［登ります］	climb
nodo	のど	throat
nokoshi-masu	のこします［残します］	leave (something)
nomi-masu	のみます［飲みます］	drink
nomimono	のみもの［飲み物］	beverage
nori-masu	のります［乗ります］	ride; get on (vehicle)
norikae-masu	のりかえます［乗り換えます］	transfer (train, bus)
nōto	ノート	notebook
nōto pasokoN	ノート パソコン	laptop computer
nugi-masu	ぬぎます［脱ぎます］	take off (clothes)
nyūiN	にゅういん［入院］	hospitalization

obasaN	おばさん	aunt
obāsaN	おばあさん	grandmother
oboe-masu	おぼえます ［覚えます］	remember (memorize)
ocha	おちゃ ［お茶］	tea (Japanese)
odori-masu	おどります ［踊ります］	dance (verb)
ofuro	おふろ ［お風呂］	bath (tub)
ohashi	おはし ［お箸］	chopsticks
oi	おい ［甥］	nephew
oishi-i	おいしい	delicious
ojisaN	おじさん	uncle
ojīsaN	おじいさん	grandfather
okane	おかね ［お金］	money
okanemochi(no)	おかねもち（の）［お金持ち（の）］	rich
okane-o tsukai-masu	おかねを つかいます ［お金を使います］	spend (money)
okāsaN	おかあさん ［お母さん］	mother
ōki-i	おおきい ［大きい］	big
oki-masu	おきます ［置きます］	put; place
oki-masu	おきます ［起きます］	wake up
okuri-masu	おくります ［送ります］	send; ship
okusaN	おくさん ［奥さん］	someone's wife
omawarisaN	おまわりさん	police officer
ōmisoka	おおみそか ［大みそか］	New Year's Eve
omiyage	おみやげ	souvenir
omo-i	おもい ［重い］	heavy
omoidashi-masu	おもいだします ［思い出します］	remember (recall)
omoi-masu	おもいます ［思います］	think (suppose)
omoshiro-i	おもしろい	interesting
onaji	おなじ ［同じ］	same

onēsaN	おねえさん ［お姉さん］	sister (older)
onīsaN	おにいさん ［お兄さん］	brother (older)
oNgaku	おんがく ［音楽］	music
oNna	おんな ［女］	woman
oNna-no hito	おんなの ひと ［女の人］	woman
oNnanoko	おんなのこ ［女の子］	girl
ori-masu	おります ［降ります］	get off (vehicle)
osara	おさら ［お皿］	plate
oshie-masu	おしえます ［教えます］	teach
oshi-masu	おします ［押します］	push
oshiri	おしり ［お尻］	buttocks
oso-i	おそい ［遅い］	late
osu	おす ［お酢］	vinegar
otearai	おてあらい ［お手洗い］	bathroom (toilet)
otera	おてら ［お寺］	temple (Buddhist)
oto	おと ［音］	sound
otoko	おとこ ［男］	man
otoko-no hito	おとこの ひと ［男の人］	man
otokonoko	おとこのこ ［男の子］	boy
otona	おとな ［大人］	adult
otōsaN	おとうさん ［お父さん］	father
otoshi-masu	おとします ［落とします］	drop
otoshimono	おとしもの ［落とし物］	lost article
otōto	おとうと ［弟］	brother (younger)
otsuri	おつり ［お釣り］	change (money)
otto	おっと ［夫］	my husband
owarase-masu	おわらせます ［終わらせます］	finish
oya	おや ［親］	parent
oyogi-masu	およぎます ［泳ぎます］	swim
oyu	おゆ ［お湯］	hot water

P

patokā	パトカー	police car
paN	パン	bread

R

raigetsu	らいげつ［来月］	next month
raineN	らいねん［来年］	next year
raishū	らいしゅう［来週］	next week
rajio	ラジオ	radio
rei	れい［零］	zero
reNji	レンジ	stove (for cooking)
reNshū	れんしゅう［練習］	practice
resutoraN	レストラン	restaurant
rētōko	れいとうこ［冷凍庫］	freezer
rēzōko	れいぞうこ［冷蔵庫］	refrigerator
roku	ろく［六］	six
Roku-gatsu	ろくがつ［六月］	June
ryōgae	りょうがえ［両替］	exchange (money)
ryōjikaN	りょうじかん［領事館］	consulate
ryokaN	りょかん［旅館］	inn (Japanese style)
ryokō	りょこう［旅行］	travel/trip
ryōri	りょうり［料理］	cooking
ryōriteN	りょうりてん［料理店］	restaurant (Asian)
ryōriya	りょうりや［料理屋］	restaurant (Asian)
ryōshiN	りょうしん［両親］	parents
ryōshūsho	りょうしゅうしょ［領収書］	receipt
ryūgaku	りゅうがく［留学］	study abroad

S

sabishi-i	さびしい［寂しい］	lonely
sagashi-masu	さがします［探します］	look for; search

saifu	さいふ［財布］	wallet
saigo	さいご［最後］	last
sakana	さかな［魚］	fish
sake	さけ［酒］	liquor
saki	さき［先］	ahead
samu-i	さむい［寒い］	cold
saN	さん［三］	three
SaN-gatsu	さんがつ［三月］	March
satō	さとう［砂糖］	sugar
se-ga hiku-i	せがひくい［背が低い］	short (person's height)
se-ga taka-i	せがたかい［背が高い］	tall (person's height)
seki	せき［席］	seat
sekkeN	せっけん	soap
sēkyūsho	せいきゅうしょ［請求書］	bill (invoice)
senaka	せなか［背中］	back (body part)
sēneNgappi	せいねんがっぴ［生年月日］	birth date
sēri	せいり［生理］	period; menstruation
sēri yōhiN	せいり ようひん［生理用品］	sanitary product (for women)
seN	せん［千］	thousand
seNgetsu	せんげつ［先月］	last month
seNkyōshi	せんきょうし［宣教師］	missionary
seNsē	せんせい［先生］	teacher
seNshū	せんしゅう［先週］	last week
seNtaku	せんたく［洗濯］	laundry
seNtakuki	せんたくき［洗濯機］	washing machine
shachō	しゃちょう［社長］	president (company)
shashiN	しゃしん［写真］	photograph
shashiN-o tori-masu	しゃしんを とります ［写真を撮ります］	take a picture
shawā-o abi-masu	シャワーを あびます	take a shower
shi	し［四］	four
shichi	しち［七］	seven

Shichi-gatsu	しちがつ［七月］	July
Shi-gatsu	しがつ［四月］	April
shigoto	しごと［仕事］	work (noun); job; business
shigoto-o shi-masu	しごとをします［仕事をします］	work (verb)
shikeN	しけん［試験］	exam
shi-masu	します	do; play (sports)
shimē	しめい［氏名］	name
shime-masu	しめます［閉めます］	close
shini-masu	しにます［死にます］	die
shiNbun	しんぶん［新聞］	newspaper
shiNgō	しんごう［信号］	traffic signal
ShiNkaNseN	しんかんせん［新幹線］	Bullet Train
shiNsetsu(na)	しんせつ（な）［親切（な）］	kind; gentle
ShiNtō	しんとう［神道］	Shintoism
shio	しお［塩］	salt
shiokara-i	しおからい［塩辛い］	salty
shiro-i	しろい［白い］	white
shita	した［舌］	tongue
shita	した［下］	under; down
shitagi	したぎ［下着］	underwear
shitsumoN	しつもん［質問］	question
shitte i-masu	しっています［知っています］	know
shizuka(na)	しずか（な）［静か（な）］	quiet
shōgakkō	しょうがっこう［小学校］	elementary school
Shōgatsu	しょうがつ［正月］	New Year
shōhizē	しょうひぜい［消費税］	sales tax
shokuji	しょくじ［食事］	dining; meal
shōyu	しょうゆ	soy sauce
shū	しゅう［州］	state; province
shū	しゅう［週］	week
shucchō	しゅっちょう［出張］	business trip
shufu	しゅふ［主婦］	homemaker

shujiN	しゅじん ［主人］	my husband
shumi	しゅみ ［趣味］	hobby
sōji shi-masu	そうじ します ［掃除 します］	clean up (verb)
soko	そこ	there (near listener)
sono	その	that (adjective; near the listener)
sora	そら ［空］	sky
sore	それ	that one (near the listener)
soto	そと ［外］	outside
Sui-yōbi	すいようび ［水曜日］	Wednesday
suki-desu	すきです ［好きです］	like
sukoshi	すこし ［少し］	few; little (amount)
sumi-masu	すみます ［住みます］	live (reside)
sūpā	スーパー	supermarket
suppa-i	すっぱい	sour
sushiya	すしや ［寿司屋］	sushi bar
sute-masu	すてます ［捨てます］	throw away
suwari-masu	すわります ［座ります］	sit
suzushi-i	すずしい ［涼しい］	cool

T

tabako	タバコ	cigarette
tabako-o sui-masu	タバコを すいます	smoke
tabe-masu	たべます ［食べます］	eat
tabemono	たべもの ［食べ物］	food
tachi-masu	たちます ［立ちます］	stand (up)
tada	ただ	free (of charge)
tadashi-i	ただしい ［正しい］	right (correct)
taifū	たいふう ［台風］	typhoon
taikutsu(na)	たいくつ（な）［退屈（な）］	boring
taisetsu(na)	たいせつ（な）［大切（な）］	important

taishikaN	たいしかん〔大使館〕	embassy
taiyō	たいよう〔太陽〕	sun
taka-i	たかい〔高い〕	tall; high; expensive
takusaN	たくさん	many; plenty
takushī noriba	タクシー のりば〔タクシー乗り場〕	taxi stand
tamago	たまご〔卵 *or* 玉子〕	egg
taNgo	たんご〔単語〕	word
taNjōbi	たんじょうび〔誕生日〕	birthday
tanomi-masu	たのみます〔頼みます〕	request
tanoshi-i	たのしい〔楽しい〕	enjoyable; fun
tanoshimi-masu	たのしみます〔楽しみます〕	enjoy
tasuke-masu	たすけます〔助けます〕	rescue; help
tate-masu	たてます〔建てます〕	build
tazune-masu	たずねます〔訪ねます〕	visit
te	て〔手〕	hand
teNki	てんき〔天気〕	weather
terebi	テレビ	television
tetsudai-masu	てつだいます〔手伝います〕	assist
- to	〜と	with - (person)
- to - no aida	〜と〜の あいだ〔〜と〜の間〕	between - and -
tō-i	とおい〔遠い〕	far away
toire	トイレ	bathroom (toilet)
tokē	とけい〔時計〕	clock; watch
tokoro	ところ〔所〕	place
tokoya	とこや〔床屋〕	barber shop
tomari-masu	とまります〔泊まります〕	stay (overnight)
tome-masu	とめます〔止めます〕	stop (halt)
tomodachi	ともだち〔友達〕	friend
tonari	となり〔隣〕	next door
tori	とり〔鳥〕	bird
tōri	とおり〔通り〕	street

tori-masu	とります［取ります］	remove; take (obtain)
tōri-masu	とおります［通ります］	pass (through)
torikae-masu	とりかえます［取り換えます］	replace
toshi	とし［年］	age; year
toshi-o totta	としをとった［年をとった］	old (age)
toshokaN	としょかん［図書館］	library
tot-te oki-masu	とっておきます	keep
tsugi	つぎ［次］	next
tsui-te iki-masu	ついていきます	follow (someone)
tsukai-masu	つかいます［使います］	use
tsukare-masu	つかれます［疲れます］	tired
tsuki	つき［月］	month; moon
tsuki-masu	つきます［着きます］	arrive
tsukue	つくえ［机］	desk
tsukuri-masu	つくります［作ります］	make
tsuma	つま［妻］	my wife
tsure-te iki-masu	つれていきます ［連れていきます］	take (a person) to somewhere
tsure-te ki-masu	つれてきます［連れてきます］	bring (person)
tsutome-te i-masu	つとめています［勤めています］	employed
tsuyo-i	つよい［強い］	strong
tsuzuke-masu	つづけます［続けます］	continue

U

uchi	うち［家］	home; house
ude	うで［腕］	arm
ue	うえ［上］	above; up; top
ugoki-masu	うごきます［動きます］	move; function
uketsuke	うけつけ［受付］	receptionist
umare-masu	うまれます［生まれます］	born
umi	うみ［海］	sea
umi-masu	うみます［産みます］	give birth

uNteN shi-masu	うんてん します ［運転します］	drive
ureshi-i	うれしい	happy
uri-masu	うります ［売ります］	sell
urusa-i	うるさい	noisy
ushiro	うしろ ［後ろ］	back; behind
usu-i	うすい ［薄い］	thin
uta	うた ［歌］	song
utai-masu	うたいます ［歌います］	sing
utsukushi-i	うつくしい ［美しい］	beautiful

W

waka-i	わかい ［若い］	young
wakari-masu	わかります	understand
warai-masu	わらいます ［笑います］	laugh
ware-te i-masu	われて います ［割れています］	broken (plate, etc.)
waru-i	わるい ［悪い］	bad
wasure-masu	わすれます ［忘れます］	forget
watashi	わたし ［私］	I
watashitachi	わたしたち ［私達］	we

X–Y

yaki-masu	やきます ［焼きます］	bake
yakusoku	やくそく ［約束］	appointment; promise
yama	やま ［山］	mountain
yame-masu	やめます	stop (quit)
yari-masu	やります	do; play (sports)
yasai	やさい ［野菜］	vegetable
yasu-i	やすい ［安い］	cheap
yasumi	やすみ ［休み］	absence; day off
yasumi-masu	やすみます ［休みます］	rest (relax); absent
yawaraka-i	やわらかい ［柔らかい］	soft

yobi-masu	よびます ［呼びます］	call (to address); invite
yōchieN	ようちえん ［幼稚園］	kindergarten
yogore-te i-masu	よごれて います ［汚れています］	messy
yōji	ようじ ［用事］	errand
yoko	よこ ［横］	side
yomi-masu	よみます ［読みます］	read
yoN	よん ［四］	four
- yori	〜より	than -
yoru	よる ［夜］	night
yowa-i	よわい ［弱い］	weak
yoyaku	よやく ［予約］	reservation
yubi	ゆび ［指］	finger
yubiwa	ゆびわ ［指輪］	ring
yūbiN	ゆうびん ［郵便］	letter; mail
yūbiN baNgō	ゆうびん ばんごう ［郵便番号］	zip code
yūbiN uke	ゆうびん うけ ［郵便受け］	mailbox
yūbiNkyoku	ゆうびんきょく ［郵便局］	post office
yuki	ゆき ［雪］	snow (noun)
yuki-ga furi-masu	ゆきが ふります ［雪が降ります］	snow (verb)
yūshoku	ゆうしょく ［夕食］	dinner

Z

zēkaN	ぜいかん ［税関］	Customs (office)
zeNbu	ぜんぶ ［全部］	all; everything
zero	ゼロ	zero

Index

Numbers

1-10 numbers, 79
10,000 and beyond numbers, 84-85
10-99 numbers, 80-81
100-9,999 numbers, 81-83

A

accounts, opening bank accounts, 209-212
activity planning
  destinations, 261
  exercises, 268-269
  guided tours, 262
  transportation, 262
  travel schedules, 263-265
  weather and climate, 265-268
adjectives
  adjective predicates
    conjugation, 50-53
    TE-form conjugation, 66
  defining characteristics, 36
  describers, 68-69
  pointing, 107-108
  shopping-related, 225-226
ages, 122-123
airport expressions
  baggage claim, 168-169
  Customs, 170-174
  immigration booths, 163-168
"also" (-mo), 37
apology expressions, 95-96
archipelago country, 12
articulating sounds, 18
asking questions
  exercises, 74
  frequently used words, 74
  introductions, 103-104
  ka, 72-73
  wh-questions, 73-74
"at" (-de), 38

B

background information
  marital status, 114
  occupations, 114-116
  personal information expressions, 113
  residence, 113
baggage claim expressions, 168-169
banking
  bills and coins, 204-207
  currency exchange, 207-209
  opening accounts, 209-212
  signs and symbols, 321
"bathroom" (ofuro), 253-255
bedtime expressions, 255-257
body-part words, 285-286
bookstores (signs and symbols), 322
bowing, 101
buffer expressions, 94
Bullet Trains, 328
bus stand signs, 326
"by means of" (-de), 38

C

calendar expressions
  dates, 191-192
  days of the week, 193
  months, 192

cashiers (signs and symbols), 324

checking in/out of hotels, 196-198

cigarette shops (signs and symbols), 323

climate and weather expressions, 265-268

clothing, 254

coffee shops, signs and symbols, 323

coin locker signs, 319

coins, 204-207

communication principles, 14-16

"company" (*kaisha*), 105

comparative questions, 236-238

complaint expressions
  hotels, 305-309
  restaurants, 309-311
  shopping, 311-313

conjugations
  adjective predicates, 50-53
  exercises, 56-58
  nouns, 53-56
  overview, 45-46
  TE-form, 59-67
    adjective predicates, 66
    noun predicates, 64-65
    verbs, 60-63
  verb predicates, 46-50

consonants
  defining characteristics, 17

pronunciation
  double consonants, 22-23
  overview, 19-21
  standalone consonants, 21-23
  tricky sounds, 21-23
syllabication, 18-19

counters
  numbers, 85-87
  shopping, 220-223

counting
  ages, 122-123
  days, 164-165
  numbers, 79-85
  people, 121-122

cuisines, 233

culture (Japanese), 13-14

currency exchange, 207-209, 321

Customs-related expressions, 170-174

D

-*de* ("by means of"; "at"), 38

dates
  calendar expressions, 191-192
  check-in-/-out dates (hotels), 191-194
  days of the week, 193
  months, 192

days
  counting, 164-165
  days of the week, 193

declining invitations, 133-135

department store floor plans, 224

describers
  adjectives, 68-69
  na-adjectives, 70-71
  nouns, 69

descriptive words, 68

destinations
  activity planning, 261
  asking for directions, 300-302
  extending invitations, 128-130
  transportation expressions, 183-184

dining out expressions, 92-93
  comparative questions, 236-238
  complaints, 309-311
  cuisines, 233-235
  etiquette, 241-243
  exercises, 246-247
  food words, 237
  menus, 238-239
  ordering, 238-241
  paying, 244-245
  taste words, 243-244

direct objects and sentence structure, 33

directions
  asking for, 300-302
  direction words, 182-183

diseases, 290

Do Not Enter! signs, 318

dochira ("where"), 105

doctors
office visits, 284-285
requests, 288-289
double consonants, 22-23
driving tips, 185-187
duration, time expressions, 158-160

E

eating. *See* dining out expressions
emergencies
exit signs, 316
nonmedical emergencies
reporting lost items, 295-297
safety facts, 293-294
thefts, 297-300
numbers, 284
endings (verb stems), 61-63
entering houses, 250-251
entrance signs, 316
etiquette (dining out), 241-243
excuse me expressions, 96-97
exercises
activity planning, 268-269
asking questions, 74
conjugations, 56-58
dining out, 246-247
in-flight expressions, 149-151
numbers, 87

personal information expressions, 123-125
shopping-related expressions, 229-230
telephone expressions, 282
exit signs, 316
expressions
activity planning
destinations, 261
exercises, 268-269
guided tours, 262
transportation, 262
travel schedules, 263-265
weather and climate, 265-268
apologies, 95-96
buffer expressions, 94
complaints
hotels, 305-309
restaurants, 309-311
shopping, 311-313
dining out
comparative questions, 236-238
cuisines, 233
etiquette, 241-243
exercises, 246-247
food words, 237
like/dislike expressions, 234-235
menus, 238-239
ordering, 238-241
paying, 244-245
taste words, 243-244
excuse me, 96-97

fixed expressions
apologies, 95-96
excuse me, 96-97
giving and receiving, 98-99
greetings, 91-97
making requests, 98
overview, 91
survival phrases, 99-100
giving and receiving, 98-99
greetings, 91-97
dining, 92-93
good-bye, 97
leaving and coming home, 93-94
nighttime, 94
thank you, 94-95
health-related, 283-292
body-part words, 285-286
diseases, 290
doctor requests, 288-289
medical departments, 289
office visits, 284-285
pharmacy, 290-292
symptoms, 286-288
house-related, 249-259
bathroom, 253-255
bedtime, 255-257
entering, 250-251
family room, 252-253
household items, 257-259

introductions, 101-108
  asking questions,
    103-104
  occupations, 104-105
  party greetings,
    106-108
  residence, 105-106
  watashi-wa XYZ-*desu*
    pattern, 102-103
  X-*wa* Y-*desu* pattern,
    102
invitations
  declining, 133-135
  extending, 127-133
  promoting, 135-137
making requests, 98
personal information
  expressions
    background
      information, 113-116
    exercises, 123-125
    family-related topics,
      119-123
    hobbies, 117-119
    traveling, 111-113
  survival phrases, 99-100
telephones, 273-282
  calling home, 275-277
  exercises, 282
  important numbers,
    281-282
  sample dialogue,
    277-281
time expressions, 153-162
  duration, 158-160
  -*kara* and -*made*
    ("from" and "until"),
    157-158

travel-related
  airports, 163-174
  banking, 204-212
  hotels, 189-200
  in-flight expressions,
    141-151
  shopping, 217-230
  transportation, 175-187
extending invitations
  common destinations,
    128-130
  -*maseN ka* pattern,
    127-130
  -*mashō* pattern, 130-132
  -*mashō ka* pattern,
    132-133

F

"family room" (*ima*), 252-253
family-related expressions
  ages, 122-123
  counting people, 121-122
  family members, 119-120
Five Golden Rules, 3-7
fixed expressions
  apologies, 95-96
  excuse me, 96-97
  giving and receiving,
    98-99
  greetings, 91-97
    dining, 92-93
    good-bye, 97
    leaving and coming
      home, 93-94
    nighttime, 94
    thank you, 94-95

making requests, 98
overview, 91
survival phrases, 99-100
flying (in-flight expressions)
  exercises, 149-151
  making requests, 141-149
foods, 237
"from" (-*kara*), 38, 157-158

G

-*ga* (subject marker), 35-36
geNkaN, 250
geographic facts (Japan),
  11-12
giving and receiving
  expressions, 98-99
good-bye expressions, 97
grammar tips
  asking questions
    exercises, 74
    frequently used words,
      74
    ka, 72-73
    wh-questions, 73-74
  conjugations, *TE*-form,
    59-67
  describers
    adjectives, 68-69
    na-adjectives, 70-71
    nouns, 69
  descriptive words, 68
  sentence structure, 32-33
greetings, 91
  dining, 92-93
  good-bye, 97

leaving and coming
    home, 93-94
nighttime, 94
parties, 106-108
thank you, 94-95
guided tours, 262

H

health-related expressions,
    283-292
    body-part words, 285-286
    diseases, 290
    doctor requests, 288-289
    medical departments, 289
    office visits, 284-285
    pharmacy, 290-292
    symptoms, 286-288
hobbies, 117-119
home delivery express
    (*takuhaibiN*), 168
homogeneous, 13
hotels
    checking in/out, 196-198
    complaints, 305-309
    reservations, 189-195
        check-in/-out dates,
            191-194
        choosing, 190-191
        room preferences,
            194-195
houses, 249-259
    bathroom, 253-255
    bedtime expressions,
        255-257
    entering, 250-251

family room, 252-253
household items, 257-259
nihoNma (Japanese-style
    room), 251

I

ima ("family room"), 252-253
immigration booths (airport
    expressions), 163-168
"in" (-*ni*), 37
in-flight expressions
    exercises, 149-151
    making requests, 141-148
        politeness, 148-149
        TE-form, 143-145
        XYZ-*ni Shi-masu*,
            142-143
indirect objects (sentence
    structure), 33
intonation patterns, 26-27
introductions, 101-108
    asking questions, 103-104
    occupations, 104-105
    party greetings, 106-108
    residence, 105-106
    watashi-wa XYZ-*desu*
        pattern, 102-103
    X-*wa* Y-*desu* pattern, 102
invitations
    declining, 133-135
    extending, 127
        common destinations,
            128-130
        -*maseN ka* pattern,
            127-130

-*mashō* pattern,
    130-132
-*mashō ka* pattern,
    132-133
promoting, 135-137

J

Japan
    communication
        principles, 14-16
    culture and society, 13-14
    geographic facts, 11-12
    population facts, 12-13
Japanese-style room
    (*nihoNma*), 251
jobs
    introductions expressions,
        104-105
    personal information
        expressions, 114-116

K

-*kara* ("from"), 38, 157-158
ka, 72-73
kaisha (company), 105
kanji, 12

L

learning tips, 4-9
    book usage guidelines,
        7-8
    Five Golden Rules, 3-7
    reasons to learn Japanese,
        8-9

like/dislike expressions (dining out), 234-235

loanwords, 24-26

long vowels, 24

lost items, reporting, 295-297

M

-*made* ("until"), 38, 157-158

-*maseN ka* pattern (invitations), 127-130

-*mashō* pattern (invitations), 130-132

-*mashō ka* pattern, 132-133

-*mo* ("also"), 37

making requests (in-flight expressions), 141-151

    exercises, 149-151

    politeness, 148-149

    TE-form, 143-145

    XYZ-*ni Shi-masu*, 142-143

marital status, personal information expressions, 114

medical conditions, 290

medical departments, 289

medical supplies, 291

medications, 291

menus, 238-239

money

    bills and coins, 204-207

    currency exchange, 207-209

    opening bank accounts, 209-212

months, calendar expressions, 192

N

-*ni* ("toward"; "in"), 37

na-adjectives, 70-71

namae ("name"), 103

names, exchanging (introductions), 101-104

    asking questions, 103-104

    watashi-wa XYZ-*desu* pattern, 102-103

    X-*wa* Y-*desu* pattern, 102

nighttime greetings, 94

nihoNma (Japanese-style room), 251

nonmedical emergencies

    reporting lost items, 295-297

    safety facts, 293-294

    thefts, 297-300

noun predicates, *TE*-form conjugation, 64-65

nouns

    conjugations, 53-56

    describers

        adjectives, 68-69

        na-adjectives, 70-71

        nouns, 69

numbers

    1-10, 79

    10,000 and beyond, 84-85

    10-99, 80-81

    100-9,999, 81-83

    counters, 85-87

    emergency numbers, 284

    exercises, 87

    important telephone numbers, 281-282

O

-*o* (object marker), 36

object markers (-*o*), 36

occupations

    introduction expressions, 104-105

    personal information expressions, 114-116

ofuro ("bathroom"), 200, 253-255

oNseN, 200

ordering at restaurants, 238-241

P

particles

    -*de* ("by means of"; "at"), 38

    -*ga* (subject marker), 35-36

    -*kara* ("from"), 38

    -*made* ("until"), 38

    -*mo* ("also"), 37

    -*ni* ("toward"; "in"), 37

    -*o* (object marker), 36

    -*to* ("together with"), 38-40

    -*wa* (topic), 40-41

    sentence structure, 33-34

party greetings, 106-108

paying at restaurants, 244-245

peace and harmony principles (communication), 14-16

people, counting, 121-122

personal information
expressions
   background information
      marital status, 114
      occupations, 114-116
      residence, 113
   exercises, 123-125
   family-related topics
      ages, 122-123
      counting people,
         121-122
      family members,
         119-120
   hobbies, 117-119
   traveling, 111-113
pharmacies
   expressions, 290-292
   signs and symbols, 320
pointing adjectives, 107-108
pointing words, 107, 223-225
police
   reporting lost items,
      295-297
   reporting thefts, 297-300
   safety facts, 293-294
police station signs, 319-320
polite requests, 148-149
post office, signs and
   symbols, 322
predicates
   adjective predicate
      conjugation, 50-53, 66
   noun predicate conjuga-
      tion, 53-56, 64-65
   sentence structure, 32-33
   verb predicate
      conjugation, 46-50
prepositions, 33

promoting invitations,
   135-137
pronunciation
   consonants
      double consonants,
         22-23
      overview, 19-21
      standalone consonants,
         21-23
      tricky sounds, 21-23
   intonation patterns, 26-27
   loanwords, 24-26
   syllabication, 18-19
   vowels
      long vowels, 24
      overview, 19-21
pull signs, 317
push signs, 317

Q

questions
   asking
      exercises, 74
      frequently used words,
         74
      introductions, 103-104
      ka, 72-73
      wh-questions, 73-74
   comparative, 236-238

R

reasons to learn Japanese,
   8-9
requests
   doctors, 288-289
   making, 98, 141-151

reservations (hotels), 189-195
   check-in/-out dates,
      191-194
   choosing, 190-191
   room preferences, 194-195
residence
   introduction expressions,
      105-106
   personal information
      expressions, 113
restaurants (dining out)
   comparative questions,
      236-238
   complaints, 309-311
   cuisines, 233
   etiquette, 241-243
   food words, 237
   like/dislike expressions,
      234-235
   ordering, 238-241
   paying, 244-245
   taste words, 243-244
restroom signs, 317
ritualized expressions. *See*
   fixed expressions
room preferences (hotel
   reservations), 194-195
rules (Five Golden Rules),
   3-7
ryokaNs, 198-200

S

safety
   facts, 293-294
   reporting lost items, 297
schedules (travel schedules),
   263-265

sentence structure
  grammar review, 32-33
  particles, 33-41
    -*de* ("by means of"; "at"), 38
    -*ga* (subject marker), 35-36
    -*kara* ("from"), 38
    -*made* ("until"), 38
    -*mo* ("also"), 37
    -*ni* ("toward"; "in"), 37
    -*o* (object marker), 36
    -*to* ("together with"), 38-40
    -*wa* (topic), 40-41
  review quiz, 42-43
  simplicity, 41-42
  word order, 31-34
shopping
  adjectives, 225-226
  complaints, 311-313
  counters, 220-223
  department store floor plans, 224
  exercises, 229-230
  expressions, 219, 226-228
  pointing words, 223-225
  types of stores, 217-218
shops (signs and symbols)
  banks, 321
  bookstores, 322
  cashiers, 324
  cigarette shops, 323
  coffee shops, 323
  currency exchange, 321
  pharmacy, 320
  post office, 322
  smoking areas, 323-324

signs and symbols, 315
  bus stands, 326
  coin lockers, 319
  Do Not Enter!, 318
  emergency exit, 316
  entrance signs, 316
  exit signs, 316
  police stations, 319-320
  pull, 317
  push, 317
  restrooms, 317
  shops
    banks, 321
    bookstores, 322
    cashiers, 324
    cigarette shops, 323
    coffee shops, 323
    currency exchange, 321
    pharmacy, 320
    post office, 322
    smoking areas, 323-324
  subways, 326-327
  taxi stands, 325
  telephones, 318
  train stations, 327-328
simplicity (sentence structure), 41-42
smoking areas (signs and symbols), 323-324
society (Japanese), 13-14
sounds (speech sounds)
  articulation, 18
  consonants, 17-18
  pronunciation
    consonants, 19-23
    double consonants, 22-23

intonation patterns, 26-27
  loanwords, 24-26
  long vowels, 24
  tricky sounds, 21-23
  vowels, 19-21
  syllabication, 18-19
  vowels, 17-18
standalone consonants, 21-23
stem endings (verbs), 61-63
stores, types, 217-218
subjects
  markers (-*ga*), 35-36
  sentence structure, 32-33
subway signs, 326-327
suffixes (conjugation)
  adjectives, 50-52
  nouns, 53
  verbs, 47
survival phrases, 99-100
syllabication
  intonation patterns, 26-27
  overview, 18-19
symptoms, health-related expressions, 286-288
synonyms, 6

T

-*to* ("together with"), 38-40
takuhaibiN (home delivery express), 168
taste words, 243-244
tasupo cards, 323
taxi stand signs, 325

taxis
   common destinations,
      183-184
   direction words, 182-183
   travel-related expressions,
      181-185
TE-form
   conjugation, 59-67
      adjective predicates, 66
      noun predicates, 64-65
      verbs, 60-63
   requests, 143-145
telephone expressions,
   273-282
   calling home, 275-277
   exercises, 282
   important numbers,
      281-282
   sample dialogue, 277-281
telephone signs, 318
thank you expressions, 94-95
thefts, reporting, 297-300
ticket reservation signs, 328
time expressions, 153-156,
   162
Time, Place, Occasion. *See*
   TPO
"together with" (-*to*), 38-40
topic particle (-*wa*), 40-41
"toward" (-*ni*), 37
TPO (Time, Place,
   Occasion), 15-16
trains
   travel-related expressions,
      176-181
   train station signs,
      327-328

transportation expressions,
   175
   activity planning, 262
   common destinations,
      183-184
   direction words, 182-183
   driving tips, 185-187
   modes, 160
   taxis, 181-185
   trains, 176-181
travel schedules, 263-265
travel-related expressions
   activity planning
      destinations, 261
      exercises, 268-269
      guided tours, 262
      transportation, 262
      travel schedules,
         263-265
      weather and climate,
         265-268
   airports
      baggage claim, 168-169
      Customs, 170-174
      immigration booths,
         163-168
   banking
      bills and coins, 204-207
      currency exchange,
         207-209
      opening accounts,
         209-212
   complaints
      hotels, 305-309
      restaurants, 309-311
      shopping, 311-313

dining out
   comparative questions,
      236-238
   cuisines, 233
   etiquette, 241-243
   exercises, 246-247
   food words, 237
   like/dislike expressions,
      234-235
   menus, 238-239
   ordering, 238-241
   paying, 244-245
   taste words, 243-244
exercises, 149-151
health-related, 283-292
   body-part words,
      285-286
   diseases, 290
   doctor requests,
      288-289
   medical departments,
      289
   office visits, 284-285
   pharmacy, 290-292
   symptoms, 286-288
hotels
   checking in/out,
      196-198
   reservations, 189-195
   ryokaNs, 198-200
houses, 249-259
   bathroom, 253-255
   bedtime expressions,
      255-257
   entering, 250-251
   family room, 252-253
   household items,
      257-259

in-flight expressions,
  making requests,
  141-149
personal information
  expressions, 111-113
shopping, 219-230
  adjectives, 225-226
  counters, 220-223
  department store floor
    plans, 224
  exercises, 229-230
  pointing words,
    223-225
  types of stores, 217-218
telephones, 273-282
  calling home, 275-277
  exercises, 282
  important numbers,
    281-282
  sample dialogue,
    277-281
time expressions, 153-156,
  162
  duration, 158-160
  -kara and *-made*
    ("from" and "until"),
    157-158
transportation, 175-187
  common destinations,
    183-184
  direction words,
    182-183
  driving tips, 185-187
  taxis, 181-185
  trains, 176-181
tricky sounds,
  pronunciation, 21-23

U–V

"until" (*-made*), 38, 157-158

verbs
  conjugation
    adjective predicates,
      50-53
    nouns, 53-56
    overview, 45-46
    TE-form, 59-66
    verb predicates, 46-50
  stem endings, 61-63
vowels
  defining characteristics,
    17
  pronunciation
    long vowels, 24
    overview, 19-21
    syllabication, 18-19

W

-wa (topic particle), 40-41
watashi-wa XYZ-*desu*
  pattern (introductions),
  102-103
weather and climate
  expressions, 265-268
wh-questions, 73-74
"where" (*dochira*), 105
words
  loanwords, 24, 26
  order (sentence structure),
    31-34

workplace
  introduction expressions,
    104-105
  personal information
    expressions, 114-116

X–Y–Z

X-*wa* Y-*desu* pattern
  (introductions), 102
XYZ-*ni Shi-masu*, 142-143

CHECK OUT THESE BEST-SELLERS

More than 450 titles available at booksellers and online retailers everywhere!

978-1-59257-115-4

978-1-59257-900-6

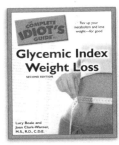

978-1-59257-855-9

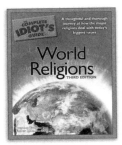

978-1-59257-222-9

978-1-59257-957-0

978-1-59257-785-9

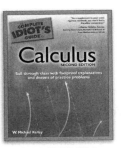

978-1-59257-471-1

978-1-59257-483-4

978-1-59257-883-2

978-1-59257-966-2

978-1-59257-908-2

978-1-59257-786-6

978-1-59257-954-9

978-1-59257-437-7

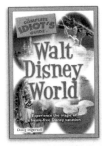

978-1-59257-888-7

ALPHA   idiotsguides.com

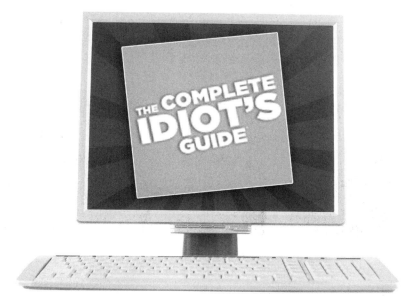

WARRANTY LIMITS

READ THE ENCLOSED AGREEMENT
AND THIS LABEL BEFORE OPENING
AUDIO PACKAGE.

BY OPENING THIS SEALED AUDIO PACKAGE, YOU ACCEPT AND AGREE TO THE TERMS AND CONDITIONS PRINTED BELOW. IF YOU DO NOT AGREE, DO NOT OPEN THE PACKAGE. SIMPLY RETURN THE SEALED PACKAGE.

This audio CD is distributed on an "AS IS" basis, without warranty. Neither the author, the publisher and or Penguin Group (USA) Inc. make any representation, or warranty, either express or implied, with respect to the audio CD, its quality, accuracy, or fitness for a specific purpose. Therefore, neither the authors, the publisher and or Penguin Group (USA) Inc. shall have any liability to you or any other person or entity with respect to any liability, loss, or damage caused or alleged to have been caused directly or indirectly by the music contained on the audio CD or by the audio CD itself. If the audio CD is defective, you may return it for replacement.